Today, economic theory is a mathematical theory, but that was not always the case. Major changes in the ways economists presented their arguments to one another occurred between the late 1930s and the early 1950s; over that period the discipline became mathematized. Professor Weintraub, a noted scholar of the modern history of economic thought, argues that those changes were not merely cosmetic: The mathematical *forms* of the arguments significantly altered the *substance* of the arguments. *Stabilizing Dynamics* is particularly concerned with the ways in which the rich and confusing talk of the 1930s evolved, over a fifteen-year period, into technical analysis of some mathematical structures. The author describes the context for the history of that change, locating it in the broader intellectual currents, and shows how the history of modern economics can be seen as a confluence of several disparate traditions. Historiographically, this book offers one of the first constructivist accounts of modern economic analysis.

Historical Perspectives on Modern Economics

Stabilizing dynamics

Historical Perspectives on Modern Economics

General Editor: Professor Craufurd D. Goodwin, Duke University

This series contains original works that challenge and enlighten historians of economics. For the profession as a whole it promotes better understanding of the origin and content of modern economics.

Other books in the series:

Stabilizing dynamics
Constructing economic knowledge

E. Roy Weintraub
Duke University

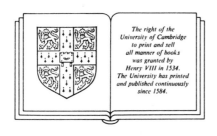

The right of the
University of Cambridge
to print and sell
all manner of books
was granted by
Henry VIII in 1534.
The University has printed
and published continuously
since 1584.

CAMBRIDGE UNIVERSITY PRESS
Cambridge
New York   Port Chester   Melbourne   Sydney

Published by the Press Syndicate of the University of Cambridge
The Pitt Building, Trumpington Street, Cambridge CB2 1RP
40 West 20th Street, New York, NY 10011, USA
10 Stamford Road, Oakleigh, Melbourne 3166, Australia

© Cambridge University Press 1991

First published 1991

Printed in the United States of America

Library of Congress Cataloging-in-Publication Data
Weintraub, E. Roy.
Stabilizing dynamics : constructing economic knowledge / E. Roy
Weintraub.
p.   cm. – (Historical perspectives on modern economics.)
Includes bibliographical references and index.
ISBN 0-521-39346-9 (hardback)
1. Equilibrium (Economics)   2. Statics and dynamics (Social
sciences)   I. Title.   II. Series.
HB145.W44   1991
339.5'09 – dc20   90-25638
                                                                CIP

British Library Cataloging-in-Publication Data applied for

ISBN 0-521-39346-9 hardback

For Nell Maxine, of course

Contents

Acknowledgments

Many individuals helped shape what is written here, because they shared their ideas, concerns, and time with me as I thought through and wrote these chapters. Most important, Neil de Marchi, my Duke University colleague, was a constant companion–guide in the journey that this book records. We talked almost daily about the issues of these histories, and my debt to him is enormous. My other Duke colleagues, Craufurd Goodwin and Bob Coats, aided this project by their willingness to comment on and criticize the unformed work that led to what is presented here. We all worked together in Duke's Economic Thought Workshop (partially funded in the past by the Sloan Foundation), along with Bruce Caldwell of the University of North Carolina at Greensboro, Dan Hammond and Mike Lawlor of Wake Forest University, and our students, chiefly Jane Rossetti and Jinbang Kim, and visitors Marina Bianchi, Mary Morgan, Aiko Ikeo, Phillipe Mongin, and Shoken Mawatari. Those regular meetings provided a forum in which I could try out new ideas.

It will become obvious that Phil Mirowski was an important influence in my rethinking of the historical issues of neoclassical economics and the role of mathematical analysis. Don McCloskey and Arjo Klamer likewise encouraged me to think in new ways about the products of economists, as did the Duke critical theorists Stanley Fish and Barbara Herrnstein Smith. I benefited from discussing these issues with Randall Bausor, Warren Samuels, David Colander, Tony Brewer, Roger Backhouse, David Hendry, Bob Heilbroner, Alex Rosenberg, Wade Hands, Nancy Wulwick, Mark Blaug, David Collard, Don Patinkin, Bob Solow, Ken Arrow, Axel Leijonhufvud, Bob Clower, Donald Bushaw, Herbert Simon, Don Lavoie, Paul Davidson, Mark Perlman, Ian Steedman, Nancy Cartwright, Analisa Rosselli, Lionello Punzo, Franco Donzelli, Harry Collins, and others at seminars and workshops in the United States, England, France, and Italy.

A year spent as a fellow at the National Humanities Center (NHC) in Research Triangle Park, North Carolina, allowed me the freedom from scheduling constraints necessary to put this work together. My NHC colleagues Joe Lowenstein, Patricia O'Brian, Sally Deutsch, Sara Maza, John Higham, and Nickolas Rupke provided an intellectual-community context for this work, and a summer grant from the National Endowment for the Humanities allowed me to forgo summer teaching while I rewrote some of the chapters.

Several parts of this book have appeared elsewhere, in somewhat different forms. Portions of Chapter 4 (dealing with Yasui and Allais) appeared as two comments in *History of Political Economy*, 19(4) 1987 and 23(3) 1991, and they are reprinted with permission of Duke University Press. Chapter 5 appeared in A. Klamer, D. McCloskey, and B. Solow (eds.), *The Consequences of Economic Rhetoric* (1988), and is reprinted with permission of Cambridge University Press. I have also drawn some smaller bits and pieces, in Chapters 1 and 8, from the following: "Methodology Doesn't Matter, but the History of Thought Might," *Scandinavian Journal of Economics,* 91(2) 1989; "Comment on Heilbroner," in Warren Samuels (ed.), *Economics as Discourse,* Kluwer Publishing Company, 1990; and "Comment on Hamminga," in Neil de Marchi (ed.), *Methodology of Economics,* Kluwer Publishing Company, 1991.

CHAPTER 1

Introduction

*[We] make constellations by picking out and putting together certain
stars rather than others [and] we make stars by drawing certain boundaries rather than others. Nothing dictates whether the skies shall be marked
off into constellations or other objects. We have to make what we find,
whether it be the Big Dipper, Sirius, food, fuel, or a stereo system.*
Goodman (1985, p. 36)

This is not the book I intended to write. I came into economics from
mathematics, and my first work in economics was in general equilibrium
theory. As is often true early in a career, concern with the worth of one's
activity is not as important as getting on with the work, and so I put aside
any interest I had had in appraisal and criticism and instead concentrated
on developing a competence in the subject matter itself. But the outsider's
perspective remained present in my thoughts. What was general equilibrium theory about? And what did "they" think they were doing in this
field? These remained open questions for me even as I proved theorems
and linked arguments. Behind the work there remained the questions.

General equilibrium theory is a problem of sorts for many different
people. Because it seems central to the discipline of economics, or at least
neoclassical economics, and because it is a high-status activity (Nobel
prizes to Hicks, Arrow, Debreu, and others), the effort to understand its
place and appraise its worth has engaged a large number of individuals.
In some sense, much is at stake. If the theory is overvalued, then the activity wastes professional resources. If the theory has defects, then the
centerpiece of neoclassical economics may be flawed, and the larger enterprise may be suspect.

General equilibrium theory has been a test case for almost all views of
what constitutes good work in economics. Milton Friedman, in his review
(Friedman 1946) of Lange's 1944 book *Price Flexibility and Employment,*
rejected that book's arguments on the basis of a methodological decision
that general equilibrium theory made no useful predictions, and so it was
not a good theory. That decision prefigured Friedman's later methodological writings. Blaug (1980) argued that because general equilibrium theory
generated no falsifiable propositions and was not itself falsifiable, it was

not a good theory. Kaldor argued that its premises, its assumptions, were false, and therefore the theory was worthless, an argument based on the methodological tenet that good theories have true premises. Alex Rosenberg, a philosopher who worries about these things, wrote that

the "cognitive status," to use an old-fashioned term, of general equilibrium theory [GET] is one of the most vexing items on the agenda of the philosophy of economics. Because of its highly abstract character, its supremely unrealistic assumptions, the alleged irrelevance of its consequences for real economies, and its centrality to economics, GET has been an interpretative mare's nest to both philosophers and economists. [Rosenberg 1986, p. 177]

Rosenberg himself first argued (1983) that general equilibrium theory was applied mathematics; more recently (1986) he has suggested that it is, instead, a process-defective explanation of price stability.

How do we assay the status of a theory? The answer has many components, but they all seem to lead to a discussion of the philosophy of science, or what in economics is called methodology. For me to try to understand the value of general equilibrium theory, it seemed that I had to understand the framework that usually was used to assess the general value of theories. Methodology beckoned at that stage in my career when I allowed my "work" to be more congruent with my interests.

In my book *Microfoundations* (1979) I first suggested that there was a way of reconstructing portions of general equilibrium theory as a Lakatosian research program, a reconstruction that facilitated appraisal because the program idea itself was created to structure discussions of the merits of scientific theories. I developed that idea further in my 1985 book *General Equilibrium Analysis: Studies in Appraisal.* There I focused on that part of the general equilibrium literature associated with the most formal mathematical presentations of the subject. In order to appraise that work, I needed to examine the history of the subdiscipline. But because no such history had ever been constructed, I had to develop it myself. I thus presented a lengthy history associated with papers on the existence of a competitive equilibrium, papers written between 1930 and 1954. That case provided the historical material I used to discuss several aspects of general equilibrium analysis. Because my interest was in the issue of appraisal, I structured the material so that it could be treated as data to be fit to one of several models of appraisal. In particular, I argued that the sequence of papers could be reconstructed as the hardening of the hard core of a Lakatosian research program, a program that was fully progressive in the Lakatosian sense.

My arguments seemed to catch the attention of individuals interested in these problems. One of the problems that surfaced in the discussion of my position was the role of empirical tests, and whether or not empirical progress could be associated with the neo-Walrasian program. As a next step in my studies, I argued that empirical progress could likewise be reconstructed from examination of a case. I presented that case study of empirical progress at a conference in Amsterdam honoring Joop Klant at his retirement (Weintraub 1988).

But all during that period I was aware that another lengthy study was waiting to be written. I had begun work in economics, in my doctoral dissertation, on questions of the stability of the competitive equilibrium. My advisor, Lawrence Klein, had been Paul Samuelson's first doctoral student. Klein was deeply interested in the possibility that random shocks in a dynamic model could produce more "sensible" time paths of the variables than would be the case in a deterministic model. In the middle 1960s, when the stability literature associated with the competitive equilibrium was still trying to find redirection in the wake of the Scarf and Gale "counterexamples," Klein thought it might be possible to stabilize, in some sense to be worked out, the unstable Walrasian system by moving to stochastic stability notions. The findings in my dissertation, however, suggested that such a hope was not realistic. Thus, my willingness to reexamine the stability literature, to do a historical reconstruction of the papers on stability from the 1930s to the late 1950s, had some basis in personal intellectual history. To come back to the literature on dynamics, as one writing a case history with a concern for appraisal of the larger general equilibrium program, seemed natural.

Recognizing that stability theory had played itself out by the late 1960s, I thought that those papers on dynamics, beginning with the Samuelson and Hicks work, continuing through the stability papers of Arrow, Block, and Hurwicz in the late 1950s, and ending with the Scarf and Gale counterexamples, would provide a case study of a subprogram, the stability program, that had degenerated in the sense of Lakatos. I thought that this case might be a natural companion case symmetric with the one on "existence" that I had already written, with progress in one part of the program set off against degeneration in another part. At any rate, that was my intent, my working hypothesis, and so I started to reread.

But what began as an attempt to examine, and appraise, the work on the stability of the competitive equilibrium has ended as something rather different, and what I now offer to the reader is not a sequel to my earlier book on general equilibrium analysis.

What has happened is that I have come to understand that knowledge is constructed, not found. This observation is two-edged: Not only is the scientist engaged in processes of construction, discovery being only one feature of the claim to knowledge, but our reconstruction of the process of science is a constructed account, not one to be found whole in the record. For economics, this means that the work of the economist is not well understood as being the work of an explorer and finder, a creator of theories and assembler of facts. But additionally, and most emphatically, histories of economics are constructed, not chanced upon. To put it another way, we have two processes, or levels, to consider: First, there is the level of the practice, in this case science or economics; second, there is the level, or metalevel, of accounting for and appraising and reconstructing that practice, specifically the history of science or the history of economics (or the sociology of science, as discussed later).

I have come to learn that among individuals concerned with the enterprise of science – philosophers, historians, and sociologists – there is a growing awareness that scientific work is knowledge creation in a context and that such knowledge is shared knowledge within a particular community. The issues are those of how the knowledge comes to be shared more widely and how the meanings are negotiated first within small groups, and then in larger and larger groups. From the view that knowledge is socially constructed comes a concern with the materials and organization of the construction. I have no interest in recapitulating here my arguments for this point of view, one that is widely shared among sociologists of scientific knowledge, nor do I wish to press this on others as a new doctrine. The point is rather that this view has some serious implications for discourse about practice, or writings about how particular work in economics came to be the way it has become.

If we do not want to argue any longer that economists attempt to test, or falsify, theoretical accounts by confronting those theories with the data, if we do not believe that such a framework can provide us with a convincing account of scientific practice, we have a problem at the metalevel as well. That is, we cannot remain convinced that our historical reconstruction is well described as confronting the actual record with the reconstructed, or theoretical, account. *If we are not falsificationist in our conceptualization of economics, we are under no compulsion to remain falsificationist about our histories of economics.* We must accept that history is not presented to us raw, as a neutral case or data source on which we can perform tests of our methodological theories of how scientific knowledge is gained. History is not "out there" waiting to answer our questions or corroborate our hypotheses. History is not found; history is written. It is an authorial construction to some purpose or other and is itself as much a creative enterprise as is the "theory" it is often "meant" to describe.

Although that came as a shock to me as an economist, it was hardly news to scholars and students in disciplines like anthropology, sociology, history, comparative literature, psychology, and archeology. I first began to understand these matters in 1986 in Amsterdam. My attempt to examine Lakatosian empirical progress had been consistent with my previous work, but in Amsterdam Don McCloskey and Arjo Klamer began to work out, publicly, the implications of McCloskey's profoundly important 1986 book, *The Rhetoric of Economics*. The discussion recorded in the conference proceedings – see the exchanges among the participants cited by de Marchi (1988) – provoked me to rethink some of my ideas. Specifically, I was taken with McCloskey's comment in the record that accepting my reconstruction of a Lakatosian program, the consequence was simply that one then could model economic analysis in a philosophically coherent framework. But what was the payoff to this linkage? What more did we know about economics? My response to McCloskey was to seek alternatives to the Lakatosian reconstruction in the sense that I wanted to "test" whether my reconstruction had implications for doing applied economics differently. That led to an invitation the next year to participate in the Wellesley conference: "The Consequences of Rhetoric." There I presented a paper in the spirit of the McCloskey book; I tried to see for myself if the ideas could illuminate some material that previously had eluded my understanding. That paper, reprinted (with minor changes) here as Chapter 5, began a lengthy process of reconsidering what I thought I knew about the nature of the activity called "doing economics," a process whose results are the chapters in this book.

What follows is not a conventional history of economic thought. That kind of history is Whiggish and magisterial; it is history as exemplar of the march of wisdom, of progress, from the dark and uninformed past to the enlightened and scientifically sophisticated present. At its best, in the books by Schumpeter, or Blaug, the grand panorama is structured by the idea of progress itself. That such narrative appears to conform to the way the historical personages conceptualized their positions (Samuelson has written, without irony, of standing like Newton on the shoulders of giants) lends a legitimacy to the historiographic choices. That kind of writing is necessarily associated with the idea that science itself, or economics, is an exemplar of knowledge growth. Knowing more, over time, means that one must provide an account of that growth, that increase. How clarity was achieved, and ignorance dispelled, frames the account's borders.

If, however, knowledge is constructed, and growth of knowledge is problematic, then history takes on different characteristics:

The realization that phlogiston and Ptolemy, ether and alchemy were actually based on quite a lot of correct observations, even though they could not be exhaustively accounted for by observation, and that neither Relativity nor Quanta – let alone quarks and quasars – could be exhaustively reduced to observation statements, brought a change. It began to dawn on philosophers that the heart of the problem was not: What is appearance and what is reality? Instead, it became: How is one to see the succession of alternative theories and how can one distinguish between them? At the moment in which the debate about appearance and reality was replaced by a debate about alternative theories, the history of sicence became part of science. [Munz 1985, p. 24]

Understanding an intellectual activity is made easier if one has knowledge of the context for that activity. Such understanding in theoretical económics is not easily gained from the "theorem-proof" structure of journal articles, which suffer from what Lakatos (1976) called the "fallacy of deductivism," the notion that mathematics and theoretical science actually develop from axioms and propositions to theorems and corollaries.

The position I am proffering takes cognizance of the fact that economics is a social activity that is carried out, is done, in communities. The conversations of economists, the "quest," in McIntyre's language (1984), is a social quest, and the conversations of the members of those communities are in outline not so different from the conversations in other "interpretive communities," such as the community of those involved in solid-state physics, the Milton community, or the sociology-of-science crowd.

Stanley Fish (1980), in his development of the idea of interpretive communities, articulated what appears to me to be central in the kinds of issues we need to address:

Interpretive communities are made up of those who share interpretive strategies not for reading but for writing texts, for constituting their properties. In other words these strategies exist prior to the act of reading and therefore determine the shape of what is read rather than, as is usually assumed, the other way around... [But] an interpretive community is not objective because as a bundle of interests, of particular purposes and goals, its perspective is interested rather than neutral; but by the same reasoning the meanings and texts produced by an interpretive community are not subjective because they do not proceed from an isolated individual but from a public and conventional point of view... [M]embers of the same community will necessarily agree because they will see (and by seeing, make) everything in relation to that community's assumed purposes and goals; and conversely, members of different communities will disagree because from their respective positions the other "simply" cannot see what is obviously and inescapably there. [Fish 1980, pp. 14–16]

I recently visited a seminar in a university economics department in which I heard a paper (van der Berg 1988) that had the following paragraph as a synopsis:

Using micro data on unemployed individuals from 1983–1985 a structural job search model is estimated. The model allows for transitions from unemployment to nonparticipation. An extended version of the model deals with the influence of on-the-job search and prospective wage increases on the search behavior of the unemployed. The empirical results show that the probability of accepting a job offer is almost one for most unemployed individuals. Still, a large portion of unemployment spells ends in transitions out of the labour force. The effects of changes in benefits on duration are extremely small.

I suggest that that paper and the world to which it is linked are fully comprehensible to members of the labor economics community, mostly comprehensible to the macroeconomics community or the microeconomics community, partially understandable to post-Keynesians concerned with Sraffa models, and incomprehensible to Milton scholars of the usual type. In order to understand that paper and the world it suggests, the world it makes, we must be as vigorous in our understanding of the community that gives meaning to that paper as we are rigorous in our criticism of the data set used by the author.

Note that I am suggesting an approach to appraising, making sense of, and discussing a particular piece of work in economics. This analysis of the particular is not based on the general "scientific method" or any other methodology or metatheory that would give simple answers, such as, True or false? or Rational: yes or no? There is no instant rationality, no test we can apply that would give us a precise judgment about the worth of a particular bit of work in economics.

This is not to say that we are entirely unconstrained in our analyses of a particular work. The poem itself provides few constraints on interpretations. Fish once said, only partly in jest, that there are potential interpretive strategies that would allow Faulkner's "A Rose for Emily" to be read as being about Eskimos, but the "Eskimo reading is wrong because there is at present no interpretive strategy for producing it, no way of 'looking' or reading...that would result in the emergence of obvious Eskimo meanings" (Fish 1980, p. 386). And there could be interpretive communities that might explain the unemployment rate on the basis of the melting of the polar ice caps.

The fundamental issue is what constitutes a good theory, and that is not a matter of comparing the theory to some standard of scientific goodness. We have to ask more complex questions of a theory and its interpretations: How was it developed? How was it presented? What do its terms mean? Who is its audience? We seek to understand the way the interpretive community has read the economy text and what makes the community more likely to respond to one interpretation rather than another. In economics we might ask about how a theory treats evidence, how it uses technical terms, and how it links problems posed in earlier papers previously valued by the community. Appraisal is a complex process of questioning and interpreting the text, or the bit of scientific practice, or the piece of economic analysis. It simply does not suffice, in the sense that it is not convincing or reasonable, to dismiss "new classical" analysis, or rational expectations, as wrong because it fails to account for Keynesian unemployment, or true dynamic uncertainty, or the class struggle, or policy effectiveness. Appraisal requires a sophisticated examination of the development of the analysis.

There is no formula for generating appraisals of work in economics. Formulas (e.g., Is it operational? Does it make predictions that can be tested? Is it falsifiable? Is it progressive?) led people to believe that there was a path to instant wisdom in economics. Although we might wish it were not so, we need to know a lot about a theory in order to appraise it.

I am left with a merely residual interest in philosophy – that being philosophizing in Sellers's sense of "an attempt to see how things, in the broadest possible sense of the term, hang together, in the broadest possible sense of the term" (Rorty 1982, p. xiv). An interest in methods has replaced concern for methodology. I am interested in criticism, or appraisal, in the broad sense of general cultural criticism, with a focus on the texts or models or theories or evidence of economists instead of the canvases of painters or the films of directors or the experiments and lab records of biologists. And because the economics of today comes from yesterday's economics, my understanding of current practice is enhanced by a perspective that embraces a context transcending the immediacy of the problem or puzzle that the analysis addresses. It is necessary to appraisal to have a context for the analysis, and that context is rooted in past work.

Writing history is not easy, and it certainly is not straightforward. Besides the choices about audience and the construction of facts, or, in sociological terms, "the nature of facticity," there are numerous issues that determine what is and what is not a source. Are the sources for the history of economics the published articles alone, or are the reminiscences of the economists sources too? Are the finished products of the scientific activity the only, or best, sources, or are they, rather, completely unreliable "texts"? Indeed, how are the texts to be read? Do we believe that the meaning resides in the writing, or that we construct the meanings of the texts in the same way that the author constructs the meanings of the phenomena? What constitutes evidence for the historian is not given, but is the result of decisions taken.

That is, science is a social activity, with certain social purposes served by the activity and the products of the activity. Just as a case study may be structured by a philosopher's concerns, that case study also may be structured by the concerns of sociologists of science. Put another way, historians of economics seem to have as an audience not only the methodology community but also a community of sociologists who study science as a social enterprise. There is not, however, a subdiscipline within economics based on the sociology of science that corresponds to that subdiscipline called methodology that is based on the philosophy of science. Whether this is because economists in the end disbelieve in sociology as, in Leijonhufvud's phrase, "a lesser tribe without a 'modl' as totem," or whether this is because it is too difficult for neoclassical economists to think about groups as social actors is in the end of no matter. There are not many historians of economics who have an interest in the sociology of the economics profession.

Of course, usually there has been some sort of sociology of science lurking in the background of the histories of economics. Citation studies, patterns of influence, who taught whom, what got published where – these were all issues of importance to the Mertonian generation of sociologists of science. That group took the products of science as given and asked questions about the production process, as it were, particularly the social or professional elements of that process. This is the sociology of science that is implicit in most case studies. But there is an alternative to this view, and that is the set of ideas associated with those modern sociologists who have redefined their field as the "sociology of scientific knowledge." That is to say, these individuals do not assume that the knowledge is "out there" and that the social process called science gathers that knowledge, so that the task of sociology is to study how that knowledge is disseminated and how rewards are to be allocated on the basis of new knowledge.

This way of looking at the scientific enterprise is again based on the idea that scientific knowledge itself is constructed socially, in communities of scientists: Knowledge is constructed, not found. From this perspective, the relevant questions to ask are not, What is the most efficient organization of science for discovery? or, Who discovered the phenomenon or fact or theory first? Rather, the analyst's attention is directed to science as an activity that produces "scientific knowledge" and asks about how that knowledge is produced: What is the role of the observer? What role do instruments play in constructing knowledge? How is knowledge agreed upon in the sense that consensus is reached on the facticity of an event or observation? How are others persuaded? How does the community train its apprentices? Writers in this tradition have been interested, for example, in how theory and data interact, exactly how experimental anomalies are treated, the rhetoric of the scientific paper, and so forth.

These are the kinds of questions I pose, and worry, in the chapters to follow. Part I contains three chapters that do history in the ways I want to see it done. The first of these, Chapter 2, reads the literature on dynamics in the 1930s from a variety of perspectives and suggests that too often the line of papers is purposefully construed as "leading" to Samuelson. That is, one can reconstruct the 1930s discussions about economic dynamics, statics, and equilibrium in many ways. However, those authors usually have been considered as moving from ignorance to understanding, from darkness to light, from prose to model. My own reading is meant to show that there are many other ways to read these papers and that it is not foolish to read the record as being discursively rich, confused, and hardly ever convergent on any coherent perspective. There are, I suggest, alternatives to the Whig reading of "out of darkness came Samuelson."

The second of these, Chapter 3, attempts to locate, or contextualize, Samuelson's *Foundations of Economic Analysis* (1947). Because this book is a classic, it may not be read much anymore, but I assume that my readers have a working familiarity with its contents. This chapter may come as somewhat of a shock to a profession accustomed to thinking that "intellectual parentage" and "influence" are simple matters of economist-antecedents. I argue that the *Foundations* is hardly a seamless weaving. Instead, various themes and subthemes, from different traditions and discourses, play themselves out in its pages. The text, read against the various contexts that occasioned it, becomes more, not less, interesting on my reading, because it becomes more nearly continuous with its time and place of origin.

The third historical essay, Chapter 4, attempts to unravel the intertwined histories of mathematical dynamics and economic dynamics, particularly in the 1940s. The issue of precursors gets a rough overhaul here, as does the notion that "tools solve problems."

The chapters in Part II are likewise related. They are loosely based on the historical material and represent some alternative approaches to the narrative structure. Chapter 5, reprinted from the Wellesley conference record (with permission), was my initial attempt to ask a "literary" question of the set of texts: "Equilibrium" turns out to have had many meanings in the same set of papers, and the role of mathematical modeling is conceptualized in a different way.

Chapter 6, my attempt to organize the historical record presented in Chapters 2–4, "reads" the set of histories of dynamics in a variety of different ways and in the end argues that the sequence of papers can be understood as an attempt to impose meaning and coherence: I suggest that the papers in that sequence impose order and thus create knowledge. I show that that process was a social process of negotiation and argument. That a rational reconstruction of the sequence of works fails to make good sense of the history of dynamics should come as no great surprise once it is clearly seen that ex post rationalizations, though they stabilize the previous history, do not themselves present their knowledge contemporaneously with the historical action and actors. Chapter 6 is best considered as an escape from the shackles of rational reconstruction and as a demonstration of the idea that although the philosophy of science can provide rules for writing the history of economics, other approaches can provide us with richer readings and deeper understandings.

This idea is viewed from a different perspective in Chapter 7. There I consider the way the history of dynamics was in fact constructed from the remarkably adept survey article by Takashi Negishi. I examine that paper in some detail and show how that particular survey article functioned in stabilizing the meaning of the series of texts in dynamics. Put another way, the Negishi survey provides a window on the transformation of discursive practice in the subdiscipline of economic dynamics, and that transformation is itself part of the history.

It is my belief, as sketched in the concluding chapter, that the history of economic thought, as a subdiscipline in economics, is, in the words of the recent song, "looking for love in all the wrong places." I argue that giving up the wish for approval from philosophers of science (methodologists) does not entail that one must seek it then from historians of science as that field is currently established. The history of economic thought, in its newer manifestations, has real richness and complexity in its matter and manner. I believe such histories are worth writing, and hence I have written this book.

From dynamics to stability

CHAPTER 2

Economists on dynamics and stability in the 1930s

The past several years have seen a number of provocative studies of the 1930s, studies that suggest the complexity and richness of the theorizing about economic dynamics. Mary Morgan (1990) showed that the early econometricians were grappling with the nature of dynamic models in order to rationalize empirical work. Kyun Kim (1989) indicated how the various models of business cycles produced in the 1930s came to be submerged by the Keynesian onslaught. The earlier heroic story, as told, for example, in Shackle's *The Years of High Theory* (1967), seems terribly oversimplified today.

The historian of economic thought, usually trained as an economist in present-day economics, naturally sees the past from the present and so reads past texts[1] against the background of current best practice. The Whig history that results is at least comprehensible and can be presented to economist-colleagues as a contribution to current debates, for the historian can assert that the confusions of the present are rooted in the mistakes of the past. As Latour and Woolgar remarked,

historians, as portrayed in historical texts, can move freely in the past, possess knowledge of the future, have the ability to survey settings in which they are not (and never will be) involved, have access to actors' motives, and (rather like god) are all-knowing and all-seeing, able to judge what is good and bad. They can produce histories in which one thing is the "sign" of another and in which disciplines and ideas 'burgeon", "mature", or "lie fallow". [Latour and Woolgar 1979, p. 107]

In what follows I shall suggest that the Whiggish reconstruction of the 1930s literature on equilibrium and dynamics is but one of a number of possible reconstructions. We can tell a story of the death of the Hayekian conceptualization, or the limitations of empirical business cycle modeling as seen by Keynesians. We can speak of the richness of the discourse about dynamics in the 1930s, or we can talk of the lack of connection with the nascent mathematical theories. There are many stories to tell.

It is always a problem, in beginning a study of a particular period, to begin at a particular time, rather than at a time a year earlier, or two years earlier, or a decade earlier.[2] In an attempt to reconstruct the controversies about the nature and meaning of "dynamics" in the 1930s, I do not intend to suggest that those who wrote in the 1920s made insignificant contributions, nor do I intend to suggest that only those authors whose contributions I shall examine played important roles in the development of the discourse. Instead, I wish simply to begin somewhere, and that somewhere will be 1930, because that year allows a discussion of some particular points that interest me. And let there be no misunderstanding here,[3] for my decision rule is clear and transparent. My focus will be on the important changes in the economics literature associated with the appearance of Samuelson's papers, in *Econometrica,* on equilibrium and dynamics, papers of the early 1940s. Those papers were to form the final part of his *Foundations of Economic Analysis,* of 1947. My reading has thus proceeded backward to include those authors, and their writings, cited by Samuelson. (In later chapters I shall also consider the "effects" on the literature of Samuelson's work.) In other words, except for the fact that some of the individuals to be discussed in what follows themselves cited some even earlier authors, whose work is also treated in these pages, I have tried to backtrack from Samuelson as a first pass at this large body of material.[4]

In what follows I shall argue that the period of the 1930s presents an array of ideas about equilibrium, statics, dynamics, and stability. I shall suggest that the complexity of the discussions of these issues is masked by readings of these texts that construe them as "pre-Samuelson." The concerns of the economists, as expressed in their writings, are not necessarily mutually congruent, nor are they consistent with the later literatures against which they often are reconstructed. I shall argue that recognizing this set of interpretive "problems" is the beginning of a more interesting historical understanding.

"Equilibrium" and dynamic analysis around 1930

Lionel Robbins's article in the *Economic Journal* of June 1930, "On a Certain Ambiguity in the Conception of Stationary Equilibrium," typifies a certain kind of writing at that time. For instance, the piece is written historically, dealing with the manner in which the classical authorities treated statics and dynamics. J. B. Clark, for example, is quoted as follows:

In any given society five generic changes are going on, every one of which reacts on the structure of society by changing the arrangements of that group system which it is the work of catallactics to study. 1. Population is increasing. 2. Capital is increasing. 3. Methods of production are improving. 4. The forms of industrial establishments are changing. 5. The wants of consumers are multiplying. [J. B. Clark, *The Distribution of Wealth*, p. 56, cited by Robbins 1930, p. 203]

Robbins goes on to comment on that passage: "These influences he [Clark] thinks are to be called dynamic. A world from which they were absent would be a static state." Robbins's Clark is thus unconcerned with price adjustment, or quantity adjustment, to equilibrium in particular markets; that presumably is not dynamic, or else those price–quantity adjustments occur so quickly that they are implicit in the notion of static equilibrium. The Clark noted by Robbins was instead concerned with a "growing" society, one in which change is present.

Robbins goes on to make what we may understand to be the major contribution of his paper, for it is the italicized lesson that is referred to prior to the point's being made, and referred to afterward as if something significant had been asserted. Robbins states that

[in] both the Clarkian and the classical construction the quantities of the factors of production are constant. *But* – and this is the fundamental difference which it is desired here to exhibit – *in the one, this constancy is the condition of equilibrium; in the other, it is simply one of the resultants of the equilibrating process.* [p. 204, italics in original]

Put directly, Robbins is asserting that constancy of labor and capital was central to the notion of equilibrium for Clark, whereas that constancy was the outcome of a dynamic process for the classical economists. The heart of this passage is the problem of the best, or most sensible, or most useful, way to think about the idea that the quantities of the factors of production are constant. Are they constant as a result of the economy's working out over time, in which case constancy is endogenous, as it were? Or is the constancy a constraint that the analyst imposes on the model of the economy's working? What is at issue really is the omnipresent problem of how the analyst is to abstract from, or conceptualize, "the economy." It is economists for whom the meaning of "the economy" is contested, and theory and analysis and discussion and data are all brought to bear on that contest for meaning. Notice that from a 1960s perspective, based on dynamic systems, Robbins can be thought of as trying to distinguish between the idea of equilibrium as a state of rest, as a static concept, and the idea of equilibrium as an outcome, a final outcome, of a dynamic process. In the former case there need be no dynamic ideas to shape the idea of equilibrium, whereas in the latter case the idea of equilibrium itself must be specified only with reference to a dynamic process that changes the state of some system.

To support such a reading of Robbins as trying to deal with distinctions about dynamics without the benefit of mathematics, one might note that Robbins drags out "the Marshallian analogy of the balls in the bowl" (p. 204) to make sense of "equilibrium."

Robbins goes on to remark that "the modern economist with even the most fleeting acquaintance with the mathematical theory of equilibrium, will recognise in the two constructions we have been examining, *not competing abstractions, but successive stages of exposition*" (p. 207, italics in original). Actually, from a modern mathematical perspective, this sentence is opaque. The idea that the constancy of the quantities of factors of production may be a condition of equilibrium and also a result of equilibrating processes can be reconstructed at present as was done earlier: "Equilibrium" has two meanings in a stable dynamic system – as a state of no motion, and as an attractor of arbitrary motions of the underlying dynamic process.[5]

If one forgets the more modern conceptualization, what Robbins is arguing is that the economist's act of making assumptions, in a model of growth, say, requires holding something constant and then seeing what emerges in equilibrium. The distinction between holding something constant and establishing the features of equilibrium seems indeed to be the "ambiguity" that appears in the title of the Robbins article. The problem that Robbins is considering is an important one, but its focal point, the making sense of the distinction between the two meanings of "constancy," is ultimately lost on a modern reader: Explaining the point got Robbins into a distinction about the nature of constancy and equilibrium that nonmathematical prose apparently cannot sustain.

I note, having made such a fuss about the difficulty we face in reconstructing Robbins's argument, that Samuelson cited Robbins's article, with the following footnote:

Leaving aside all analogies with other fields, there has necessarily been within the main corpus of economic theory a preoccupation with dynamics, if only implicitly. The Classical economists from Smith to Mill had theories of long-run movements of population and accumulation. [Samuelson 1947, p. 313]

Samuelson was reading Robbins as concerned with dynamics, and as likely confused about the proper way to distinguish among static equilibrium, stationary equilibrium, and dynamic equilibrium. I contend that the Robbins argument, presented in its own context, was read by Samuelson as "familiar" in its concern with understanding distinctions among terms like "statics," "dynamics," "stationarity," "stability," and so forth. That that appropriation of Robbins may misread Robbins is not to the point. Of course Robbins's argument was taken and used by Samuelson for his own purposes. The point in 1990 is rather that it is difficult to read Robbins without the *Foundations* filter. Reading Robbins on dynamics requires contextualizing Robbins and his work, and Samuelson's 1947 *Foundations* certainly was not a context for Robbins's 1930 article.[6] In any event, Robbins's work was shaped by a complex and involved set of influences and interests. The 1930 contests over the meaning of "equilibrium" can hardly be approached today by simple citation of past works, together with an argument that the past is prologue; such reconstruction of the past misleads a modern reader by assuming a coherence that was not historically present.

Ragnar Frisch

Two papers by the exceptional Norwegian mathematical economist Ragnar Frisch figured prominently in Samuelson's discussions of dynamics and provided a locus classicus for the 1930s distinctions among such concepts as equilibrium, disequilibrium, stability, instability, and stationary state. The first paper usually is credited with making the distinctions that, in econometrics, were to allow study of the business cycle, whereas the second paper introduced the ideas that were to allow mathematical economists to link their concerns with those of mathematicians. I shall thus take up these papers in the reverse order of their appearance.

Frisch's paper "On the Notion of Equilibrium and Disequilibrium" appeared in the *Review of Economic Studies* in 1936.[7] Frisch there introduced the language that a relation was to be considered dynamic if "it contains at least one of the variables as related to *different points of time*" (p. 100, italics in original). The variables were themselves distinguished as to their form, with the instantaneous form given at an instant as x_t, and the dynamic form given in any other way, as, for example, $\dot{x}_t$ or $x_{t-\theta}$. Frisch was thus able to note that "the study of the evolution, in particular the study of the time shape of the curves $x_t, y_t, z_t \ldots$ can, in most cases, be done directly from the nature of the structural equation without introducing any notion of 'equilibrium' values of the variables" (p. 101). Further, given a point in time (t) and all instantaneous forms of the variables, such as x_t, y_t, z_t, and so forth, if the evolution of the system is such that those instantaneous values do not change, then those values define a stationary state, or stationary equilibrium. Thus, all dynamic variables, such as $\dot{x}_t$, must be zero in such a state. If "no tendency to change exists . . . [the] system may then be said 'to be in equilibrium'. Otherwise it may be said to be in 'disequilibrium'. In the latter case the system would, if left to itself, change its configuration as time goes on" (pp. 101–2).

For equilibrium states, or even given configurations, Frisch considered that the system could be specified so that outside forces, not modeled by the system, could intrude on the theory, and thus he was led to examine the effects of such shocks to the given system:

Now, suppose that we have a situation which is a stationary equilibrium . . . and suppose that a small disturbance is introduced. . . . If the system, after being exposed to such a small disturbance[,] tends back to the original equilibrium situation, or to another equilibrium situation close to the original one...then the equilibrium in question is stable. Otherwise it is unstable. [p. 102][8]

This distinction between stability and equilibrium was to be very important in later work, especially Samuelson's work, for *the idea of stability thus created conceptualized the economy as a system subject to small shocks, and thus the issue of importance was whether or not the system would return to equilibrium.* There are, of course, other possible ideas. We could ask whether, after a shock, the system would simply remain within certain bounds, or we could characterize the motions of the system as, perhaps, oscillatory, and ask whether, after a shock, the system would remain oscillatory. More important, we could ask about revolutionary change, or sharp breaks, or cataclysms. That Frisch conceptually grounded the language of equilibrium in the small disturbances that leave the underlying structures whole is not accidental to our story here. This language is rooted, of course, in Hamiltonian perturbation theory. All the alternative systematizations would have had to be formalized, to stabilize linguistic practice, in ways different from those that were used. The point here is simply that the idea of stability identified by Frisch was exactly the idea of stability in the sense of Liapunov. The Liapunov definition was associated with a distinct mathematical tradition, although the general idea was present and had been fully worked out in a large and well-developed mathematical literature going back well into the nineteenth century. This mathematical definition was embedded in a theory somewhat refocused from the nineteenth-century approaches. However, for our investigation here, it suffices to recognize that the Frisch definition was not really different from the definition of stability that mathematicians at the time were used to considering.[9]

Frisch also authored, in that period, the even more famous "Propagation Problems and Impulse Problems in Dynamic Economics," originally an essay in *Economic Essays in Honor of Gustav Cassel* (Frisch 1933). (My copy is a reprint of that essay as distributed by Universitetets Okonomiske Institutt, Oslo, Norway, 1933.) That paper was primarily concerned with the theory of business cycles, and it adopted a point of view that was to become of major importance to econometricians over time. Frisch conceived the economy as characterized by a system that oscillated under the influence of certain exterior impulses. The problem thus became, in macroeconomics, to separate out two primary motions of the economy: a motion associated with the internal dynamic structure of the economy, and a motion associated with the external shocks.

The paradigm was the idealized pendulum: The frictionless system itself produced oscillations of a certain form, magnitude, and amplitude:

[The] length of the cycles and the tendency towards dampening are determined by the intrinsic structure of the swinging system, while the intensity (the amplitude) of the fluctuations is determined primarily by the exterior impulse. An important consequence of this is that a more or less regular fluctuation may be produced by a cause which operates irregularly.... The propagation problem is the problem of explaining by the structural properties of the swinging system what the character of the swings would be in case the system was started in some initial situation. This must be done by an essentially dynamic theory. [Frisch 1933, p. 1]

The metaphor of the economy as a closed physical system, as a pendulum, structures the first twenty-seven pages of this thirty-three-page essay. Frisch explores several kinds of dynamic models involving simple differential equations for such things as the rate of change of the capital stock and the rate of change of *encaisse désirée,* the desire for cash-on-hand. Frisch is then able to produce, using some essentially economic arguments about the timing of decisions, a pair of mixed differential-difference equations that have, as their solutions, or motions, some quite complicated damped oscillations.[10]

The final few pages of the paper, beginning with Section 5, "Erratic Shocks as a Source of Energy in Maintaining Oscillations," concern the impulse problem that arises from the observation that although reasonable models of the economy give rise to damped oscillations, the observed cycles (time series) in economic data are not characterized by such damping. Frisch suggests that analysts study "what would become of the solution of a determinate dynamic system if it were exposed to a stream of erratic shocks that constantly upsets the continuous evolution, and by so doing introduces into the system the energy necessary to maintain the swings" (Frisch 1933, p. 27). He cites the metaphor introduced by Wicksell: "If you hit a wooden rocking-horse with a club, the movement of the horse will be very different from that of the club" (p. 28).

The major point is more sophisticated, for Frisch provided an entry to the study of systems that, as the later econometric models were to make clear, mixed deterministic and random components. Citing mathematical work on generalized harmonic analysis and the idea of differential equations subject to error, by Norbert Weiner, Frisch considered a second-order differential equation for a damped pendulum. Frisch showed that the general solution, the time path of motion of the pendulum, depended on the sum of two terms: The first was weighted by the initial position, and the second was weighted by the initial velocity. Suppose the pendulum had been started at

time t_0, and that it is hit at the points of time $t_1, t_2 \dots t_n$ by shocks which may be directed either in the positive or negative sense and that may have arbitrary strengths.... The essential thing to notice is that at the point of time t_k the only thing that happens is that the velocity is increased by a constant e_k. . . . In other words, the fact of the shock may simply be represented by letting the original pendulum move on undisturbed but by letting a new pendulum start at the point of time t_k with an ordinate equal to zero and a velocity equal to e_k. [Frisch 1933, pp. 30–1]

Thus, the solution of the shocked system is the sum of three components, each with weights: Basically, the first is a trend component (associated with the first-order term of the equation), the second is a damped sine-wave component or oscillatory component (associated with the second-order derivative), and the third is a cumulation-of-shock term, a summing or smoothing of the random errors. The weight operator for this last term *"will simply be given by the shape of the time curve that would have been the solution of the deterministic dynamic system in case the movement had been allowed to go on undisturbed"* (p. 31, italics in original).

Frisch had thus untangled the ideas of trend, cycle, and fluctuation in economic time series and had shown how one could develop models to represent such series. He had produced a systematic framework for examining notions of equilibrium and stability in dynamic models of the economy. However, the mathematical notation he used was specific to the business cycle problem, and his definitions and discriminations were likewise problem-specific.

The Frisch taxonomy was developed in a business cycle framework. As Mary Morgan argues in her history of econometrics (Morgan 1990), Frisch was concerned with "the following problem: what should a model look like which accounts not only for cycles in economic variables but does so in a way that can be reconciled with observed economic data?" The context for Frisch's work was, in fact, more from the data side than from concern with theoretical puzzles like the meanings of "equilibrium" and "stability." Frisch had, all through the 1920s and early 1930s, written about and studied time-series problems. His belief that such series, because of the mutual interactions among the variables, their confluence, as he called it, made least-squares estimation problematic led him to different approaches to the study of time series. His work on "bunch maps" was his attempt to solve those problems. His theoretical studies themselves came from his conceptualization of time series as overlays of many different component cycles. Morgan shows that, for Frisch,

the economic system has its own path (consisting in his model of the combination of three damped, but *fixed,* component cycles) which provide a set of weights. This acts as a linear operator on the random shocks in a cumulative fashion to produce a combination of *changing* component cycles like those he had observed in real economic variables. [Morgan 1990, p. 96]

Put another way, Frisch's theoretical analysis of dynamics emerged from the issues of time-series analysis, specifically the problem of linking empirical work with the theory of endogenous business cycles. The work was sophisticated in its treatment of dynamics. The subject was conceptually complex because it concerned process and intertemporal linkages of many economic variables, with those variables conceptualized temporally to allow the theory to build in time organically. For instance, the three variables used by Frisch in his paper were "consumption," "capital starting," and "carry-on activity." These stabilized the field of inquiry in a particular fashion; they created the intrinsic dynamics as process. There is little in "income" and "consumption" and "investment" that is dynamic in the usual macroeconomic theory. Investment, supposedly forward-looking in the theory of Keynes, is modeled as a short-run income flow: In the usual IS-LM picture the variables are undated and static. That the business cycle literature of the 1930s was a literature of process, not a literature of fixity and magnitude, is often forgotten.[11]

This having been said, it is worth noting that there is a tension in Frisch's writing on dynamics based on the alternate conceptual worlds he inhabited. The pendulum is not a process, but a closed mechanical device. The time series of economics are thought of as closed pendulum systems at a cost, and that cost is a certain coherence of metaphor and model. The econometric approach of process and the physical approach of mechanics are combined in Frisch in the interplay among the various cycles, the ideas of trends and cycles and shocks.[12]

Mary Morgan has suggested that the econometric program associated with the Frisch conceptualization was submerged by the probabilistic "revolution" ushered in by Haavelmo's work and that it is a mistake to read the Frisch time-series papers as being of a piece with modern time-series analysis (Morgan 1987). I am suggesting that the same situation obtains with respect to Frisch's theorizing about dynamics. That the stability literature, as it developed in Samuelson's work and in the literature based on the *Foundations,* did not necessarily concern business cycles is rarely mentioned. But the Frisch concern with untangling the systematic from the accidental, trend from cycle, was a long way from the issues associated with market problems like the nature and robustness of particular price–quantity configurations. Again, the desire on the part of later writers to see Frisch as leading to Samuelson, because Samuelson used the Frisch work in his own analysis, forced the past to look more like the present.

Paul Samuelson (1987) recently insisted that the only sensible way to read past economic writings is as early manifestations of the current understanding of economics. I suggest that one of his colleagues at the Massachusetts Institute of Technology is nearer the mark in suggesting that first, there are many ways to read a text, and the ways most accessible to a modern are often inappropriate when applied to the past. Second, that plasticity of texts does not place all ways of reading on a par.... I offer [students] a maxim: When reading the works of an important thinker, look first for the apparent absurdities in the text and ask yourself how a sensible person could have written them. When you find an answer...you may find that more central passages, ones you previously thought you had understood, have changed their meaning. [Kuhn 1977, p. xii]

Jan Tinbergen

Mary Morgan's historical studies (1987, 1990) suggest that a number of elements in process-type analysis of business cycles are obscured by Keynesian macrodynamics. Macroeconomics, rooted in a general equilibrium framework, cannot easily pose the various dynamic problems associated with statistical analysis of business cycles. Even more clearly than in the case of Frisch this can be seen in the work of Jan Tinbergen. For this Dutch scholar there was a consistent intertwining of the ideas of dynamics, equilibrium, and econometrics. As an exemplar of Tinbergen's views on the issues of dynamics and his understanding of the problems, consider his 1935 *Econometrica* paper "Annual Survey: Suggestions on Quantitative Business Cycle Theory" (cited by Samuelson in his discussion of dynamic issues in the *Foundations*).

The paper is simple, in one respect. Tinbergen asserts, early on, that he is adopting the distinctions Frisch introduced regarding the meanings of "statics" and "dynamics": "a theory [is] being called 'dynamic' when variables relating to different moments appear in one equation" (Tinbergen 1935, p. 241). It is a bit unsettling to realize that for Tinbergen, dynamic analysis is already preassumed to be mathematical analysis, as there is no prior mention, in the article, of mathematics or equations. For Tinbergen, the mathematical understanding of dynamics is the only understanding of dynamics. For Tinbergen, the only really significant issue is the untangling of the problems associated with different dynamic notions. He needs to distinguish between mechanisms and exterior influences and between the propagation and impulse problems that concerned Frisch.[13]

And it "is also important to distinguish between the *mathematical form* of the mechanism, i.e. of the equations defining it, and the *economic sense* of those equations" (p. 242, italics in original). That is, "the mathematical form determines the nature of all possible movements, the economic sense being of no importance here" (p. 242). Hence, the mathematics can provide an array of possible solutions to a well-posed problem, but only some among those solutions will be economically meaningful. Any solution to a dynamic equation, any solution of difference, differential, or mixed differential-difference equations, defines a path or motion.

Tinbergen seems to be asserting that prior information about paths is not relevant to the mathematician, but is crucial to the economist in selecting certain motions and calling them economically meaningful equilibria.

This disjunction between his view of the role of mathematics and the role of the economist in a real analysis was perhaps shaped by his own background, for he was trained as a physicist. He had received his doctorate in 1929, and he recalled that "I liked physics and mathematics very much and I also felt that was the thing I was perhaps strongest at, but at the same time I had already come to the conviction that [being a socialist and a member of the Socialist Party] I could probably be more useful to society by being an economist" (Tinbergen 1987, pp. 118–19). That doctorate had been earned as a student of the distinguished physicist Paul Ehrenfest, who had been doing brilliant work in statistical mechanics. As Chakravarty (1987, p. 653) notes, "Ehrenfest was influential in directing Tinbergen's attention to mathematical formulations of economic problems and Tinbergen's dissertation dealt with minimum problems in physics and economics."

That view shaped his paper. The second section, called "The Facts," sets out a variety of dynamic considerations, relationships among economic concepts and categories, that can be used to structure the analysis of a dynamic equation or a set of equations. And lest it be forgotten, Tinbergen is interested primarily in statistical models of the business cycle, and so he is especially concerned with magnitudes of influence, correlated movements of variables together. He pays attention to the idea that some variables move before other variables, that causes and leads and lags are relevant to any explanatory theory, a view fairly standard at that time in the United States, a view associated with Wesley Claire Mitchell. For Tinbergen, the role of the dynamic theories is to allow comprehension of the process, of the system's behavior over time and in time.

The third section of the paper is an interesting attempt to provide a mathematical dynamic system to interpret the mechanisms of the "recent theories" of such traditional theorists as Hayek and Keynes and the more mathematical theorists like Kalecki, Frisch, and Roos. Tinbergen uses the ideas of these authors, as well as the dynamic "facts of economic life" set out in his preceding section, as building blocks for relatively formal dynamic systems of equations. For example, in treating Kalecki, whose ideas were themselves presented mathematically, Tinbergen notes that the argument leads to a

mixed difference and differential equation. Kalecki shows that one of the components which this system may show – and the one which is economically the most important – is a periodic movement with a period which, assuming realistic values for the constants, turns out to be 10 years. [Tinbergen 1935, p. 269]

The Tinbergen program was rooted in the statistical analysis of economic behavior, "process analysis," as it was then termed. Such analysis required that the economic data be realized as points on economically meaningful paths or motions of the system, where the system had to be structured as a set of equations relating the relevant economic variables. Dynamics, for Tinbergen, was associated with mathematical theory, as the nature of economic data, in time, required theories to be dynamic, to be presented generally as dynamic systems. Tinbergen's training in physics may have determined his perceptions and understandings of these issues, but the fact is clear that for Tinbergen, a dynamic theory was a mathematical theory based in mathematical physics, and the language of dynamic systems was the appropriate language in which to frame the economic problems.

Of course, that language had to be supplemented with real economic understanding at two points. First, the system itself was to be constructed from the building blocks suggested by the "facts" of dynamic economic life (e.g., the decision to produce precedes the output of the production process). Second, when a suitable mathematical equation was found and used to model the problematic phenomena, only one, or a small number, of the many paths or solutions to the equation would be economically meaningful; it was the economist's problem to use economic theory to elicit the appropriate solutions from the model. For example, each of the possibly infinite number of eigenvalues of a mixed differential-difference equation corresponds to a particular frequency and thus a cycle length, but only some of those cycle lengths make economic sense.

The Tinbergen survey thus helps define one component of a status quo ante for understanding dynamic theory, where the ante is "before Samuelson." If Robbins was mathematically unsophisticated, some others were not. Frisch was concerned with reconstructing realistic time paths of economic variables statistically, as was Tinbergen. The latter, however, was embedding his concern within the larger issues of business cycle research, enabled by his training in physics, particularly statistical mechanics. "Dynamics" and "equilibrium" meant different things to Robbins and Frisch and Tinbergen. But this point may be more clearly recognized by considering Keynes.

Keynes: statics and dynamics

That the 1930s contested "equilibrium" and "dynamics" is nowhere clearer than in the subsequent disputes over the nature and meaning of Keynes's *The General Theory of Employment, Interest, and Money* (1936). The exegetical literature is immense, and it was only partly as a joke that in an earlier book I presented a model of that theory as "the 4,827th reexamination of Keynes's system" (Weintraub 1979). In keeping with the emphasis on the study of history as a hermeneutical, not discovery, activity, I want now to raise a linked set of issues regarding Keynesian theory, though I shall not pretend to settle any of them.

The usual American "Keynes" is reconstructed out of Hicks's SI-LL (or IS-LM) presentation, as simplified by the later Modigliani model, and refurbished thereafter by Patinkin; this is all supplemented by a student version associated with Samuelson's elementary textbook and the 45° line. In this reconstruction, Keynes's theory is static, not dynamic. From such a view, one of the historical problems, or rather one of the problems for the historian of economic thought, becomes the "shift" in Keynes's views between the *Treatise on Money* (1930) and the *General Theory,* for it is generally argued that the *Treatise* is a book in the business cycle tradition of argumentation about the connections, in a temporal process analysis, among various real and monetary variables. At that time the links were through the different versions of the quantity theory of money. Why, it is asked by some Keynesians, did Keynes find the process theory of 1930 inadequate, and why did he move to the theory of the 1936 book? This inquiry is associated with the idea that Keynes, in his genius, left a bad tradition for a new theory of his own creation, so the interpretive issue is one of discovery, or knowledge growth, or creativity. There is thus a large literature that attempts to date Keynes's "awakening" somewhere between 1931 and 1935.

For some other scholars, however, the issue is different. Finding the *General Theory* of the IS-LM reconstruction objectionable, or politically anathema, Keynes is conceptualized as Shackle, or as Robinson, or, the post-Keynesians would suggest, as a theorist concerned with time and expectations and other dynamic issues as set out in his 1937 restatement of his theory. The historical problem for these writers, then, is to suggest that there was no break between the *Treatise* and the *General Theory,* but rather a suppression of some of the dynamic components of the former in the exposition of the latter, purely for convenience.

The text of *The General Theory of Employment, Interest, and Money* remains unstable, contested, and problematic. I have no superior wisdom to share on this issue directly, but I would like to suggest that the unsettled nature of Keynesian theory, historically considered, is linked to the issues I have been considering here, particularly the transmogrification of the 1930s "conversation" about statics and dynamics and equilibrium by the instrumentality of mathematical systems theory as it was introduced by Samuelson in the *Foundations.*

To suggest this point is easier than to argue it fully: I would need another book to unpack the contests over the meaning of Keynesian theory. Here I shall simply indicate how such an argument might proceed.

Keynes wrote, in his Chapter 18 of the *General Theory* ("The General Theory of Employment Restated"), that

thus our four conditions together are adequate to explain the outstanding features of our actual experience; – namely that we oscillate, avoiding the gravest extremes of fluctuation in employment and in prices in both directions, round an intermediate position appreciably below full employment and appreciably above the minimum employment a decline below which would endanger life. [p. 254]

The four conditions are called "stability conditions" and include, for example, the following:

(i) The marginal propensity to consume is such that, when the output of a given community increases (or decreases) because more (or less) employment is being applied to its capital equipment, the multiplier relating the two is greater than unity but not very large. [p. 250]

This language of oscillation, fluctuation, above and below, increase and decrease, stability, and equilibrium as intermediate position is striking. We have here a set of terms that require interpretation. A modern reader simply uses the systems model and asks whether the marginal propensity to consume being less than 1 is a stability condition for the "true underlying dynamic model." The first modern reader was, of course, Paul Samuelson, who constructed exactly that model in the *Foundations,* in the section "Analysis of the Keynesian System" (pp. 276–83). Or consider the following well-known passage (p. 257):

It would have been an advantage if the effects of a change in money-wages could have been discussed in an earlier chapter. For the classical theory has been accustomed to rest the supposedly self-adjusting character of the economic system on an assumed fluidity of money-wages; and when there is rigidity, to lay on this rigidity the blame of maladjustment.

Interpreting this passage, or at least its implicit understanding of movement and change, we have a counterposition between the "classical" notion that the system, or the economy, was self-adjusting in the sense that if it were not to be in a Marshallian equilibrium, it would soon become so if money wages were to be "fluid" or able to move. To this Keynes suggests, in the remainder of the chapter called "Changes in Money-Wages," that movements in money wages have a variety of effects, and those effects are not necessarily associated with increases or decreases in employment, so that self-adjustment to positions of full employment of labor is not necessarily connected to the nonrigidity of money wages.

The modern systems reconstruction of this argument, the neo-Walrasian or neoclassical reconstruction, is in terms of a static equilibrium model of several equations (IS-LM) and a comparative statics argument first constituted by Don Patinkin in his *Money, Interest, and Prices* (1965). That line of approach held that the Keynesian argument had to be interpreted as pertaining to disequilibrium, or dynamic adjustment, because the static framework simply could not produce the less-than-full-employment position. Keynes has been interpreted, has been read, on this view as having a dynamic idea embedded in a static conception.

I am not suggesting that this reading of Keynes is wrong or right. *I am suggesting that this reading interprets and reconstructs in the same way that every reading of a text is an interpretation, a reconstruction.* The point goes to the heart of the Keynesian theory disputations. The construction of texts is always in context, and the context in which a modern economist-reader reads is one shaped by the economic world of Samuelson's *Foundations.* Keynes's dynamics, statics, stability, and equilibrium are difficult to recontextualize apart from the dynamic systems vision introduced to economists in the 1940s. Historical reconstructions, like that of Axel Leijonhufvud, that locate Keynes's theorizing about equilibrium in a Marshallian context thus have much to recommend them; they stabilize the text by linking it to earlier texts, not later ones.

If Keynes's dynamics can be reconstructed from Marshallian concerns and his personal intellectual development, and if Frisch's dynamics were associated with the generation of "realistic" time paths of economic variables, and if Tinbergen's dynamics was associated with his training in physics and his interest in econometric approaches to the business cycle literature, what can we make of the claim that the pre-Samuelson literature on dynamics and equilibrium "led" anywhere in particular? Specifically, it is part of the folklore of the history of dynamics that this literature led to Hicks's *Value and Capital,* which was then "done right" by Samuelson. Because I intend to address this reconstruction directly, let me turn now to Hicks's approach to these issues.

Hicks and dynamics

One of the major sources cited by Samuelson in his treatment of dynamics and stability was John R. Hicks's *Value and Capital* (1939). But in contrast to Frisch and Tinbergen, Hicks came to dynamics from economics. As one of his autobiographical pieces noted, he had had some mathematical training before going to Oxford, and in his first year at Oxford he took more mathematics, but

I took P.P.E. [the honors degree in politics, philosophy, and economics] in the second year of its existence, when the necessary teaching was far from having taken shape. My tutor was a military historian, who had no interest in the subject.... I turned to economics after I had taken my degree, through a fortunate contact I had with Graham Wallas, and through him with LSE [London School of Economics]. [Hicks 1977, p. 134]

In 1926, the first of Hicks's LSE years, Hugh Dalton "said to me 'you read Italian, you ought to read Pareto.' So it was reading the *Manuale* which started me off on economic theory. I was deep in Pareto before I got much out of Marshall" (Hicks 1984, p. 282). As a result of that, when Robbins came to take up his post at LSE in 1929, Hicks was asked to lecture on general equilibrium theory. Hicks shared the point of view of the Robbins men:

> The faith in question was a belief in the free market, or "price-mechanism" – that a competitive system, free of all "interferences," by government or by monopolistic combinations, of capital or of labour, would easily find an "equilibrium.". . . Hayek, when he joined us, was to introduce into this doctrine an important qualification – that money must be kept "neutral" in order that the mechanism should work smoothly. [Hicks 1982, p. 3]

The other major area of Hicks's interest at that time was "risk," and through the alliance, more real than imagined, among LSE, Chicago, and Vienna, he began to lecture on risk in 1929 using Frank Knight's book.

The progression of Hicks's thinking that led to *Value and Capital* has been traced by Hicks several times, but the best place is probably in the essay "LSE and the Robbins Circle." The starting place for Hicks's work was the model of Hayek, for

> I remember Robbins asking me if I could turn the Hayek model into mathematics. . . . I couldn't do it. . . . It was claimed that, if there were no monetary disturbances, the system would remain in "equilibrium." What could such an equilibrium mean? . . . The [Pareto and Wicksell] equilibrium was a static equilibrium in which neither prices nor outputs were changing [while the Hayek] "equilibrium" must be a progressive equilibrium, in which real wages, in particular, would be rising. . . . The next step, in my thinking, was to pick up a hint that I had found in Knight – equilibrium with perfect foresight. [Hicks 1982, p. 6]

Thus, Hicks noted that equilibrium, in a world of intertemporal choice, required that expectations never be disappointed, so perfect foresight was required. That meant that if people were not omniscient, there was no place for neutral money; Hicks had taken a major step away from Hayek as a result. That kind of view led Hicks to a portfolio theory of money, presented in his "Suggestion for Simplifying the Theory of Money," read in 1934 and published in 1935, a paper that Keynes noted was similar to the liquidity preference notions of his soon-to-be-published *General Theory*.

But the other main line of development for Hicks was through the Swedish economists. Hicks had reviewed the German version of Myrdahl's book, and that review appeared in 1934. Further, Lindahl was in London in the summer of 1934, and again in 1935, and Hicks had direct contact with that father of social-accounting theory and, through him, the ideas of the other Swedish economists (Hicks 1977, p. 143). Hicks tried to discuss, in his review of Myrdahl, the introduction of expectations as explicit variables in a formal equilibrium theory (Hicks 1977, note 11). The problem was beginning to define itself as follows: In a static general equilibrium model there are n markets and n prices for the various goods. Because by Walras's law one of those market equilibrium conditions is redundant, there are $n-1$ market-clearing equations to solve for the n prices, so that $n-1$ relative prices can be determined. But when the future is introduced, because the future expected prices may influence today's markets, there are n additional expected prices as variables, for each of m periods, so there are mn additional variables, but no more equations. The system will be in equilibrium if the expectations are equivalent to perfect foresight, so that relative prices remain constant. With money, or uncertainty, this cannot happen:

One can then show, straight off, as I think I did show, that the use of money is enough in itself to make a free market system potentially unstable; and that the higher the degree of development, or sophistication, that it exhibits the greater does the degree of instability become. [Hicks 1982, p. 9]

The problem was the way in which expected prices, one for each good for each period, could be linked to the market supplies and demands for that first period in which the agents made their intertemporal plans. That, of course, led to the idea of temporary equilibrium in the 1939 *Value and Capital* and was the focus of the work Hicks was doing all through the middle and late 1930s. That also made it possible for him to be sympathetic to the Keynes of *The General Theory of Employment, Interest, and Money* (1936), for the message of the lack of automatic market adjustments back to equilibrium, in a monetary economy, was a message that Hicks had already adopted and passed on, through his having had to come to terms with, and reject, the *Prices and Production* (1931) model of Hayek.

Hicks, then, was grappling with the meaning of equilibrium from early in the 1930s. He believed that the nature of equilibrium in a monetary economy was problematic if it was associated with market clearing in what was then the usual way of modeling a market by an equation of supply with demand. Hicks was thus forced, by that kind of thinking of balance, to ask about the ways that a balance could fail to be achieved or, in his thinking, the ways in which the system could fail to be in, or fail to reach, equilibrium. That language led Hicks to the language of stability, because the Hayekian and Wicksellian stories that the models were supposed to tell or cast light on were stories of "real" markets subject to monetary disturbances. That introduced the language and metaphors of equilibria being stable or unstable into a problem context in which the shocked system either did or did not return to equilibrium. As Hicks looked back on that period of writing, he spoke in exactly those terms:

Monetary institutions... can then be introduced as a means of checking, or moderating, the instability. When they are introduced in this way... one can see that they are imperfect safeguards against instability, and are themselves liable to be infected by it. [Hicks 1982, p. 9]

Hicks, in framing the problem in that way, was explicit about what dynamics was concerned with; he was contemporaneously aware of Frisch's definition of dynamics as presented in the 1933 paper. He noted that according to that definition, "Hayek's model does engender a [dynamic] process; some kind of lag (or lags) must therefore be implicit in it" (Hicks 1967, p. 207). That, for Hicks, was always the meaning, in economics, of dynamic theory:

The essays I have chosen for this second volume are those concerned with what used to be called *economic dynamics*. I do not nowadays care for that description, since the mechanical analogy is not one which I would care to emphasise. And it seems to have gone out of fashion. Its place has been taken by *macro-economics*. [Hicks 1982, p. xi]

Money is important in a world of uncertain tomorrows and expectations based on the present and the past, but not held with certainty. This leads to potential "instability" or failure to achieve equilibrium of full employment of resources, including labor. Dynamics is thus a feature of macrotheorizing in the Keynesian sense, whereas neutral money features in static, or classical, or nonmonetary general equilibrium models of the economic system, a non-process-oriented system out of time.

To a modern reader, this last set of arguments is clear, for its clarity is that of *Value and Capital*. We are comfortable with such an argument to the degree that we are living in a conceptualized economy created, at least in part, by Hicks. Is this not why Nobel Prizes in economics are awarded? But what is a bit less clear is the way in which the mathematics that Hicks used structured his argument in certain ways and constrained him to ask certain questions and to accept certain features of the problem situation as salient, while characterizing and then rejecting others (no less significant in the economics) as uninteresting. To argue this case, I must reconstruct the Hicksian mathematics, for the techniques are themselves suggestive of the underlying thought processes in ways that may lead us to say that Hicks's post hoc recollections are potentially misleading documents of intellectual history.

Hicks's mathematics

There are two primary sources for examining the mathematics that Hicks used in creating his equilibrium and stability theories. The first is the monograph *Théorie mathématique de la valeur en régime de libre concurrence,* published in 1937; the second is *Value and Capital,* published in 1939. The mathematical appendixes of the latter were essentially the text of the former, though *Théorie mathématique* used all statements of the analyses in elasticity terms, whereas *Value and Capital* used the variables and their derivatives and partial derivatives instead. The latter was thus more mathematical in the sense of mathematical theorems, though it would appear that Hicks was more of an economist and tended to think in elasticity terms. In fact, the major solution to the temporary equilibrium problem adumbrated in the last parts of *Value and Capital* consisted in the creation of the elasticity of expectations, no doubt attempted as a solution because of the success Hicks had had in his *Theory of Wages* with the new definition of the elasticity of substitution.

In ordinary language, Hicks posed the problem as follows:

What do we mean by stability in multiple exchange? Clearly, as before, that a fall in price of X in terms of the standard commodity will make the demand for X greater than the supply.... i) Granted that the market for X is stable, taken by itself (that is to say, a fall in the price of X will raise the excess demand for X, all other prices being given), can it be rendered unstable by reactions through the markets for other commodities? ii) Supposing that the market for X is unstable, taken by itself, can it be made stable by reactions through other markets? [Hicks 1939, pp. 66–7]

The appendixes to the chapters on exchange give that, for commodity r, where X_r is demand and $\bar{X}_r$ is the fixed amount to be exchanged, then "if the system is to be in equilibrium, the demand for every commodity must equal the supply. [Therefore] $X_r = \bar{X}_r$ $(r = 1, 2, 3, \ldots, n)$" (p. 314). And

since $\bar{X}_r$ can be taken as constant, the conditions for stability of exchange can be got by examining the sign of dX_r/dp_r. In order for equilibrium to be perfectly stable, dX_r/dp_r must be negative (1) when all other prices are unchanged; (2) when p_s is adjusted so as to maintain equilibrium in the market for x_s, but all other prices are unchanged; (3) when p_s and p_t are similarly adjusted, and so on, until we have adjusted all prices, excepting p_r (and of course p_n, which is necessarily 1). [p. 315]

The stability conditions, in Hicks's words, take the form

$$
\left| \frac{\delta X_r}{\delta p_r} \right| \quad
\begin{vmatrix} \dfrac{\delta X_r}{\delta p_r} & \dfrac{\delta X_r}{\delta p_s} \\[2ex] \dfrac{\delta X_s}{\delta p_r} & \dfrac{\delta X_s}{\delta p_s} \end{vmatrix} \quad
\begin{vmatrix} \dfrac{\delta X_r}{\delta p_r} & \dfrac{\delta X_r}{\delta p_s} & \dfrac{\delta X_r}{\delta p_t} \\[2ex] \dfrac{\delta X_s}{\delta p_r} & \dfrac{\delta X_s}{\delta p_s} & \dfrac{\delta X_s}{\delta p_t} \\[2ex] \dfrac{\delta X_t}{\delta p_r} & \dfrac{\delta X_t}{\delta p_s} & \dfrac{\delta X_t}{\delta p_t} \end{vmatrix}
$$

which are Jacobian determinants, or determinants of the principal minors of the Jacobian matrix of the first-order conditions, or equilibrium conditions. The stability condition is that these minors have determinants that alternate in sign. This is, of course, well known now and then to be simply the statement that the Jacobian matrix is negative definite as a quadratic form, and this is associated with the fact that the equilibrium is a maximum.[14] Thus, the stability conditions are equivalent to the proposition that the consumer is maximizing utility at an exchange equilibrium. This is made explicit early in the appendix:

In order that u should be a true maximum it is necessary to have not only that $du = 0$... but also that $d^2u < 0$. Expanding these expressions, and writing u_{rs} for the second partial derivative, as u_r for the first, we have

$$du = \sum_{r=1}^{r=n} u_r dx_r,$$

$$d^2u = \sum_{r=1}^{r=n} \sum_{s=1}^{s=n} u_{rs} dx_r dx_s.$$

This latter expression is a quadratic form... consequently the conditions for $d^2u < 0$ for all values of $dx_1, dx_2, ..., dx_n$, such that $du = 0$ are that the determinants... should be alternatively negative and positive. [p. 306]

Now Hicks, to be sure, is primarily interested in certain economic arguments, chief among them the characterization of the demand relationships; he is thus primarily interested in the implications, for the behavioral characterization, of the *assumption* that there is a stable equilibrium.[15] That is, if there is a stable equilibrium, in the sense he uses the phrase, then the substitution matrix (associated with the Jacobian matrix noted earlier) must have certain properties, and those properties can be interpreted behaviorally.

It is thus a remarkable feature of Hicks's argument that calling his system "stable" is fundamentally irrelevant to his argument: His results flow directly only from the first- and second-order conditions that there be a utility maximum in the case of the consumer. This result carries through to the exchange case without any modification (pp. 314–19) in the mode of argument. In the case of a firm, the argument simply goes to net income maximization; the same second-order conditions are used, and there again they are called stability conditions. In the general equilibrium case for production and exchange, Hicks reduces the problem to the two previous cases of exchange and the firm and argues, after suggesting that all previous results must continue to hold, that

consequently the further analysis of the general equilibrium of production is identical with that of the general equilibrium of exchange; and all of the propositions... can be reinterpreted in a wider sense. [p. 325]

This line of argument is important, so it is well to paraphrase it so that we do not lose sight of what is at issue: (1) The agent is in equilibrium. (2) In equilibrium, certain relationships must hold, else the meaning of equilibrium is unclear. (3) If the agent is maximizing (utility or profit, etc.), then a position away from equilibrium is intolerable, and there are forces set in motion to return the position to one of equilibrium. (4) A stable equilibrium is one in which there is a tendency for small displacements from the equilibrium position to be counteracted by movements back to equilibrium. (5) Thus, stability analysis is linked to maximization conditions, for it is the idea of maximization that, for Hicks, sets up a tension that the system must resolve by a return to the equilibrium state.

Ultimately there was no need for Hicks ever to have used the language of stability, for he only specified, in his mathematics, the characteristics of the equilibrium position itself, namely, that it was a position behaviorally defined by the agents' maximizing behaviors. Formally, Hicks's use of the Jacobian meant that the underlying dynamic system that the mathematics induced was associated with a symmetric matrix. Because such matrices have real eigenvalues, the stability theory of the related dynamic system is trivial indeed to establish. It was the general case that was problematic. Stability, in the mathematical literature, was well defined as a characteristic of dynamic systems in the sense that the language of stability–instability implied the presence of a process relating the laws of motion of the system, how states of the system changed or evolved, to particular states or motions of the system called equilibrium states or motions. Stability, in that literature, was associated with a relationship between a particular state and other nearby states, where that relationship was defined by the dynamic laws that governed the transformation from state to state. *For Hicks, stability was process-independent; the formal analysis (as opposed to the verbal exposition) was entirely concerned with the character of equilibrium positions.*

This set of observations is connected to the curious separation between Hicks and the later stability literature, a discontinuity seldom understood by neo-Walrasian theorists. But recall that Hicks was at Cambridge from 1935 to 1938, and it was during that time that he wrote *Value and Capital,* a "systematisation of the work I had done at LSE.... My own dynamic model...owes much more to what I had got from the Swedes, from Myrdahl and Lindahl [than it did to Keynes]" (Hicks 1984, p. 286). Hicks moved on to other concerns, during the war years, particularly to social accounting; but *Value and Capital* had gone out to the rest of the English-speaking world not yet involved in the war that had come to England in 1939. The book got distributed throughout the world before the War broke out. But I was there-after cut off from the reactions that were forming to it; it was only after the War that I found out what had been happening. [A footnote continues the remark by noting that] Years after, when visiting Japan, I was assured that my book had been a set book at Kyoto University since 1943. I was astonished, and asked them how it could have been possible for them to get copies. They said that until De-cember 1941 they could import through America; and then, they said, we cap-tured some in Singapore! [Hicks 1984, p. 287]

Though Hicks's *Value and Capital* was frequently cited in the literature on stability that developed in the 1940s and 1950s, Hicks himself, as indi-cated, was uninterested in those issues. Not only was his interest different, he was profoundly unsympathetic to the way the literature was developing:

[In America in 1946] at Cambridge I met Samuelson; in New York I met Arrow; and at Chicago Milton Friedman and Don Patinkin. I did not know them, but they knew me; for I was the author of *Value and Capital* which...was deeply influencing their work.... But I am afraid I disappointed them, and have con-tinued to disappoint them. Their achievements have been great; but they are not in my line. I have felt little sympathy with the theory for the theory's sake, which has been characteristic of one strand in American economics...and I have little faith in econometrics on which they have so largely relied to make their contact with reality. [Hicks 1984, p. 287]

Hicks was not a participant in the developing literature, following Sam-uelson, on stability and dynamics, despite his thinking of his own work as dynamic. Hicks was interested in capital theory and that kind of dy-namics in a generic sense of intertemporality. That the ideas that Hicks introduced into economics, or that were taken by Samuelson and others as Hicks's contributions, were different from those ideas that Hicks him-self believed to be important is not such an unusual happenstance in sci-ence. The point is rather that two related sets of ideas were present in *Value and Capital* concerning equilibrium and stability. First, there was the general idea of intertemporal coherence. Second, there was the idea of a return to a market-clearing position of equilibrium. It was this latter notion that was formalized mathematically, although it was the former notion that gave the idea its power in economic argumentation. But the mathematical form allowed the ideas to be stabilized as the mathematics was refined and developed. We see that from Hicks there was a bifurca-tion of the dynamics literature into two separate lines, lines that were not to be even partially reintegrated until the 1960s: The two lines concerned (1) the stability of a competitive equilibrium and (2) growth dynamics and capital theory. Samuelson's unpacking of the Hicksian stability analysis by using both the Frisch taxonomic guidelines and the mathematical struc-ture of what was in fact Liapunov stability theory of dissipative dynamic systems emphasized the former at the expense of the latter, and it was that move that influenced the subsequent literature. What has been less well understood is the way that that move "changed" the earlier literature also, as the texts, such as *Value and Capital,* increasingly came to be understood as precursors, or imperfect attempts to get it right, or near misses, or confused nonmathematical ramblings.

Problems and reading lessons

One story that is suggested by my reading concerns the interplay between alternative conceptualizations of the economy and alternative formalizations of that economy's representations. How, in other words, does the "economy" provide a context for reading about the theoretical structures that "model" that economy?

> ...within the negotiation of meanings that turn individual proposals into intersubjective realities, we find ambient nature passively constraining possible meanings through active experience that is inseparable from the language use.... Similar constraining processes occur in all discourse communities.... Various discourse communities appeal to various kinds of experience as touchstones for their negotiations of communal meaning.... Science, however, has taken empirical experience as its major touchstone, so that in the process of negotiation of meaning, empirical experience not only constrains the range of possible meanings but is actively sought in the attempt to establish stable meanings from the negotiation. [Bazerman 1988, p. 312]

I have suggested that alternative visions of the economy shaped the conceptual worlds of Frisch, Tinbergen, and Hicks. As a consequence, reading Hicks, say, from the world-picture we have inherited from Samuelson's *Foundations* is not wrong, nor is it necessarily misleading, for it leads somewhere, and no "where" is specially privileged.

What I have presented here is a set of questions, problems really, for the historiography of economic thought. Meaning does not reside in texts, not is it to be found. Meaning is provided by readers who come to a text with histories of their own, both personal and social. How is it possible to read texts without interpreting them? It should not be contentious to assert that the reader of Samuelson's *Foundations* is presented with at least two ways to reconstruct the 1930s papers. Either the earlier literature was diverse, diffuse, and different from what was to emerge in the post-*Foundations* period, or it was a coherent line that was to lead to the overarching conception of dynamic theory presented in the *Foundations.* If the former was the case, then that dynamic theory is not fundamentally coherent, in that the conceptual streams it merged were not necessarily consistent, and so one should in fact expect that a variety of tensions remain unresolved by the new formalism. One such "problem" might be the fracture of dynamic analysis into multimarket stability theory and capital theory, and the loss of endogenous business cycle theory.

Alternatively, if the earlier literature was coherent and was a stepping-stone to the *Foundations,* then Samuelson's work itself should have permitted all of the past concerns to be represented in the later literature. That such was manifestly not to be is the strongest case that can be made for reading the pre-*Foundations* work as complex and diverse and for seeing the dynamic theory set out in the *Foundations* as a rich, rambling, and necessarily imposed structure, one that created orderliness out of the writings in the disorderly past.

CHAPTER 3

The foundations of Samuelson's dynamics

The origins of a work like Samuelson's *Foundations of Economic Analysis* (1947) are of some interest, beyond a search for precursors, for the light they can shed on problems that the work raises; some problems of the later literature that grew out of the work are otherwise obscure without a reader's comprehension of the context of the original contribution. The *Foundations,* which set out the issues of statics and dynamics and equilibrium in economic theory, creates some special concerns. For example, the theory of stability of economic equilibria appears to have been generated by that work, but the line of such work had thinned out by the late 1950s. In terms created by the philosopher Imre Lakatos, the sequence of papers on the stability of a competitive equilibrium might be considered a scientific research program that was progressive during the 1940s and early 1950s, but degenerated after that time. If so, then a reexamination of the prehardened state of the program, before Samuelson's *Foundations,* might suggest the reasons for the degeneration. Alternatively, certain features of the theory set out in the *Foundations,* particularly its mathematical structure, have shaped the ways in which economists and their audiences have interpreted experience or created the terms and observations of that experience itself. Is unemployment an equilibrium or disequilibrium phenomenon? This question has implications for policy as well as cognition, but the associations of "equilibrium" and "instability" are, for modern economists, the associations and ways of experiencing that are consistent with the mathematical theory laid out in the *Foundations.* As a consequence, reconstructing the context in which that book was written can aid our understanding of the world it created, a world that in some measure we still inhabit.

I shall argue in what follows that there were two major mathematical streams that nourished the *dynamic* theory outlined in the *Foundations.* One of those streams ran from applied mathematics via biology, and the other flowed more directly from the nineteenth-century mathematics literature, mediated by physics and physical chemistry. Each of those streams directed the course of the argument, and each has created some problems for the modern reader. Additionally, I shall attempt to uncover some less obvious connections, seldom remarked upon, associated with the general

39

resurgence of equilibrium notions in social theory current at the time and place of Samuelson's writing of the *Foundations*.[1] In this chapter I shall identify themes and point out connections.

This is not, however, a study that would argue that Samuelson was influenced either directly or indirectly by one or another person or book or article. Such searches for influence are seldom clear and usually are unconvincing. My own interest is rather more diffuse, and consequently my task is simpler. I seek to locate Samuelson's *Foundations* in some context, to provide a way to read it as continuous with its time and place. What I shall present, then, is a study of how a set of ideas in economics was intertwined with related work in pure and applied mathematics and work being done in other, more "distant" disciplines.

I need to caution the economist-reader, however, that the argument of this chapter is not consistent with the self-construction that Samuelson has put forward over the years of his great fame; his autobiographical treatment of the issues that concern me here hardly mentions the topics that I consider to be important, and his recollections of influence focus on themes I ignore. This is not so unusual as it might seem:

The significance of autobiography should therefore be sought beyond truth and falsity, as these are conceived by simple common sense. It is unquestionably a document about a life, and the historian has a perfect right to check out its testimony and verify its accuracy. But it is also a work of art, and the literary devotee, for his part, will be aware of its stylistic harmony and the beauty of its images. . . . We may call it fiction or fraud, but its artistic value is real: there is a truth affirmed beyond the fraudulent itinerary and chronology, a truth of the man, images of himself and of the world, reveries of a man of genius, who, for his own enchantment and that of his readers, realizes himself in the unreal. [Gusdorf 1980, p. 43]

The exemplar of this must certainly be Samuelson's "Economics in My Time" (1986b). This paper is rhetorically remarkable: The posturing and presentation of self as both brash and Olympian are less entertaining than disclosing; the section of most psychological interest begins as follows: "Here briefly, in the third person for objectivity, is a superficial outline of my scientific career" (p. 65). Although such tensions are understood in politics – we know that all presidential candidates were not born in log cabins, no matter what hokum their flacks put out – economists, and the scientists they seek to emulate, more generally present their own histories as *veni, vidi, vici*. It is curious indeed that economists, who are professionally attuned to social blarney ("We can have more defense, lower taxes, and less unemployment with more growth and less inflation if you vote for me, my friends."), should be so gullible about the recollections of senior economists that create the mythic past of the discipline. I am not suggesting that Samuelson was or is a confabulator, nor am I going to argue that his writing (e.g., Samuelson 1972) sets out to reconstruct reality differently from a true reality. Autobiographical truth is a complicated issue:

> The content of an autobiography is not alone sufficient to create truth. What actually transforms content into truth of life is the context that contains the content. By the context I mean the writer's intention to tell the truth; the ratification through the actual choices he makes word by word, as well as in his tone, style, and organization; the assumptions that permeate the book, giving rise to content while overlapping the reader's own sense of lived experience in the world. I would argue that it is the reader's willingness to experience and cocreate this context that allows autobiography to speak the truth. [Mandel 1980, p. 72]

The historian-reader must surely chuckle at this kindergarten reminder that first-person accounts must be read with attention to the way in which the author reconstructs and reinterprets the world. A historian understands from experience, both professional and personal, that the found world is a constructed world and that contemporary accounts are not necessarily more useful for all purposes than later accounts. Because all accounts interpret, the issue is always one of the more or less useful interpretations for the particular purposes of the rhetor.

In what follows, then, I shall develop several contexts in which Samuelson's *Foundations* can be located. My argument is simply that this placement allows the richness of the *Foundations* to be better understood. Before proceeding, however, I must point out that my context reading of the *Foundations* here is based on the simple idea that if Samuelson cited a work in the *Foundations,* then that work can be taken as part of the context of the *Foundations.* This "methodology" places a constraint on my reading.

A. J. Lotka and physical biology

Herbert Simon (1959, p. 493) recalled that "a sect – and by any reasonable definition, mathematical social scientists formed one – needs arcana, as source both of its special wisdom and of passwords by which its members can recognize each other. In the Thirties, a person who had read Lotka's *Elements of Physical Biology* and Richardson's *Generalized Foreign Politics,* and who was acquainted with the peculiar empirical regularities compiled by Zipf, was almost certainly a fellow sectarian." Despite such notice, and despite a more recent discussion by Joel Cohen (1987) in *The New Palgrave,* the fact remains that one of the most curious and generally unnoted relationships in economic literature is between Alfred J. Lotka's *Elements of Physical Biology*[2] and Paul A. Samuelson's *Foundations of Economic Analysis.*

There are, in fact, only three references to Lotka in the Samuelson work, all in the later stages of the book. The first appears in a section on the logistic law, on pages 291–4 in the *Foundations*. The second reference to Lotka, in a footnote on page 309, cites an article by Lotka on applications of certain integral equations to "industrial replacement"; this reference occurs in a digression section titled "Other Functional Equations." The third Lotka reference appears in the section "Stationary States and Their Generalization," in Chapter XI ("Some Fundamentals of Dynamical Theory"), which was mostly reprinted from a 1943 Samuelson article. This last reference is to a method of successive approximations that can be used to solve certain kinds of dynamic market problems. Samuelson notes that his own discussion is "essentially identical with the moving equilibrium of a biological or chemical system undergoing slow changes" (1947, p. 323). The footnote citation of Lotka's book after this sentence simply states that "this [Chapter XXI of the Lotka book] contains numerous references."

Three references to an apparently obscure,[3] and quirky, treatise in biology hardly provide a structure on which to hang a thesis, but I shall suggest, in the pages that follow, that the relationship between the two books is profound and natural. However, it is not my claim that Lotka's book shaped Samuelson's book. Instead, what I shall be arguing is that there is much to be gained by attending to Lotka's book. The detail into which I shall go will measure not the direct importance of any problematical borrowing but rather the context of the literature with which Samuelson was concerned. A detailed reading of Lotka, then, will provide a first look at some themes that will surface repeatedly in the *Foundations*.

The plan of the *Elements of Physical Biology*

Lotka's plan was to provide a new systematization of biological processes, and his approach was self-consciously mathematical. He conceived of physical biology as an overarching framework of ideas, and his Table 1 (p. 53) suggests the systems structure of his conception. Each level, or branch, of the program is associated, in the book, with a set of mathematical ideas, and Lotka presents a set of examples for each idea introduced.

After a study of growth processes based on the simple differential equation

$$dX/dt = aX$$

Lotka considered more complicated equations. He noted that the general form for such processes was

$$dX/dt = a + bX + cX^2 + \cdots$$

which led quickly to attempts to find simple models of this type. Thus, one contribution that Lotka believed he had made was in the identification of the "law of population growth," a theory based on the differential equation

$$dX/dt = aX + bX^2$$

which has as its solution

$$X(t) = (a/b)/[1 + \exp(-at)]$$

which yields the logistic curve. Lotka spent a great deal of energy in the book in finding corroborations, in various data sets, of the "truth" or "validity" of this law, data including the U.S. population, fruit-fly populations, growth of bacterial colonies, and so forth. The insight was a good one, because the differential equation is based on the idea that the growth of a population is associated positively with the level of the population, and growth stops when some absolute limit is reached.[4]

Part 1 of the book is associated, then, with introductory ideas, and the focus is on evolution, which Lotka defines as *"the history of a system undergoing irreversible changes"* (p. 24, italics in original).

Lotka was aiming at a law of evolution that would function in the same way, with the same degree of generality, as the laws of thermodynamics, in particular the second law of thermodynamics.... The law established a single direction for the processes occurring in an isolated system and could therefore be considered a law of evolution. Lotka's understanding of evolution...echoed a discussion of the second law put forth by the physicist Jean Perrin in 1903.... Lotka's "law" of evolution was a restatement of the law of natural selection, expanded to answer the larger question: to what end did natural selection lead with respect to the energy flow of the organic system taken as a whole. [Kingsland 1985, pp. 37–8]

The subject, or program, is presented in terms of the differential equation

$$dX_i/dt = F_i(X_1, X_2, \ldots, X_n; P, Q)$$

Lotka remarks that "the very form of these equations suggests, as the first and most elementary problem, the treatment of the case of evolution under constant conditions, as defined by constant P's and Q's" (p. 51). Thus, for fixed parameters, the system is an autonomous system of first-order equations. Such a system was identified, in economics, with the equations describing the multiple-market system, if the X's are prices and the F's are excess-demand functions. For Lotka, "the *Statics* of evolving systems," or what an economist would call comparative statics, was associated with slowly evolving parameters, slowly changing P's and Q's: "This branch is, in a sense, a special division of the Kinetics of Evolution, namely that which concerns itself with systems in which velocities of transformation [the dX_i/dt in the preceding equation] are zero, so that there is *Equilibrium,* or, to be more exact, a *Steady State*" (p. 51). If *P* and *Q* are fixed, zero velocity is associated with equilibrium, whereas if *P* and *Q* are changing, even slowly, the system's zero velocity, or no change in the state variables, is termed steady-state behavior. These distinctions, of course, are identical with those introduced by Samuelson in the *Foundations* and the earlier articles out of which the *Foundations* grew. For example, page 261 of the *Foundations* reminds us that "stationary or equilibrium values of the variables are given by a set of constants... which satisfy [a set of functional] equations identically." Because the functional equations are dynamic, or time-dependent, they include differential equations like those of Lotka as special cases, and the terminology is directly applicable.[5]

For our interest in economic dynamics, the most important idea, however, is that the underlying model, the framework within which the differential equations are interpreted, is that of *dissipative dynamic systems.* That is, the usual physical systems are conservative in that some quantity, usually energy, is conserved along paths or motions of the system. Lotka points out that these systems are reversible, so that time can be run backward, as it were, to solve for earlier positions of the motions. A physical system to model the motions of the orbiting planets can be solved forward to find a future position of Mars, or backward to find out a previous position. Lotka, as an evolutionary biologist, was concerned to develop classes of mathematical models that were irreversible, that could not be "run backward." The idea of equilibrium for such a system was not that of a periodic motion appropriate to the solar system, nor to similar physical equilibria, but rather to a dissipative system, a sort of solar system with friction, with heat loss, with a unidirectional flow through time. Biological entities die, organisms evolve. For Lotka, the social sciences, too, must be modeled by such dissipative systems.[6] Thus did Lotka anticipate the general systems point of view (von Bertalanffy 1973), with its distinctions between open and closed systems, and their associated, and different, notions of equilibria.

Part 2 of Lotka's book, on kinetics, is primarily concerned with the simple equation of growth and the resulting logistic curve. The chapters concern various populations and examples of the growth law. Samuelson, of course, takes this discussion over in pages 291–4 of the *Foundations,* and he has one reference to Lotka there, citing pages 64–8. Samuelson has, as well, a section on population theories (pp. 296–9) that is similar to the material in Lotka's next fifty pages on population growth.

In Part 3, on statics, Lotka is concerned with equilibria, with zeros of the function $F_i(X_1, X_2, \ldots, X_n)$. He notes that from the viewpoint of kinetics, an equilibrium (or a stationary state) is a state in which velocity, dX_i/dt, is zero. Alternatively, a dynamic conception of equilibrium is associated with a balance of forces, and he notes that this meaning is tied etymologically to the spelling of the word "equilibrium" as "aequa libra," the poised balance. More interestingly, he notes a third meaning, in terms of energetics, in which

a system in dynamic equilibrium is found to be characterized by the attainment of a minimum (or sometimes a maximum) of certain functions having the dimensions of energy; a state in which the virtual *work done* in any small displacement compatible with the constraints *vanishes*. [p. 144, italics in original]

On such a view, a steady state, in which some motion in the parameters can be defined, is a misnomer, though he allows that by an abuse of language those states can be termed equilibria as well.

The most interesting feature of this discussion is the analysis of the case $n = 2$ and the presentation of the results of treating the various eigenvalue conditions (both roots positive real, both complex conjugates and real parts negative, etc.). The six types and five subtypes (associated with purely imaginary eigenvalues of the characteristic polynomial) allow one to draw the familiar sources, sinks, saddles, spirals, and closed loops of the motions of two-dimensional linear dynamic systems.[7] These analyses recall Samuelson's discussion of these ideas in Chapter XI of the *Foundations* ("Some Fundamentals of Dynamic Theory"), as well as Samuelson's famous paper on the multiplier and accelerator (Samuelson 1939), even though that analysis was conducted in terms of difference equations, not differential equations. Most of the rest of Lotka's Part 3 is concerned with specific cycles (e.g., carbon dioxide, nitrogen, water, phosphorus) and attempts to discuss them using the language of equilibria of dynamic systems.

This part ends with three interesting chapters (XXI–XXIII): "Moving Equilibria," "Displacement of Equilibrium," and "Parameters of State." The first of these chapters concerns equations like

$$dX_i/dt = F_i(X_1, X_2, \ldots, X_n; P)$$

where the P evolves slowly as $P(t)$, so that solutions, or equilibria, derived under the assumption that $P = $ constant are continuously linked in the case P is not a constant, but is rather a slow variable (slow with respect at least to the dynamic process relating the X_i). Chapter XXII is primarily concerned with the Le Chatelier principle, which is quoted by Lotka, from an English translation of the French, as

Every system in chemical equilibrium, under the influence of a change in any single one of the factors of equilibrium, undergoes a transformation in such a direction that, if this transformation took place alone, it would produce a change in the opposite direction of the factor in question. *The factors of equilibrium are temperature, pressure, and electromotive force,* corresponding to three forms of energy – heat, electricity, and mechanical energy. [Lotka 1956, p. 281, italics in original][8]

Most of his discussion represents an attempt to make sense of this, in terms of systems he has set up. And the final one of these chapters, "Parameters of State," is as well a discussion of the effects on equilibria of changes of parameters, and it gives form to the discussion by economists of comparative statics.

Samuelson, of course, was the one responsible for bringing Le Chatelier's principle to the attention of economists, and he used this set of ideas in discussing costs and production and noted that his "method employed here is that which underlies Le Chatelier's Principle in physics. By making use of Professor E. B. Wilson's suggestion that this is essentially a mathematical theorem applicable to economics, it has been possible to gain increased generality without increased complexity and emptiness" (p. 81).[9] The other mentions of the principle, in the *Foundations,* include the primary reference, which gives, in a footnote, a reading of the physical statement in a rough form as Lotka's quotation from Le Chatelier and applies it to state a general theorem concerning the effect on equilibrium of changing a parameter in the presence of constraints, and it is this form, as given on page 38, that the Le Chatelier principle has taken in later economic analysis.[10] Pointing to the connection between Lotka and Samuelson, Simon (1959, p. 494), notes that "in these chapters we see many of the sources of Samuelson's analysis of the relations of statics and dynamics in his *Foundations* – a debt which Samuelson acknowledges. We also see from the examples Lotka uses that he was familiar with the literature of mathematical economics, and there are references to Cournot, Edgeworth, Jevons, Pareto, and others."

Energetics

The final Part 4, "Dynamics," of the *Elements of Physical Biology* begins by setting up the equation

$$dX_i/dt = F_i(X_1, X_2, ..., X_n; P, Q)$$

where Lotka notes that by considering the X_i as aggregates of living organisms, those state variables are, in fact, "energy transformers," and so "the dynamics which we must develop is the dynamics of a system of energy transformers, or *engines*" (p. 325, italics in original).

That conception is what, in later years, earned Lotka the title of "father of ecology," for his idea suggested that

we may form the conception of a *system of transformers* comprising, in the most general case, individual single transformers, aggregates of composite transformers, and coupled transformers.... It is precisely such a system of transformers that is presented to us, on a vast scale, in nature, by the earth with its population of living organisms. Each individual organism is of the type of the simple transformer, though it does not operate with a single working substance, but with a complex variety of such substances. [Lotka 1956, p. 329, italics in original][11]

This set of ideas leads Lotka to consideration of economic systems and to a most general conception of general equilibrium, one in which value and utility are related to the "embodied" energy and in which exchange is a kind of zero-energy transformation. He notes that his ideas have value for

the light they throw, quantitatively, upon the biological foundations of economics, in the relations which they reveal between certain biological and certain economic quantities. It must be remembered that the mathematical method is concerned, not only, and indeed not primarily, with the calculation of numbers, but also, and more particularly, with the establishment of relationships between magnitudes. [p. 354]

And this sentence ends with a footnote to Irving Fisher's introduction (1897) to A. Cournot's *Researches into the Mathematical Theory of Wealth.* The idea is that "the life contest, then is primarily a competition for available energy.... Energy in this sense and for this reason *has* value for the organism – which is a very different thing from saying (as some have said or implied) that economic value *is* a form of energy" (Lotka 1956, p. 355).

The next several sections consider the energetics approach to social evolution and economic organization. The issue is not that of Lotka's economic insights, which are sparse, but rather that his views were shaped by the energetics approach of W. Ostwald. Lotka, after receiving an undergraduate degree in physics and chemistry in 1901 from the University of Birmingham, in England, had gone to Leipzig, in Germany, for advanced training.

The founding father of the energetic approach to chemistry, Friedrich Wilhelm Ostwald, was then the director of the new Physical-Chemistry Institute which had opened in Leipzig in 1897. During the year that Lotka was there (1901–1902) Ostwald delivered a series of lectures, later published under the title *Vorlesungen über Naturphilosophie,* in which he propounded the idea that energy was the central organizing concept of the physical and biological sciences. It was one of those lectures that started Lotka on the train of thought that culminated in the *Elements.* [Kingsland 1985, p. 28]

Lotka was indeed concerned with economic ideas themselves, and it is a bit odd that his influence on economics was indirect, through his mathematical modeling, and not direct, through his analysis of the economy of nature. Despite ideas, akin to those of Jevons, that individuals could "maximize" their adaptations by distributing their efforts at the margin in appropriate ways, he was not notably successful in applying the neoclassical ideas with exactitude.

His interests were mainly in the human animal: when he dabbled in economic biology, he thought like an economist and not like a biologist.... Lotka's idea that the tendency of individual economic behavior was to maximize reproduction and growth was of interest to him only in that it explained the tendency of the whole system to maximize energy flow in the course of evolution. [Kingsland 1985, p. 44]

The final chapters concern psychology and philosophy. They deal with consciousness itself and attempt to locate consciousness in the dynamics of coordinated systems. The early references to Freud and Bertrand Russell suggest that Lotka not only was well read but also was an intellectual squirrel, storing up nuts and tidbits for the longer-term project: "He knows...that he has been born in a large, complex, unexplored world where every new view brings a surprise. This compound of surprise and wonder, this naive curiosity that delights in examining every shining stone – shows forth on each page of Lotka's book" (Simon 1959, p. 495).

Learning mathematical dynamics in the 1930s

If Lotka's book suggests that the applied mathematics literature was a deep well out of which Samuelson could drink dynamics, the mathematical literature itself directly nourished Samuelson's investigations into dynamic theory. The difficulty that economists had with dynamics in the late 1930s – economists' confusion about equilibrium, stability, and dynamics – was not matched by similar confusion in the mathematics literature. Indeed, we shall see that it was the very lack of confusion in the mathematics community that made the Samuelson contributions so clear and cogent. Again, let me be clear that it is not important, for my project here, to ask, What did Samuelson know about dynamics, and when did he know it? Instead, I am interested in bringing out, in "surfacing," material related to another question: What mathematical dynamics *could* he have known at the time he was learning the mathematics that was to shape the *Foundations of Economic Analysis?*

There is, however, a real problem in discussing the history of dynamics in the mathematical literature in the 1930s, and that problem is that the subject has not been one explored in any detail by historians of mathematics. As Simon Diner has written, "it is a pity that all the histories of mechanics which exist nowadays end with Henri Poincaré and Alexandre Lyapunov.... *One must wish that historians of science begin to work on the history of the renewal of mechanics in the XXth century*" (1986, p. 282, italics in original).

The only useful general study of which I am aware appeared in the same volume with the Diner piece, though it was only twelve pages long: "Some Historical Aspects Concerning the Theory of Dynamical Systems," by the French mathematician Christian Mira (1986). I shall use this study as a guide to the mathematics, though I shall have to break into the mathematics directly. We shall thus be concerned with the major writings on the subject of dynamics and stability, and that will lead us to what were the canonical works in the field, the books of Picard and Birkhoff. But before we begin to examine these works in detail, it will be useful to recall the major themes that drove the concerns of these authors.

As Birkhoff noted, in a review of Poincaré's collected works,

[Consider] $dx/X = dy/Y$, $(x, X, y, Y$, real).... Fundamental in Poincaré's treatment of [this] case is the geometric representation of (x, y) as a point of the plane or surface, while the equation [just written] determines the direction of the corresponding integral curve. This direction becomes indeterminate at the singular points $X_i = 0$, $(i = 1, ..., n)$. [Birkhoff 1934, p. 364]

Birkhoff was the intellectual heir of Poincaré and was recognized as such at the time. Birkhoff's long mathematical career, spent almost entirely at Harvard, was one of the major forces that shaped American mathematics in this century. His intellectual debt to Poincaré, whose point of view toward differential equations he adopted, was real and acknowledged. That approach to dynamics was very explicit and concerned the following set of issues. Consider a system of differential equations of the form

$$dx_i/dt = X_i(x_1, ..., x_n) \qquad (\text{for } i = 1, ..., n)$$

As Birkhoff noted,

The final aim of the theory of the motions of a dynamical system must be directed towards the qualitative determination of all possible types of motions and of the interrelationship of these motions.... For a very general class of dynamical systems the totality of states of motion may be set into one-to-one correspondence with the points, P, of a closed n-dimensional manifold, M, in such wise that [we have the equation given earlier that describes the motions].... The motions are then presented as curves lying in M. One and only one such curve of motion passes through each point P_0 of M.... As t changes, each point of M moves along its curve of motion and there arises a steady fluid motion of M into itself. By thus eliminating singularities and the infinite region we are directing attention to a restricted class of dynamical problems.... However, most of the theorems for this class of problems admit an easy generalization to the singular case.... *The differential equations of classical dynamics are more special, and in particular possess an invariant n-dimensional integral over M.... Poincaré proved that in general the motions of such more special dynamical systems will recur infinitely often to the neighborhood of an initial state, and so will possess a kind of stability "in the sense of Poisson."* [Birkhoff 1927, pp. 189–90, italics added]

Birkhoff was fundamentally concerned with understanding the motions of dynamic systems. In the general case, those systems take the form of $dx_i/dt = X_i(x_1, \ldots, x_n)$ for $i = 1, \ldots, n$. In the case of a single variable, so that $n = 1$, we would have $dx/dt = X(x)$. If X is a linear function, of course $dx/dt = ax$. In this case the motions are motions on the line that stands for the manifold M, and the line "flows" into itself as the rate of flow at a point x is equal to ax for some real number a. In the plane, we have, in the linear case, $dx/dt = ax + by$ and $dy/dt = cx + dy$, where nonsingularity requires that $ad - bc \neq 0$. In matrix terms,

$$d\begin{bmatrix} x \\ y \end{bmatrix} \bigg/ dt = \begin{bmatrix} a & b \\ c & d \end{bmatrix} \begin{bmatrix} x \\ y \end{bmatrix}$$

The picture of this system is represented in the phase plane, the x–y plane. The origin is the equilibrium, because $X(t) = 0$ for $X(t) = [x(t), y(t)]$ means that $dX/dt = 0$, so there is no movement of the system if it is in this state. Through any other point in the plane, however, there is a line of force, as it were, a curve of motion given by the differential equation. There are several cases in the plane, if the system is linear. If the matrix is nonsingular and is denoted by A, either there are two real eigenvalues or there is one pair of complex conjugate eigenvalues. In the former case, if the eigenvalues are both negative, then the plane is covered by lines pointing into the origin. If the eigenvalues are real and positive, then the plane is covered by lines pointing out from the origin. The former case identifies the origin as a "sink," the second case as a "source." If the eigenvalues are real and of opposite signs, then the picture is of a saddle point at the origin. If the eigenvalues are complex, the real parts are both zero, both positive, or both negative. If positive, we have spirals out from the origin; if negative, we have spirals into the origin; if zero, we have concentric circles around the origin.

In the general case, where $X(x_1, \ldots, x_n)$ is not linear, matters are much more complicated. If the function X is analytic, then X has a power-series representation at least locally, and the linear analysis can be generalized. If, however, X has singularities, then new issues arise, and the flows may be complicated indeed. Characterizing the motions for X arbitrary, even in the plane, is a major task. The analyst is led to ask whether, in the general case, some more specificity is usefully imposed. As Birkhoff noted, if the system arises from a real physical system, it usually will be true that the minimization (or maximization) associated with the dynamic system will be linked to an invariant integral, where that integral represents a conservation law.

Now the main line of analysis of dynamic systems for Poincaré, as for Birkhoff, was the characterization of motions that had physical significance. The basic idea was that some motions of a system were special because they attracted other motions:

A causal system [like the foregoing differential equation] will be said to be non-recurrent in case there is not a general tendency for the system ultimately to return to the near vicinity of an arbitrary initial state.... Such a system possesses certain "central motions" which all other motions tend to approach.... It is a very interesting fact that the central motions are necessarily periodic or recurrent in type. [If it is recurrent] Poincaré said that such a system is stable in the sense of Poisson. [More specifically, variational systems are associated with the minimization of some physical construct.] The classical [forms] in which the variational systems have been embodied are the equations of Lagrange and Hamilton...all purely dynamical systems in which there is no dissipation of energy [e.g., conservative systems] fall under this variational type. [Motion of such systems] may be roughly characterized by saying that it is either periodic, or uniformly recurrent, or approaches and recesses from a set of uniformly recurrent motions at longer and longer intervals of time. [Birkhoff and Lewis 1935, pp. 308–12]

From this perspective, the idea of stability is easy to broach:

The fundamental fact to observe here is that this concept [of stability] is not in itself a definite one but is interpreted according to the question under consideration.... Certain parts of the phase space are regarded as "regions of stability," the other regions as regions of instability. A motion will then be said to be "stable" if, after the instant in question, its curve of motion forever lies in the stable part of the phase space...this definition is so general that it can hardly be called a definition at all. Nevertheless any less elastic definition will fail.... The region of stability of phase space may be taken to be a small region containing within its interior an equilibrium point. The equilibrium point is called stable if, no matter how small this region of stability has been chosen, any motion initially sufficiently near the equilibrium point will remain in the region of stability indefinitely. [For variational systems] the points of stable equilibrium correspond to points where the potential energy is a minimum. [Birkhoff and Lewis 1935, pp. 314–15]

These ideas are associated, in Birkhoff's writing, with interest in the stability of other forms, and he stressed, even apart from the mathematical theory, the applicability of the ideas to biological systems, population, social theory, and personality as stable or integrated. He closed this article with the observation that although "the possible types of stability are infinitely numerous and varied ... [the] most significant types ... from the standpoint of practical application are the stability of recurrent and non-recurrent systems about the positions of equilibrium and in the neighborhood of periodic motions in the case of variational systems" (Birkhoff and Lewis 1935, p. 333).

In a summation view of Birkhoff's contributions, written as an obituary and appearing as an introduction to his collected works, we find the distinguished Marston Morse (1946, p. 370), a Birkhoff student, writing as follows:

As with Poincaré the history of Birkhoff's researches in dynamics is one of successes which are partly complete and partly incomplete. The grand aim was to give a formal normal reduction of a dynamical system which distinguishes equilibrium points as to stability, and enables one to pass from these forms to a complete qualitative characterization of the system. Hamiltonian and Pfaffian systems formed the central core [of his work] with the restricted problem of three bodies a typical example.

Lastly, with regard to Birkhoff, we note that his major book on dynamics, specifically the end of Chapter IV, on stability of periodic motions, contains this interesting penultimate paragraph:

Finally a type of "unilateral stability" in which the displacements remain small for $t > 0$, and in general tend to vanish as t increases indefinitely, has been considered by Liapounoff and others. [A footnote here by Birkhoff refers the reader to Picard (1st ed., 1896), Volume 3, Chapter 8.] It is easy to demonstrate that if the m multipliers [i.e., eigenvalues] possess negative real parts, this kind of stability will obtain. Furthermore it is necessary for this kind of stability that none of the real parts are positive. In the case of the equations of dynamics, however, the real parts of the multipliers can not all be negative, since with every multiplier λ_i is associated its negative. Thus the only possibility of unilateral stability in dynamics is seen to arise when the multipliers are pure imaginaries [i.e., eigenvalues with zero real parts, as before in the linear case giving rise to concentric circles, or periodic orbits]. In this case the proof of unilateral stability would lead to the proof of permanent stability. [Birkhoff 1927, p. 122]

On Samuelson's relations with Birkhoff, we have in Samuelson's 1972 memoir only the curious footnote on anti-Semitism, associated with the popular story (here being denied by Samuelson) that *that* explained Samuelson's move from Harvard to the Massachusetts Institute of Technology (MIT):

[Among bigots] one could, so to speak, have one's cake and eat it too by believing – as did the eminent mathematician George D. Birkhoff and, to a degree, the eminent economist Joseph Schumpeter – that Jews were "early bloomers" who would unfairly receive more rewards than they deserved in free competition. Again, lest I be misunderstood, let me hasten to add the usual qualification that these men were among my best friends and, I believe, both had a genuine high regard for my abilities and promise. [Samuelson 1972, p. 12]

In any event, Samuelson cited Birkhoff extensively in the *Foundations* (six footnote references, five variously to the dynamic systems book, and one to the article with Lewis), and we can assume that Birkhoff, at Harvard, was not unimportant for Samuelson's learning about dynamic systems, even if an influence was indirect, through Wilson's guidance to the literature. But before we examine the possibilities available through Wilson's mentoring, we must look at the other mathematician whose work Samuelson cited in his *Foundations*.

Picard's analysis

The one additional source in the mathematical literature that the written record suggests helped to shape Samuelson's *Foundations* is the three-volume work by the eminent French mathematician Emile Picard. Volume III of *Traité d'analyse* is concerned with the theory of differential equations, and this remarkable book was readily available on publication of the third edition, even though it was not translated. Samuelson has three references to Picard's book. His first reference, supposedly to a result on the relationship between eigenvalues and solutions of linear differential equations, is to Picard's page 185. This must, however, be an error, because page 185 contains some unimportant argumentation concerning certain periodic solutions of differential equations. It is more interesting, however, to examine his third reference to Picard's Volume III, because it is that reference that occurs in the section "Concepts of Stability" in Chapter XI, titled "Some Fundamentals of Dynamical Theory," which was, Samuelson states, reproduced with a few alterations from his 1943 *Review of Economics and Statistics* article "Dynamics, Statics, and the Stationary State."

This reference to Picard is important, so I shall quote from it at length:

A very common use of stability in nonconservative physical systems is the one which I have termed *stability of the first kind*. It holds when every motion approaches in the limit the position of equilibrium (and every other motion). It is not reversible in time; going backwards, all stable systems become unstable. [Samuelson 1947, p. 334, italics in original]

This Samuelson paragraph has a footnote, number 31, which states that

this might be termed stability in the sense of Liapounoff. (See E. Picard, *Traité d'analyse*, III, p. 200.) It is also shown there that instability of the first order rules out stability in this sense. Birkhoff has termed this [i.e., Liapunov stability] unilateral stability. [Samuelson 1947, p. 334]

Samuelson goes on to note that

First order stability of the first kind prevails when certain sufficient conditions hold; namely, when the linear terms in the expansion of our functional equations taken by themselves yield a system which is perfectly stable. We have been concerned almost exclusively with this definition of stability. [Samuelson 1947, p. 334, italics in original]

This is interesting, and we turn to Picard (1928, p. 200) to examine the reference:[12]

Nous dirons avec M. Liapounoff que *c'est une solution stable* si, pour tout nombre positif *l*, quelque petit qu'il soit, on peut assigner un autre nombre positif ϵ, tel que l'on ait

$$|x_1| < l, |x_2| < l, ..., |x_n| < l$$

pour toutes les valeurs positives de *t*, dès que l'on prend pour les valeurs initiales (correspondant à $t = 0$) $\alpha_1, \alpha_2, ..., \alpha_n$ de $x_1, x_2, ..., x_n$ des valeurs réelles quelconques satisfaisant aux inégalités

$$|\alpha_1| < \epsilon, |\alpha_2| < \epsilon, ..., |\alpha_n| < \epsilon$$

This passage by Picard itself has a footnote reference, to wit: "A. Liapounoff, *Sur l'instabilité de l'équilibre dans certains cas où la fonction des forces n'est pas un maximum (Journal de Jordan, 5° série, t. III, 1897)*."

The Samuelson chapter goes on to develop the various results concerning Liapunov stability, including the theorems concerning the relationship between this kind of stability and instability and the eigenvalues of the linear system associated with a given dynamic system.

This was the Samuelson reference, in the *Foundations,* to the stability he was to make famous as "stability of the first kind." The more important issue, as in the Sherlock Holmes story "Silver Blaze," is the dog that did not bark, or in this case the reference that was not present, for in the work of Picard (1928, Chapter XIV, pp. 382f.) we find a section that could have saved Samuelson and other economists from twenty years of fumbling around not knowing how to prove stability theorems about economic equilibria.

To make the argument quite specific, we shall have to quote from those pages in the work of Picard. Because the passages are lengthy, I reproduce the French text in the Appendix to this chapter. Briefly, those pages by Picard set out the general set of *n* linear differential equations, with the origin as an equilibrium motion. The argument goes on to show that there is a relationship between the eigenvalues of the original system and a related quadratic form, and that quadratic form may be used as a measure of the discrepancy between an arbitrary motion and the equilibrium motion. The form is, of course, a Liapunov function, and Picard attributes the theorem about Liapunov functions and their properties in relation to stability of linear systems to Liapunov himself; Picard further provides the precise reference to Liapunov's proofs, citing the 1908 French translation from the Russian.

Some questions

To put matters baldly, Picard, in the book so well known that it was already in a third edition in 1928, not only gives the complete reference to the French translation of Liapunov's stability theory, and thus the location of the material on the indirect method of stability analysis, but goes even further and gives one of the main theorems of Liapunov theory. It is unfortunate that Samuelson, who had already noted that the Liapunov definitions of stability were to be the most important for his own work, so important that he renamed the idea "stability of the first kind," did not note those later chapters in Picard and therein find the method of Liapunov, with a Euclidean norm function as a Liapunov function, used to establish a result.

Frank Hahn has commented upon Samuelson's perspicacity in seeing the issues of Liapunov-type mathematics. Hahn states that "on one occasion [*Foundations*, p. 302] he used the methods of Lyapounov...without naming them as such. He was here within a hair's breadth of a development that did not occur for another ten years" (Hahn 1983, pp. 50–1). Hahn makes this remark because Samuelson analyzed a gradient process like $\dot{x}_i = F_i(x_1, \ldots, x_n)$, where F_i was an ith partial derivative of some function F that attained a maximum at $x_i = 0$ for all i. Samuelson used this, and the fact that for small x, $\sum F_i(0, \ldots, 0) < 0$, to infer the monotonic decrease of the function $\frac{1}{2} \cdot \sum x_i^2$ for $x \neq 0$. "No other economist, as far as I know, had employed a Euclidean norm in stability analysis before Samuelson. His technical mastery and insights make it a pleasure to read these early and vital contributions" (Hahn 1983, p. 51).

This leads to several related questions: If Samuelson did not read the relevant pages in the work of Picard, why did he not? If Samuelson read the relevant pages in the work of Picard, why did he not cite them in the same manner in which he cited the other passages from Picard? And if he did read the relevant pages in Picard's book, why did he not read Liapunov, for Picard's footnote gave a clear reference in French to the major work of Liapunov?

The answers to these questions would not modify one's view of Samuelson's contributions, which are immense, but rather would aid an understanding of the interrelationships between the mathematical literature and the applied literature, relationships often noted but imperfectly understood because there are too few case studies available for historians of the social sciences to use.

These questions can be answered on several levels. The first level, the more surface level, is fairly easy to set out. It is simply that Samuelson was not very comfortable with the French language. In speculating on this matter in response to my question to him, Nobel laureate Robert Solow, Samuelson's colleague, suggested that

if Paul had read more of Picard he would surely have cited him; Paul is one of the more compulsive citers in history. My guess is that he never read on, may barely have read the sentence cited, because his ability to read French is less than epsilon, where epsilon is.... A better high school education might have saved the profession twenty years. I suppose Wilson or somebody told him there was a passage in Picard, so he dutifully wrote it down. *I don't have to tell you that I have just made up the story. It is, however, utterly plausible.* [Solow, 1988, italics added]

At a somewhat deeper level, I would like to suggest that Samuelson did not address the issues of Liapunov stability directly because *he was not directly interested in stability except as a tool for comparative statics analysis.* That is, Samuelson was concerned to examine equilibrium positions and to compare the properties of equilibria with respect to one or another parameter shifts. His correspondence principle, on which he placed great emphasis, was that the *assumption* of stability placed restrictions on the static equilibrium conditions and that it was the stability assumption that allowed determinate comparative statics results. As a conjecture, Samuelson suggested that such determinate results would obtain in stable systems. On this point, Herbert Simon has suggested that

in spite of the opening paragraph of Chapter IX of the *Foundations,* the early interest in dynamics had little to do with proving [the] Walrasian general equilibrium to be stable. Rather – as is shown by the remaining four paragraphs of that section – the interest was in using second-order conditions of equilibrium, derived in turn from the conditions of dynamic stability, to draw inferences in comparative statics. (Note that this whole section of Chapter IX comes verbatim from Samuelson's April 1941 *Econometrica* paper.) Hence, in my view, the reason that Samuelson didn't pay much attention to the general method of Liapunov is that it was irrelevant to the questions he was then asking – he wasn't trying to prove global optimality of a system having appropriate convexities. [Simon 1988]

This observation seems to me to be accurate. It is consistent with Samuelson's not ever having written directly on the Walrasian general equilibrium system, or, more precisely, the existence-of-equilibrium problem, during the period when such mathematical investigations were proceeding quickly. Neither did Samuelson continue writing in the stability literature after the material in the *Foundations* appeared; the contributions of the late 1940s, and through the 1950s, cited Samuelson's early work, but he himself had moved on. It makes sense to claim that because his interest was in the properties of equilibrium, and the comparative statics propositions that could be inferred from a stability argument applied to a particular system, he had little or no interest in a purely formal stability analysis of the general Walrasian system.

That said, there remains the deeper question of why Samuelson was so much more interested in the comparative statics of equilibrium, so little concerned with the stability theory. Saying that that was the case does not address the issue of why that was the case. To attempt to explain a negative, which in this case would be Samuelson's lack of concern with formal stability theory, is never easy, and the explanation can never be completely satisfying. Should we bring in Samuelson's childhood, his religious training, his education, his mentors and peers, and so forth? Should we explain by calling attention to larger issues, or more personal ones? The structure of my argument to this point suggests that Samuelson can be read against the background of those whom he cites, and the written record defines the actual context of the *Foundations*. My discussion of Lotka and Birkhoff and Picard suggests that a narrative locating Samuelson in his times is well achieved by linking Samuelson's writing with the writings of others whom he obviously read (and cited). This makes his writing part of an intellectual fabric and both draws out the extensions of the tradition at the edges and suggests the essential continuity of his contribution with those of others. It uses the written record, and little else, to read Samuelson in context.

But context is more complex and richer than a set of citations and references. Even leaving aside the personal psychological basis of Samuelson's construction of material to study and problems to see and solve, leaving aside the personal background in what we may term, following Nelson Goodman, world-making, there remain other bases on which we may claim to contextualize Samuelson's *Foundations*. The world of the *Foundations,* I have argued, is rooted in a concern with dynamics, and stability plays an important role in those discussions. But stability was not emphasized to the extent that it had been in the mathematical sources Samuelson cited, particularly Birkhoff and Picard. To explain this negative leads into a complex and difficult set of issues that this chapter cannot hope fully to address. Additionally, I have no single easy answer to give. Nevertheless, I am convinced that one line of argument satisfies several requirements, but especially the requirement of coherence, which, after all, is one of the ways we appraise more general narratives. To that argument I now turn.

E. B. Wilson and the Gibbs tradition[13]

Samuelson (1972, p. 7) notes that he heard lectures by the mathematician Gilbert Bliss at Chicago. But the most important influence on his mathematical education probably was the mathematical physicist turned statistician E. B. Wilson. As Milgate (1987, pp. 922–3) notes, "Wilson's relatively few contributions to economics in the interwar years...were not without their influence in Harvard economic circles." From his position as professor of vital statistics at the Harvard School of Public Health he was fully aware of the work on population dynamics by Lotka and Volterra, and indeed he had had a long-running feud with Lotka's Johns Hopkins mentor, Raymond Pearl, over the logistic curve (cf. Kingsland 1985). It is reasonable to assume that Samuelson came to Lotka through Wilson, and he certainly had access to the mathematical community through him. Wilson himself, with an interest in economics, was the kind of applied mathematical generalist who would have been intellectually attractive to Samuelson. It was Wilson to whom Samuelson has referred as

...my revered teacher of mathematical economics and statistics. [He] was the last of the universal mathematicians. He was Willard Gibbs's favorite student, and one of the first to do work in a variety of fields: vector calculus, functionals, mathematical physics, aeronautical engineering, vital statistics, psychometrics, and, most important for me, mathematical economics. He was also the only intelligent man I have ever known who loved committee meetings. He also loved to talk and we had hours of conversation following his lectures. [Samuelson 1972, p. 11]

This noted, the only actual reference to E. B. Wilson in Samuelson's *Foundations* is the remark, on page 81 (in the chapter on the theory of cost and production), that "the method employed here is that which underlies Le Chatelier's principle in physics. By making use of Professor E. B. Wilson's suggestion that this is essentially a mathematical theorem applied to economics, it has been possible to gain increased generality without increased complexity and emptiness." In the Introduction to the enlarged edition of the *Foundations,* in 1983, Samuelson refers to Wilson as "Gibbs's disciple and my master."

Mirowski argues that Wilson was crucial to the "scientific" program in economics, where "science" was interpreted as a mathematization similar to that of physics, or at least the physics of an earlier time when Wilson had been receiving his education. Wilson himself

bounced from discipline to discipline, really a bit of a dilettante, starting in math with Gibbs, doing some forgettable work in physics then aeronautics at MIT (he managed to dislike both Einstein's relativity and Planck's quantum hypothesis); was given a chair in vital statistics at Harvard without really knowing anything about it, and began to get involved with the business of the Harvard Economics Department in the later 1920s. [Mirowski 1989c]

I shall argue that Samuelson's mathematical dynamics reflects in large measure the beliefs and prejudices of E. B. Wilson. Consequently, it will be useful to sketch some of Wilson's background and views.

Wilson (1879–1964), as Willard Gibbs's last Ph.D. student (he received his degree in 1901),[14] was well positioned to cross many disciplinary boundaries. Gibbs's own work was seen as the most important scientific work done by an American: His biographer wrote that "Gibbs's work forms a completed whole in whose framework the developments of the succeeding three-quarters of a century in the fields it covers appear for the most part as necessary and inevitable consequences. Like Sir Isaac Newton's *Principles,* this work of Willard Gibbs stands out in the history of man's intellectual progress as an imperishable monument to the powers of abstract thought and logical reasoning" (Wheeler 1952, p. 69). The distinguished historian Cynthia Eagle Russett (1966, p. 17) wryly notes that this passage, "even allowing for biographical hyperbole, [provides a] verdict [that] is essentially just."

It would take me too far afield to assay the influence of Gibbs's work in all fields. His lengthy paper "On the Equilibrium of Heterogeneous Substances" (Gibbs 1906), which was finished by 1878, was a remarkable construction of thermodynamic theory and demonstrated the power and value of the equilibrium notion in physical dynamic systems. The ideas of conservation and maximization play themselves out in a variety of physical-model contexts, and the mathematical structures of seemingly disparate problems are revealed to be essentially coherent.

What he did, essentially, was to add to the independent variables, entropy and volume, of the prime [thermodynamic] equation, a specific number of other independent variables or energy terms equal to the number of components in the system. The new concept he introduced in this connection, called the chemical potential, performs the same function in chemical systems as temperature and pressure do in mechanical systems. Here lay the key to the vast field of chemical equilibrium. In an isothermal (constant temperature) complex system, equilibrium exists when the chemical potential is at a minimum.... Gibbs had pioneered a new scientific field, that of physical chemistry. [Russett 1966, p. 18]

Wilson was Gibbs's man. A "polymath," his interests began with the vector and multilinear algebra book done with Gibbs, but were not to be limited by pure mathematics. His hostile commentary on Einstein's revision of relativity theory, in 1914, suggested that he was unafraid of taking on the lions. In 1908 he solved a problem of an oscillating chain suggested by Osgood, and "he prepared two papers giving a systematic exposition of the work of Gibbs on statistical mechanics" (Hunsaker and Mac Lane 1973, p. 292). This apparently led him away from purely mathematical problems. He went on to work in aerodynamics. An interest in statistics developed out of his position at the Harvard School of Public Health, and that led him to economics. More interestingly, he was the managing

editor of the *Proceedings of the National Academy of Sciences* for fifty
years, from its first issue in January 1915 until his death in December 1964.
The range of his interests made a fine match for that distinguished journal.

In a letter to the Harvard economics chairman, H. H. Burbank, dated
March 23, 1934, Wilson wrote that in a projected course he would offer
for economists, "I should not attempt to teach economics but simply
mathematical economics which in many respects is a different thing. I
couldn't teach the steam engine but I have taught thermodynamics and
the analogy is about the same."[15] That course was actually a physics course
of a type and variety that reflected his own training; it had no contact
with the modern physics of the 1920s and 1930s, the quantum physics that
overturned the verities of the earlier, Gibbs-trained, youthful Wilson.
In a subsequent letter, again to Burbank concerning another revision of
Wilson's course for economists, and *most probably a course either taken
by Samuelson or whose readings were studied by Samuelson,* Wilson wrote
the following:

Schumpeter has suggested that it would be particularly well for me to give as I
gave last time a general theory of equilibrium such as this is understood by physical
chemists including the phase systems of Willard Gibbs. Most of our equilibrium
theory in economics really has for its background the notions of equilibrium which
arise in mechanics. Although Pareto was certainly quite familiar with the types of
equilibrium which arise in physical chemistry and are necessary in fact for the
study of the steam engine he doesn't use this line of thought in economics. [Wilson
1938a]

Related to that argument, Wilson suggested, in a letter to P. A. Sorokin
on that same day, that

it has always seemed to me that the analogies used by people in the social sciences
which were drawn from physics were limited to mechanics. In the early days physical chemistry was treated on the analogy to mechanics and the treatment was
most often awkward and ignored some of the most striking phenomena. It was
only with the slow infiltration of Gibbs's notion about phases into the general
teaching about physical chemistry that physical chemists came to extend equilibria
and quasi-equilibria on a broader basis than they could be understood from mechanical analogies.... I am inclined to believe that sometime in the discussion of
social phenomena it [may be] necessary to have some concepts even more general
than that of the phase system.... [Wilson 1938b]

More directly, ten days later Wilson wrote to Samuelson with critical
comments on a paper by Samuelson:

Moreover, general as the treatment is I think that there is the possibility that it is
not so general in some respects as Willard Gibbs would have desired. [In] discussing equilibrium and displacements from one position of equilibrium to another position he [Gibbs] laid great stress on the fact that one had to remain within

the limits of stability. Now if one wishes to postulate the derivatives including the second derivatives in an absolutely definite quadratic form one doesn't need to talk about the limits of stability because the definiteness of the quadratic form means that one has stability. . . . I wonder whether you can't make it clearer or can't come nearer following the general line of ideas [that] Willard Gibbs has given in his Equilibrium of Heterogeneous Substances, equation 133. . . . [Wilson 1938c]

I submit that this argument by Wilson is significant, because it suggests an entire framework for thinking about the relationship between stability and equilibrium. Wilson, attributing the line of attack to Gibbs, links Gibbs and the thermodynamic approach of late-nineteenth-century physics to Samuelson and the mathematical economic analysis of the middle twentieth century.[16] Wilson's view that stability analysis itself is not nearly as important as analysis of equilibria is reflected in the concentration on comparative statics by Samuelson. I do not mean to suggest that Samuelson was doing Wilson's bidding, nor do I mean to suggest that Samuelson's contribution was not original with him. What I am arguing, however, is that the prejudices of E. B. Wilson, a world-view shaped as a student of Willard Gibbs, were congenial to Samuelson's own program of making economics scientific by presenting the essential propositions of the subject in a mathematical, and thus clearly analyzable, form. That the particular form taken by those mathematical propositions made the extended analysis of stability less interesting than comparative statics, and that that led Samuelson away from a concern with Liapunov theory and later developments in the mathematical economics literature on competitive equilibria, was incidental.

Of course, there are two references to Gibbs in the text of the *Foundations*. The first, a footnote on page 21, appears attached to the italicized statement by Samuelson of his general method of obtaining determinate results from solutions to maximum or minimum problems. The note is as follows:

It may be pointed out that this is essentially the method of thermodynamics, which can be regarded as a purely deductive science based on certain postulates (notably the First and Second Laws of Thermodynamics). That such abstract reasoning should in the hands of Gibbs and others lead to the validity of fruitful theorems testifies to the validity of the original hypothesis. [Samuelson 1947, p. 21n]

The second reference to Gibbs appears in the discussion of marginal productivity equilibrium conditions, as a footnote:

There is an intersting discussion of an exactly analogous equilibrium system in the famous paper of J. Willard Gibbs, "The Equilibrium of Heterogeneous Substances," *Collected Papers*, I, 55–349. [Samuelson 1947, p. 70n]

Actually, there is another reference to Gibbs, but it is not to be found in the index. If one opens the book to the title page, directly under the Harvard "Veritas" seal one finds the italicized headstone quotation for the entire book: "'Mathematics is a Language' – J. Willard Gibbs."

My brief discussion can be indicative only, but it suggests that the following argument cannot be easily dismissed: *One of the major reasons why Samuelson was concerned less with stability than with comparative statics was that the thermodynamic tradition of Gibbs, embodied in the equilibrium system of interest to physical chemists, was not so concerned with stability theory as it was with the equations defining, and the properties associated with, equilibrium states of the relevant system.* Liapunov theory, like the stability theory of dissipative dynamic systems, was of relevance only to the extent that one remained, for the duration of an equilibrium argument, or comparative statics argument, "within the limits of stability," meaning the region of the phase space in which the system was stable. Because Samuelson was concerned, generally, with local results, he could use the conditions of stability to argue that there was no limit to stability in the sense of Gibbs, and thus he had no need to concern himself with the difficult issues of the region of stability, or the basins of attraction of particular motions, which formed the corpus of stability theory that was of interest to mathematicians and those control engineers concerned with either nonlinear systems or oscillations.

Samuelson, on this reading, was triply bound by his training: as an imperfect translator of Picard, as an economist, and as a mathematical economist influenced by Wilson and the thermodynamic tradition of Gibbs. He had an interest in statics and dynamics, as well as equilibrium and comparative statics, and those interests led him to a limited concern with stability. The fact that his interest in and comprehension of the contemporaneous mathematical stability literature were neither intense nor detailed does not appear so surprising in retrospect.

L. J. Henderson and the Harvard Pareto circle

Although the Harvard sociologist Pitirim Sorokin took early notice of the theories of the economist-sociologist Pareto, the English translation of Pareto's *Trattoro,* called *The Mind and Society,* did not appear until 1935. However, it had an immediate impact on American social thought. The reason was that a Harvard professor of biological chemistry, Lawrence Joseph Henderson, had become enchanted with Pareto's arguments in the late 1920s and had managed to interest a large group of people in Pareto's social theory. It is well to recall that those ideas were based on the idea of society as a system:

Having framed society within a "system" schema, Pareto could facilitate his work enormously by establishing determinate conditions within it, conditions, that is to say, which did not vary at random but were completely described with reference to some general laws. Probably the commonest means to this end in the physical sciences is the use of some definition of equilibrium. Pareto had used just such a definition years before as a student at Turin. Bearing in mind his student experience, Pareto now invoked a definition of equilibrium not unlike the one set forth in his thesis: equilibrium was "such a state that if it is artificially subjected to some modification different from the modification it undergoes normally, a reaction at once takes place tending to restore it to its real, its normal, state." This particular formula was very close to that of Le Chatelier in physical chemistry. [Russett 1966, p. 91]

This is not the place to examine the way in which Pareto did or did not believe that equilibrium was an empirical or theoretical entity, or whether social processes were sufficiently akin to the pure economic processes analyzed and described by Walras and Pareto to permit general equilibrium analysis to extend to social systems. It suffices, rather, to note that such extensions were seen by others as important contributions to understanding social processes and that the idea of a social system, with its concomitant baggage of equilibrium notions, stability theorizing, and well-defined system boundaries, allowed an alternative to the Marxian vision of struggle and revolutionary unheaval. Pareto's social theory was, for the turbulent 1930s, a fully worked out conservative social theory.

To see that this noneconomic Pareto was, and is, deemed to be conservative in nature, I need only recall to the reader a remark by H. Stuart Hughes (1961, p. 82) that Pareto was "justly celebrated as the greatest rationalizer of authoritarian conservatism in our time." This point comes out even more clearly in Barbara Heyl's 1968 history of Harvard's "Pareto circle," which concludes that the Pareto period in American sociology ended by the early 1940s, at least in part because of "the Second World War which made the Soviet Union our ally and altered the ideological situation within American sociology. Marxism seemed less of a threat and more of an historical antecedent to sociology" (Heyl 1968, p. 334).

But this races ahead too quickly, for in the preceding decade the spectre of communism had indeed stalked, if not the land, at least the American intellectual community. Pareto provided an alternative vision of society. And L. J. Henderson was such a visionary:

After majoring in physical chemistry as a Harvard undergraduate [he] had received his M.D. degree from Harvard Medical School in 1902. He continued his studies in biological chemistry at Strasbourg for four semesters and then returned to a lectureship in Harvard College. The following year he became a regular instructor in both college and medical school where, as instructor, then assistant professor and professor, he continued to teach biochemistry until his death in

1942.... In Henderson the two basic equilibrium models met and fused, for Henderson was adept in both the physical and life sciences.... In particular Henderson owed heavy intellectual debts to...Joseph Willard Gibbs in physical chemistry and Claude Bernard in physiology. [Russett 1966, p. 112][17]

By the late 1920s, the confusion of the times apparently led Henderson to read Pareto:

As my familiarity with the work has increased, I have become convinced that my acquaintance with Pareto's analysis of facts, with his synthesis of results, with his methods, and with some of his theorems is at present indispensable for the interpretation of a wide range of phenomena, whenever and wherever men act and react upon one another. [Henderson 1935, p. vi]

From the point of view taken here, the importance of Henderson's reading Pareto at that time cannot be ignored:

He decided to conduct a seminar on Pareto, and early in the 1932 academic year he began recruiting faculty members to be participants. Schumpeter, Brinton, and Parsons all came. Henderson's good friend Charles P. Curtis, Jr., a Boston lawyer and a Harvard Fellow, gave him some assistance in running the course. Henry Murray, Clyde Kluckhorn, and Robert Merton also attended, and Henderson personally invited [George Caspar] Homans, who was in his first year of graduate school, to join the seminar. Henderson conducted the seminar for two years, from 1932 to 1934. Apparently most of the same men attended regularly throughout its duration. [Heyl 1968, p. 318]

There was another line of Henderson's influence, and it led directly to Samuelson:

Henderson was also the first chairman of the Society of Fellows at Harvard, established in 1933, whose members, besides receiving scholarships to study whatever they wished, dined together once a week. Among the early members were C. M. Arensberg, B. F. Skinner, W. F. Whyte, and G. C. Homans. They soon became familiar, through their conversations, with Henderson's views. [Homans 1968, p. 351]

Samuelson, of course, was a member of the Society of Fellows:

Before his SSRC fellowship [to study economics at Harvard beginning as a graduate student in 1935] gave out, he overcame the opposition of the Society of Fellows to economics and rode on the shoulders of Vilfredo Pareto into the sacred circle of Junior Fellows. The philosopher Willard van Orman Quine, the mathematician Garrett Birkhoff [son of the Harvard mathematician George David Birkhoff], the double-Nobel physicist John Bardeen, the chemists Bright Wilson and Robert Woodward, the polymath Harry T. Levine were his companions in arms in the Society of Fellows. There he hit his stride and began to turn out articles faster than the journals could absorb such quasi-mathematical stuff.... His *Foundations of Economic Analysis,* written mostly as a Junior Fellow but usable later for the Ph.D. union card.... [Samuelson 1986b, p. 66]

The best first-person account I have been able to find of the Society of Fellows in that period is the autobiography written by the eminent sociologist George C. Homans. Following Chapter 6, mostly on Henderson, he recalled, in Chapter 7, his lengthy intellectual connection to Pareto and gave a detailed account of the workings of the Henderson seminar:

The seminar met for a couple of hours late in the afternoon for the better part of the academic year in, I think, the junior Common Room of Winthrop House.... Henderson worked slowly through the *Traité,* providing his exegesis of selected passages. After each of these he would ask for questions. If there were none, he would go on. Except from Sorokin, I do not remember there was much argument.... Towards the end of the first year of the seminar Charlie Curtis approached me and suggested that we collaborate in writing an introduction to Pareto's sociology for American readers. [Homans 1984, p. 105]

Homans was a member of the Society of Fellows, as a junior fellow, during the Samuelson years, and Homans recalled with fine detail how he was selected:

I had run as a poet [in 1934] and had rightly been rejected. My candidacy for the second year was quite another matter. By that time *An Introduction to Pareto* had been published; I had demonstrated my Paretian faith; I was Henderson's man and Henderson was chairman of the society. [Homans 1984, p. 121]

The only curiosity in the chapter on the Society of Fellows was that although everyone whom Samuelson recalled was discussed in detail by Homans, Samuelson himself was mentioned only in the context of Homans hearing from him about "the Keynesian revolution, which was only then just gathering force in economic theory" (Homans 1984, p. 127). Homans also noted there that it was the anthropologist Conrad Arensberg who "advocated Percy Bridgeman's operationalism in the definition of scientific concepts" (p. 127), a line of argument that played a major role in Samuelson's *Foundations,* composed at that time and place.

One last connection, from Homans: On his leaving the Society of Fellows, and needing a regular job, the possibility of a position in the Harvard Sociology Department arose:

The Sociology Department had few tenured professors and I suspect that President Lowell did not altogether trust Sorokin's uncontrolled judgment. Accordingly he had set up a committee to make the main administrative decisions. [The] committee included scholars from elsewhere in the university who were supposed to be interested in sociology. Among the outsiders were Henderson (no surprise), Mayo, Edwin B. Wilson, an old ally of Henderson's and a distinguished statistician at the School of Public Health. [Homans 1984, p. 131]

The circle is completed, and virtually unbroken: Gibbs to Wilson, Gibbs to Henderson, Poincaré to Birkhoff, Pareto to Henderson, energetics to

Lotka to Wilson – roll them all together in the Harvard of the 1930s, add one young and scientifically open-minded Samuelson eager to please his senior fellows, simmer in the Society of Fellows, and the *Foundations* emerges, contingent as it must be on its context.

A concluding note

I have tried to suggest that several lines converged in Samuelson's *Foundations of Economic Analysis,* or, more precisely, in the papers of the late 1930s and early 1940s that were to form the *Foundations.* Those lines reflect currents then strong, ideas then powerful, and concerns then compelling. The mathematics of dynamic systems, through Birkhoff and Picard, the applied mathematical analysis of systems from Lotka, the thermodynamics of the late nineteenth century through Gibbs via Wilson, and the confused literature on economic dynamics of the 1930s all shaped the way Samuelson constructed his arguments in the *Foundations.* Those influences were not entirely consistent one with another, and the dissimilarities in their visions of the shapes of the natural processes at work led to a tension in Samuelson's own work on dynamics and stability, a tension that was resolved by his movement away from formal analysis of existence and stability of competitive equilibria in abstract Walrasian systems. That the context in which ideas are developed can illuminate the tapestry of the form in which those ideas are presented is hardly news. But the myth that the vision of a single individual, instantiated in a classic scientific work, is a coherent whole must be resisted, even in such a case as Samuelson's *Foundations.*

Appendix[18]

[Consider the first-order linear system given by]

$$\frac{dx_1}{dt} = a_{11}x_1 + a_{12}x_2 + \cdots + a_{1n}x_n$$

$$\frac{dx_2}{dt} = a_{21}x_1 + a_{22}x_2 + \cdots + a_{2n}x_n$$

$$\cdots\cdots\cdots\cdots\cdots\cdots\cdots$$

$$\frac{dx_n}{dt} = a_{n1}x_1 + a_{n2}x_2 + \cdots + a_{nn}x_n$$

les a étant des fonctions réelles de la variable réelle *t*. *Je suppose que tous les a soient limités,* c'est-à-dire moindres qu'un nombre fixe M pour t compris entre t_0 et ∞. Posons $x_i = y_i e^{\lambda t}$ $(i = 1, 2, ..., n)$, λ étant une constante pour le moment arbitraire.

Le système devient

$$\frac{dy_1}{dt} = (a_{11} - \lambda)y_1 + a_{12}y_2 + \cdots + a_{1n}y_n$$

$$\frac{dy_2}{dt} = a_{21}y_1 + (a_{22} - \lambda)y_2 + \cdots + a_{2n}y_n$$

$$\cdots\cdots\cdots\cdots\cdots$$

$$\frac{dy_n}{dt} = a_{n1}y_1 + a_{n2}y_2 + \cdots + (a_{nn} - \lambda)y_n.$$

En multipliant ces équations respectivement par $y_1, y_2, \ldots, y_n$ et ajoutant, nous aurons

$$\frac{1}{2}\frac{d(y_1^2 + y_2^2 + \cdots + y_n^2)}{dt} = (a_{11} - \lambda)y_1^2 + (a_{22} - \lambda)y_2^2 + \cdots + (a_{nn} - \lambda)y_n^2$$

le second membre étant une forme quadratique en $y_1, y_2, \ldots, y_n$. Si nous prenons pour λ une constante α suffisamment grande, le second membre sera une forme quadratique définie et négative, et nous aurons par suite

$$\frac{d(y_1^2 + y_2^2 + \cdots + y_n^2)}{dt} < 0.$$

Par suite, quand t augmentera de t_0 à $+\infty$, la fonction

$$y_1^2 + y_2^2 + \cdots + y_n^2$$

ira en diminuant. Il en résulte que $y_1, y_2, \ldots, y_n$ restent en valeur absolue moindre qu'un nombre fixe, et, par suite, les produits

$$x_1 e^{-\alpha t}, x_2 e^{-\alpha t}, \ldots, x_n e^{-\alpha t}$$

seront limités.

The footnote, of real importance, reads as follows:

Cet intéressant théorème est dû à M. Liapounoff, qui l'a fait connaître dans un Mémoire important publié en langue russe (Liapounoff, 1892) dans le Bulletin de la Société mathématique de Kharkoff. Ce Mémoire très étendu vient d'être traduit en francais dans les *Annales de la Faculté des Sciences de l'Université de Toulouse,* 2° série, t. IX, 1908. [p. 385n]

CHAPTER 4

Liapunov theory and economic dynamics

The literature on the stability of the competitive equilibrium that came to fruition in the late 1950s was woven of three specific skeins in earlier work. First, there was the 1930s literature that had attempted to untangle statics from dynamics, and equilibrium from disequilibrium; that analysis had been done by Frisch, Tinbergen, Hicks, and others, though later writers would claim that the issues had finally been framed by Hicks's *Value and Capital* (1939). That book directed economists to the microfoundations-of-macroeconomics "problem" and suggested that the stable–unstable distinction could make sense of the dissimilar Keynesian and classical positions on unemployment. Second, there was a 1930s literature on equilibrium and stability whose lineage traced back to Pareto, social-systems analysis, and the social application of mechanical ideas. That tradition, with roots in physics, the physical chemistry of Willard Gibbs, and the evolutionary biology/ecology of A. J. Lotka, found expression in Paul Samuelson's writings in the late 1930s and early 1940s and provided the basis for his *Foundations of Economic Analysis* (1947). Third, the story of the introduction of modern stability theory into economics featured the interrelationship of two disciplines, mathematics and economics, that were linked in serendipitous ways in the 1940s. In this chapter I intend to tell this last story.

The tale is complex, however, and many seemingly peripheral issues take on special meaning. For instance, there have been conflicting priority claims regarding the first uses of certain mathematical techniques in economics. Further, there have been some troubling issues regarding the interactions of tools and reasoning methods, issues that have led some economists to look with suspicion on what emerged as dynamic economic theory. This chapter will present a narrative of the developments, but also will treat the issues of precursors and priority claims. To begin, it may be helpful to set the scene by describing some of the concerns of one portion of the mathematics community in the United States and elsewhere in that period.

Without going into great detail on the state of mathematical research on differential equations in the 1930s, I note that one of the significant teaching and research texts used by American mathematicians in the pre-1940 period was Emile Picard's three-volume *Traité d'analyse*.[1] That book, mostly composed prior to 1920, contained sufficient introduction to the work of the distinguished Russian mathematician A. M. Liapunov to allow that work to find its way to the mainstream literature in differential equations.[2] Nevertheless, Liapunov's mathematical ideas, though not unknown in the West, were not part of an ongoing research tradition. Instead, much of the research on stability and equilibrium in the Western mathematical literature was concerned with what can roughly be termed "the Poincaré program," a research tradition that was concerned with the stability of conservative dynamic systems and thus focused on maintained cycles, particularly the limit-cycle behavior of dynamic systems. The alternative discussion of dissipative systems had a decided engineering flavor – a sense of heat loss through friction, the wearing down of mechanical parts – and was not highly theoretical in origin. The classic concern of equilibrium theory and stability analysis in the mathematical literature was with the Newtonian problems of the stability of the solar system: Do the maintained limit cycles give rise to the orbits of the heavenly bodies?

Indeed, "in 1887 King Oscar II of Sweden offered a prize of 2,500 crowns for an answer to a fundamental question in astronomy. *Is the solar system stable?* We see now that it was a major turning point in mathematical physics" (Stewart 1989, p. 60). That was the modeling problem, and that was the origin of the mathematical interest in stability theory. Such conservative dynamic systems were at the heart of the nineteenth-century mathematical interest in stability problems and appear to have been at the root of Poincaré's interest in such matters, for Poincaré won King Oscar's prize with his memoir in French, the title of which translates into English as

On the Problem of Three Bodies and the Equations of Dynamics. It was published in 1890 and it ran to 270 pages in the original. The first part establishes general properties of dynamical equations; the second applies the results to the problem of arbitrarily many bodies moving under Newtonian gravitation. [Stewart 1989, pp. 66–7]

A. M. Liapunov

Within twelve years, from Poincaré's *Mémoire sur les courbes définies par une equation différential* (1881–86) to Lyapunov's thesis *Obshčaya zadača ob unstoičivosti dviženiya* (1892), the qualitative theory of differential equations emerged almost from scratch as the core of a new field of mathematics; both Poincaré and Lyapunov were motivated by problems in mechanics, celestial mechanics above all. . . . Lyapunov developed from 1888 to 1892 a theory of dynamical stability which makes his 1892 thesis both a pioneering piece of work and a classic. [Henry 1987, p. 256]

These were the two classic works in dynamic systems, and one of them was more accessible to Western mathematicians. That is, the American disciple of Poincaré was G. D. Birkhoff, and through his position in American mathematical circles he was able to influence the work of those young mathematicians interested in dynamic systems. It was not as if the work of Liapunov was lost, or unknown, but rather that the American interest in dynamics developed in the Poincaré-Birkhoff tradition. That tradition was concerned primarily with classical problems in mechanics. The flavor of Birkhoff's concerns comes through clearly in a "philosophical" paper he wrote in the mid-1930s:

A causal system [like the differential equation given earlier] will be said to be non-recurrent in case there is not a general tendency for the system ultimately to return to the near vicinity of an arbitrary initial state. . . . Such a system possesses certain "central motions" which all other motions tend to approach. . . . It is a very interesting fact that the central motions are necessarily periodic or recurrent in type. [If it is recurrent] Poincaré said that such a system is stable in the sense of Poisson. [More specifically, variational systems are associated with the minimization of some physical construct.] The classical form in which the variational systems have been embodied are the equations of Lagrange and Hamilton. [All] purely dynamical systems in which there is no dissipation of energy [e.g., conservative systems] fall under this variational type. [Motion of such systems] may be roughly characterized by saying that it is either periodic, or uniformly recurrent, or approaches and recesses from a set of uniformly recurrent motions at longer and longer intervals of time. [Birkhoff and Lewis 1935, pp. 307–12]

That is, the kinds of systems of concern to Birkhoff, and those of interest to the Poincaré program, were conservative systems. Dissipative systems were different, and of less concern.

Matters were quite different in the Soviet Union:

[S]oon after the Revolution, mathematical research experienced an almost explosive growth. At once a number of front-rank figures appeared in the Soviet Union. [In addition to the work associated with Urysohn, Alexandrov, and Pontrjagin, under] the influence of Liapunov. . . the Soviet mathematical physicists have made signal contributions to the general theory of differential equations and their application to oscillatory phenomena. A whole school of research on oscillatory phenomena has developed in Moscow, and one of the books issued by that school [was] *The Theory of Oscillations,* by Andronov and Chajkin. [Lefschetz 1949, p. 140]

The history of that mathematical school is not well known among economists, but E. S. Boĭko (1983) has recently published a discussion of the development of that Moscow group, sometimes called the Andronov school. Of course, some of the discrepancy between the influence of Poincaré and that of Liapunov may be traced to the fact that French was generally understood by all American mathematicians, whereas Russian was hardly understood at all. Although Liapunov's original work was translated into French in 1907 by the Mathematical Society of Toulouse, the work of the Soviet mathematicians writing in the 1930s was not readily available in the United States in the same way that Birkhoff's work was available.[3] Furthermore, as the Soviet mathematical work developed, its intellectual vitality was continually replenished by connections with engineering applications of a sort not generally associated with pure mathematical research in the United States; that "impurity" also reduced its potential readership. The impurity, of course, was associated with the fact that the systems were dissipative and were modeling actual, not classical celestial, mechanical problems.

But the timing of these new mathematical developments are also of interest, for

after Poincaré and Liapunov, the theories which they had developed stagnated for many years. The first sign of a revival came in the early twenties from an applied mathematician named Van der Pol with his study of the famous equation which bears his name. Before long, quite a large group of pure and applied mathematicians in the Soviet Union took up the cudgels. They divided up, curiously enough, into two sets, the first grouped around the Institute of Oscillations in Moscow, and the second consisting of the very prolific pair of Kryloff and Bogoliubov in Kiev. The two groups had actually nothing in common and by and large seemed to have ignored one another's existence. [The Moscow group was organized around 1930] under the direction of the late Mandelstam, a distinguished mathematical physicist, and it included L. S. Pontrjagin. [The group] dealt almost exclusively with problems of [differential equations of] the first and second orders [and] the content of the new ideas, over and above Poincaré and Liapunov is meager to say the least [, though they] knew how to apply [the older techniques] in the most efficient manner. [Lefschetz 1953, pp. 71–2][4]

The other group, in Kiev, "attacked the problem of nonlinear oscillations in the same spirit as physicists and engineers, unhesitatingly making every possible approximation and thus went forward where the strict methods of general theory were stopped" (Lefschetz 1953, p. 73). The major work describing that group's research was translated into English by Lefschetz in 1943, as discussed later.

During the war the Kiev group broke up, and the Moscow group became more diffuse in their interests, increasingly focusing on control problems, which led to work in the 1950s on the Pontrjagin maximum principle.[5] In some measure the Soviet tradition was to become international because of the particular background and situation of an American mathematician. Solomon Lefschetz was to be responsible, in large part, for introducing Western, particularly American, mathematicians to the work of the Soviet mathematicians on differential equations and for reintegrating the traditions of Poincaré and Liapunov. But before picking up that thread, let us consider the state of play in mathematical economics at that time, specifically the kind of work concerned with dynamics that was being introduced by individuals interested in economics.

Griffith C. Evans

Mathematical Introduction to Economics, by Griffith C. Evans, was published in 1930 by the reputable McGraw-Hill. Evans was, at that time, a mathematics professor at Rice Institute in Houston.[6] We must first recognize that the mathematical economics considered useful by most economists was that of Bowley's dreadful *The Mathematical Groundwork of Economics* (1924). That book showed how to count equations and unknowns in order to see if it would be feasible to solve sets of simultaneous nonlinear (!) equations by the method of "successive elimination."[7] In such an environment, Evans's book was remarkable indeed.

Evans was a real mathematician. Herbert Simon notes that

it is likely that his initial contact with mathematical economics took place in Italy and France [while a postdoctoral student of Vito Volterra at the University of Rome around 1910] for he shows great familiarity with the work of such writers as Pareto, Amoroso, and Divisia [while among] earlier writers he mainly cites Cournot and Jevons; among his contemporaries, Irving Fisher, Henry Schultz, and Henry Moore. [Simon 1987, pp. 198–9]

Though there are many interesting points to examine in Evans's book, concern with dynamics leads me to several pages in particular. Evans discusses, in an early chapter on competition and cooperation, the issue of modifying cost factors:

Up to this point we have been considering situations in which time was not a determining factor. They have been steady states, or states of equilibrium. The rates of production, prices, costs, etc., have been connected directly through equations among themselves without any need of introducing the time as a variable. But we can conceive of the desirability of investigating situations which are not in equilibrium, in order to see where they tend, and how rapidly. [Evans 1930, p. 33]

This remark leads to the next chapter (IV), "Cases of Variable Price," in which Evans notes that "we shall not have an adequate picture of economics until we invent likely hypotheses which will make the price vary with time, and enable us to determine it for various times, that is as a function of time" (p. 36). This leads to a remarkable discussion in which he creates a dynamic law of demand in which quantity depends not only on price but also on the time rate of change of price. This differential equation is set against an equilibrium of supply and demand to yield a general solution of price as

$$p(t) = p_1 + C \exp[-(\alpha - a/\gamma - h)\cdot t]$$

Thus, the result is that the coefficients of the demand and supply curves, the a, α, γ, and h in the equation, determine whether the price will converge to the equilibrium value. In other words, the true dynamic stability of the equilibrium is associated with the limiting behavior of the arbitrary solution of the differential equation of price change. The next page contains a real phase diagram, a vector field, and the following page 41 contains a diagram of vector fields converging and diverging from an equilibrium price. This sort of explicit treatment of stability of equilibrium was not to reappear again until Samuelson wrote a dozen years later. In brief, the Evans book provided an explicit treatment of equilibrium and the stability of that equilibrium in terms of the differential equations needed to discuss change, and with reference to which the ideas of change and process could be developed in a mathematically coherent fashion.

It is a fact that the Evans book was not specifically cited by Samuelson in the text of the *Foundations,* nor by Hicks or other writers on these problems. One would have supposed that a book purporting to be a mathematical introduction to economics would have been cited frequently, because Evans was not unknown to Roos, Fisher, Hotelling, and other early members of the Econometric Society.[8] But even without citations, the book was read. As Simon points out,

Evans's books and his articles were an important resource for early American students with an appetite for mathematical economics, who prior to their publication found an extremely sparse literature on which to graze. Samuelson, for example, mentions Evans [in the Preface to the second reprinted edition of the *Foundations*] as one whose works he "pored over." [Simon 1987, p. 199]

It is tempting to praise Evans as a "precursor" of modern dynamics, or an early pioneer. That would necessitate my asserting that the mathematical literature was well advanced compared with the economics literature, a viewpoint that would give an entirely Whiggish reading to that period's texts. Because the concerns of economists developed from economic problems or, more precisely, problems that concerned other economists, a distinct mathematical literature could never be either more or less advanced; such a literature, while it remains separate, does not even exist for the economics community. After the economics literature began to develop by incorporating elements of a mathematical literature, it then became possible for a Whig historian of economics to reconstruct the earlier mathematical literature as historically continuous with the later economics literature. In truth, however, there were no points of connection. That the economists of the 1940s and 1950s read the 1930s economics literature on dynamics as the story of a great struggle toward the Samuelsonian stability liberation movement is probably inescapable. That the earlier mathematical literature on stability made good sense to readers in the 1950s and 1960s, in ways that the earlier economics literature on stability did not, should not cause surprise either. Suppose we ask ourselves *not* to think about an elephant for the next minute. We cannot. And neither can most *economists* today think about stability and disequilibrium *without* differential equations, without a dynamic adjustment mechanism, without feeling at one with Evans; indeed, Samuelson's message was exactly that stability problems required formal specification of adjustment mechanisms. But that economists cannot think so easily about such matters is no reason that historians cannot think about them, with the result that their exhilaration at finding precursors, such as Evans, is mitigated by the harsh fact that Evans was unconnected. As Latour noted,

since the status of a claim depends on later users' insertions, what if there are no later users whatsoever? This is the point that people who never come close to the fabrication of science have the greatest difficulty in grasping. They imagine that all scientific articles are equal and arrayed in lines like soldiers, to be carefully inspected one by one. However most papers are never read at all. No matter what a paper did to the former literature, if no one else does anything else with it, then it is as if it had never existed at all. You may have written a paper that settles a fierce controversy once and for all, but if readers ignore it it cannot be turned into a fact; it simply cannot. [Latour 1987, p. 40]

The formal structure of the new stability theory

It will be helpful in keeping issues in this narrative in perspective to remind ourselves that stability analysis was changing in the United States during the 1940s under the influence of the Soviet mathematical theories that Lefschetz and others were introducing to American mathematicians and engineers. The theory of the qualitative behavior of dissipative dynamic systems was thus coming to be well understood, and applications were already finding their way into the various literatures by the early 1950s. To be clearer about the nature of these moves, and the connections among the problems studied in mathematics and economics, we need to be clear about the formal structure of the analysis as it was developing. As we shall see, claims about "discovery" and "first use" of Liapunov theory in economics have led to a number of problems of "assigning credit" in traditional histories of economic thought, and so it will be necessary to be clear about the nature of that theory.

The mathematical structure was associated with a system generally given by

$$\dot{x} = X(x,t); \qquad X(0,t) = 0$$

where x and X are vectors of dimension n, $x = 0$ is an equilibrium solution usually denoted x_e, and any $x(t)$ satisfying the equation is called a trajectory or path or motion of the system. If the equation is such that

$X(x, t) \equiv X(x)$, then the system is called an autonomous system; such systems do not have their "laws of motion" depending explicitly on time. We note immediately that this mathematical formulation differs from that of Samuelson's book in that the Samuelson version was characterized, in its generality, by functional equations like $F^i[X_1(t), ..., X_n(t)] = 0$, where each X_j could be a differential expression of arbitrary degree, say.

In the language and notation that was becoming standard in the 1940s, the analyst investigated the system in the form

$$\dot{x} = Ax + f(x)$$

where the matrix A was $n \times n$ constant, and the components f_i of f were power series of degree at least 2 in the components x_j of x, so that the original autonomous system had had an analytic right-hand side. Stability analysis investigated the local stability properties of the system by analysis of the A matrix: If and only if A had eigenvalues with negative real parts, then the system possessed local stability, for example. Analysis would proceed to examine such systems with purely imaginary eigenvalues, or a zero eigenvalue, or various boundedness conditions on the asymptotic growth of the nonlinear $f(x)$, and results might be of the form "if f satisfies conditions $A, B, ...$, then the autonomous system is globally asymptotically stable."

Now, all of this analysis was present in the original Liapunov treatise, and it was the difficult problem of generalizing the results to more complicated functions f, or more delicate eigenvalue properties, that had been the contribution of the Moscow school:[9]

Whatever Liapunov obtained by the preceding method of solution [i.e., solving the differential equation directly and establishing the motion's asymptotic behavior by computing its limit as $t \to \infty$] is referred to by him and his successors as his *first method*. Liapunov also introduced in his mémoire a *second method* which is in high favor in the Soviet Union but not outside. If $V(x; t)$ is a function of x and t with continuous first partials near the origin then along a trajectory of $[\dot{x} = X(x, t)]$

$$V = \sum_i X_i \frac{\delta V}{\delta x_i} + \frac{\delta V}{\delta t}.$$

If one can find a V such that for x small $V > 0$ while $\dot{V} < 0$ for $t > \tau$ then the origin is stable.... Roughly speaking $V = $ const. represents a family of ovals surrounding the origin which shrink along the trajectories when the origin is stable and expand when the origin is unstable. Other criteria of this nature were developed by Liapunov and later also by Malkin and Persidsky. They are all inspired by the classical condition of stability of equilibrium, according to which the potential energy must be a minimum. It is important to observe regarding the second method of Liapunov that it does not impose analyticity on the X_i, and thus has a much larger theoretical range of application than does the first method. [Lefschetz 1953, p. 70]

I note, for the record, as it were, that the Liapunov theory is directly associated with systems in which energy is conserved. Equilibrium carries with it all the connotations of the minimization of potential energy. Mirowski (1989a) has made the significant claim, which I find convincing, that the structure of neoclassical economics was provided by the structure of field theory, of energetics. *The energy metaphor, from field theory, is at the heart of the neoclassical conception of optimization; with the Liapunov theory the mathematical structure of stability analysis was thus wholly reconciled with the intellectual structure of economic equilibrium theory. What I am suggesting here is thus consistent with the Mirowski thesis, for the rapid acceptance of Liapunov theory in economic dynamics is simply the "long-awaited" linking of field theory's dynamics with field theory's statics.*

What is a precursor?

This discussion permits me to open up a historiographic can of worms. Since the major theorem on the stability of a competitive equilibrium was established in the late 1950s there has been a series of claims about the early moves to that theorem, or early forms of that theorem, in the writings of economists. But because the proof of the strong theorem required Liapunov theory, or the second or indirect method of Liapunov, the claims frequently have concerned the first use, or first near-use, or independent discovery of the content of, the Liapunov theory. Specifically, for Liapunov analysis and economic stability theory, the first Liapunov-function-based proof generally is said to have been that by Arrow, Block, and Hurwicz in 1959. But Yasui and Morishima, writing in Japanese, used Liapunov functions as early as the late 1940s. Hahn (1983, pp. 50–1) claims that Samuelson's discussion on page 438 of the *Foundations of Economic Analysis* (1947) "was within a hair's breadth of a development [Liapunov's method] that did not occur for another ten years." Now, in one sense, this is all very curious. Why should economists be making claims for independent discovery or first use by an economist, in the 1940s or 1950s, of a mathematical theory that was developed in the 1890s and was common textbook knowledge (e.g., Picard) in the 1920s? Further, I have noted that the theory is intrinsic to the structure of neoclassical optimization theory, being its dynamic component, so the first near-use is simply a matter of Annie Oakley's "doin' what comes naturally."

Of course, there is a troublesome problem embedded in every discussion of scientific discovery. As the eminent historian of science Thomas S. Kuhn (1977, p. 166) remarked,

To make a discovery is to achieve one of the closest approximations to a property right that the scientific career affords. Professional prestige is often closely associated with these acquisitions. Small wonder, then, that acrimonious disputes about priority and independence in discovery have often marred the often placid tenor of scientific communication. Even less wonder that many historians of science have seen the individual discovery as an appropriate unit with which to measure scientific progress and have devoted much time and skill to determining what man made which discovery at what point in time.

In economics, where discovery is less problematic than is success in solving some recognized problem, or resolving some apparent paradox, the questions of priority are no less acrimonious, and the claims made on behalf of particular economists are no less strident (Merton 1957). My previous studies in the modern history of general equilibrium analysis have proved to pose more of a minefield than I had expected: The "simultaneous" nature of the proofs of existence of a competitive equilibrium by Arrow and Debreu and by McKenzie – they were publicly presented within twenty-four hours of each other (Weintraub 1985, p. 104) – and the fact that both Arrow and Debreu have been awarded Nobel Memorial Prizes based on that work, whereas McKenzie has not, and the fact that there are those who refer to the Arrow–Debreu model, whereas others refer to the Arrow–Debreu–McKenzie model, should have alerted me to the presence of unresolved issues.

It is this context that has sensitized me to the fact that the 1988 Nobel Memorial Prize awarded to the eminent French economist Maurice Allais has been associated with some problematic claims made on his behalf. Because this chapter is concerned with the development of the literature on dynamics and stability, with a focus on the period from 1939 to 1958, and because claims made on behalf of Allais concern priority for his work in stability theory in that period, it is possible to bring the discussion into sharper focus.

The central problem can be simply stated: In *The New Palgrave,* Bernard Belloc and Michel Moreaux, the authors of the entry on Allais, write that

it is impressive that the research programme defined at the start in Allais (1943) has been almost wholly fulfilled, even though some of the initial basic assumptions have been drastically revised.... Allais [(1943)] gives the earliest formulation of an intertemporal general equilibrium and, in particular, all the arbitrage conditions between capital goods and land are made explicit. *Then the first results on global stability of Walrasian tâtonnement are proved by means of Lyapunov's second method under assumptions equivalent to gross substitutability (cf. Negishi,* Econometrica *(1962), for a report in English).* [Belloc and Moreaux 1987, pp. 78-9, italics added]

Further, the distinguished mathematical economist Jean-Michel Grand-mont wrote, in his "Report on M. Allais' Scientific Work" (Grandmont 1989, p. 5), that

M. Allais proved stability of equilibrium under assumptions which, taken to-gether, are essentially the same as *gross substitutability,* and through an argument that in fact uses Lyapounov stability method (1907). This discovery occurred well before K. Arrow and L. Hurwicz' innovative study of the issue (1958). M. Allais' priority is in particular established by T. Negishi in his survey (1962, p. 656).

This passage is then footnoted as follows:

Allais' proof was not entirely correct, as the Lyapounov function he used was not differentiable everywhere. He may be forgiven, perhaps, for having over-looked this technical point... [ellipsis in original].

Because this claim about Allais's work is based on a particular way in which history is constructed, it is important to be clear not only about that claim but also about the historiographic issue from which it follows. My claim, which I repeat now, is that the history of economic analysis is con-structed, not found, and that historians construct by providing reinterpre-tations of apparently "fixed" texts. So, too, "priority" is constructed, not discovered and then awarded. In what follows, my discussion of Allais's work on stability, and a shorter discussion of Yasui's contribution, will provide the case study for discussion of the historiographic problem.

Negishi on Allais

Section 6 of Negishi's "The Stability of a Competitive Economy: A Sur-vey Article" (1962) was titled "A Contribution of Maurice Allais." It is im-portant to be explicit about Negishi's notice of Allais's work, because the claims of Belloc and Moreaux, and that of Grandmont, rest on Negishi's authority:[10]

A brief comment may be appropriate on the significance of the rather neglected contribution to this field [of stability theory] of M. Allais in 1943. [Here Negishi cites Allais (1943), pp. 486–9.]
    The stability of the Walrasian tâtonnement is discussed. It must be mentioned first that the original model of the tâtonnement due to Allais is not our tâtonne-ment process (T) in the sense that price adjustment is assumed to take place not simultaneously in all markets but successively in one market after another.... Secondly, it must be noted that Allais did not assume gross substitutability (S) explicitly but made assumptions which, taken together, are essentially the same as gross substitutability (S).
    Admitting these points, we can reconstruct Allais' argument in terms of our own model (T) under assumptions (S) and (W) [where (W) is Walras's law]. It will be shown that Allais' argument, if properly reformulated, is the proof of the

stability by the method of Lyapunov, i.e., by the use of a function decreasing through time. [Negishi 1962, p. 656]

We can be quite clear here. Negishi nowhere claimed that Allais proved the major stability theorem relating gross substitutability to stability of the tâtonnement process. Neither did Negishi claim that Allais had rediscovered, or even used, Liapunov theory. Negishi, however, was able to reconstruct one of Allais's arguments in terms of the modern treatment of stability via Liapunov's indirect method. Such a reconstruction is equivalent to a restatement of a Marxian argument in terms of a three-sector linear model – such a reconstruction is not, however, a demonstration that Marx proved, or knew, the second fundamental theorem of linear programming. Belloc and Moreaux, and Grandmont, cite Negishi to support their own claims for Allais's "priority." *Negishi nowhere states anything that allows such a claim to be made, nor does his own treatment of Allais's work on "stability" permit such an interpretation.*

If there is a claim to be made on behalf of Allais, then it must be made by examining Allais's work itself; an argument from Negishi's authority is impermissible.

Allais looking back on his contribution

Perhaps Negishi was wrong; perhaps Allais had in fact proved what Grandmont and Belloc and Moreaux claimed he had proved. That he might have done so is not unreasonable, on the face of it, for he was certainly able enough, and interested enough, to have done so. Further, he had access, in a way English-speaking economists did not, to the dynamic analysis of Poincaré and Liapunov, whose original Russian thesis had been translated and published in French in 1907. (Or might he have had a working knowledge of Picard's books in a way that Samuelson did not?) One of the ways in which we can assess the possibility that Allais "almost" rediscovered Liapunov theory is to consider what Allais believed he had contributed to economic analysis. We have available to us the remarkable document *Contributions à la science économique: Vue d'ensemble, 1943–1978,* published in Paris in 1978 by the Centre d'Analyse Economique, under the auspices of the Centre National de la Recherche Scientifique (CNRS). In this volume Allais reviews his own writings, over the thirty-five years of his published work, and presents what he believes to be his significant contributions to the many fields and subfields, problems and analyses, in which he worked so brilliantly.

We are concerned here with Part II of that book: "Theories de l'évolution et de l'equilibre économique general, de l'efficacite maximale et des fondements du calcul économique." In that part, Allais summarizes and reemphasizes the important results he had obtained in his various writings: The topics are laid out systematically, and within each topic section Allais traces chronologically his own writings on the topic. In this Part II he begins, after an overview, with his reassessment of the major work at issue here, his 1943 book *A la recherche d'une discipline économique. Première partie: l'économie pure.*

He begins reconstructing his contributions by noting that he has gone through the exercise before, in the Introduction to the 1952 reprint edition of the 1943 book:

Dans l'*Introduction* á la deuxième [édition] de 1952, j'ai analysé les *apports originaux* que je pense avoir présentés dans cet ouvrage et je ne puis qu'y renvoyer. Cependant, je crois devoir mentionner ici ceux de ces apports qui, avec le recul du temps, m'apparaissent comme les plus importants. [Allais 1978, p. 32]

(In the Introduction to the second edition of 1952 I analyzed those original contributions that I think I presented in that work. . . . However, I believe that I ought to mention here some of those contributions that, with the passage of time, appear to me as the most important ones.)[11]

He then goes on to list, in order, those ideas and arguments and contributions that he believes to have been significant. Sixth on the list is "démonstration de la stabilité de l'équilibre dans le cas d'une économie walrasienne" (demonstration of the stability of equilibrium in the case of a Walrasian economy). This is followed by a footnote reference to the 1943 book's pages 486–93. He concludes the section with this sentence: "*Sur tous ces points, il s'agit de contributions entièrement nouvelles pour lesquelles il n'existe rien d'équivalent dans la littérature antérieure*" (On all these points, these contributions were entirely new, and there existed no equivalent work in the previous literature) (Allais 1978, p. 34, italics in original). To this Allais appends the following footnote:

Quelques favorables qu'aient été les analyses de mon ouvrage de 1943, leurs auteurs n'ont pas apercu la plupart des apports originaux que je viens de rappeler. Cependant cette circonstance n'est paradoxale qu'en apparence. La raison en est en effet l'incapacité des critiques d'apprécier tout apport que leur réflexions antérieures ne leur ont déjà pas permis d'apercevoir plus ou moins confusément. [Allais 1978, p. 34]

(However favorable were the discussions of my 1943 work, the authors did not notice most of the original contributions that I have recalled here. Yet this is not as paradoxical as it may appear. The reason is essentially the inability of the critics to appreciate any contribution that their own thinking at the time does not already allow them to understand more or less confusedly.)

Allais certainly believed that he had demonstrated the stability of equilibrium for a Walrasian multimarket system. Just as certainly he appears to have believed that his contribution was original, an improvement, and a break with the past work, which in this case must have meant the work of Samuelson and Hicks, not Pareto and Walras. Was that the case?

Before addressing this issue, I want to reiterate that nowhere in this 1978 reconsideration does Allais claim that he used, or understood, or even was aware of Liapunov theory. In his set of strong claims about originality and priority, there is no mention whatsoever about the technique used to prove stability. Failing to find such a claim made on his own behalf, in a context in which such a claim would have been natural, must make one suspicious of the claim made for him by Grandmont and Belloc and Moreaux.

The 1943 stability analysis

It remains, then, to examine the claim that in his 1943 book Allais (1) used explicit Liapunov methods and/or (2) used the indirect Liapunov methods implicitly and/or (3) provided a proof of the stability of the Walrasian multimarket system.

The first claim can be easily dismissed. In Allais's pages 486–93 there is no mention of Liapunov theory, and no function or analysis is identified as Liapunov's indirect method.

Negishi was correct, however, in noting that Allais's analysis could be redone using the language of Liapunov theory. (Indeed, Hicks's stability analysis could be so reconstructed, likewise for Samuelson, even Walras, etc.) To see this, and to appraise the claim that Allais had, twenty-five years before Arrow, Block, and Hurwicz, proved the stability of a Walrasian multimarket system, it is necessary to take up Allais's 1943 analysis in a bit more detail.

Allais begins in Section 193 by arguing that

Le principe de cette démonstration est essentiellement le suivant: Si l'on considère la somme

$$\mathcal{H} = \sum_B |\mathcal{B}_i - \mathcal{B}|$$

des valeurs absolues des différences entre les valeurs des offres et celles des demandes, il est possible de montrer, sous certaines conditions vraisemblables, que cette somme que nous appelerons "fonction caractéristique," ne peut que décroître, lorsqu'un marché élémentaire quelconque évolue conformément à la loi d'évolution des prix. [Allais 1943, pp. 486–7]

(The main idea of this proof is essentially the following: If one considers the sum $\mathcal{H}$ of the values of supply and demand, it is possible to show, under certain reasonable conditions, that this sum, which we call the "characteristic function," can only decrease when one arbitrary market evolves in conformity with the law of the evolution of price.)

It is immediately obvious that this sum, over all markets, of the differences in value between supply and demand, what Allais calls a "characteristic function," is or can be construed as a Liapunov function, and his comment that it will be seen to decrease over the time of operation of the law of markets (the tâtonnement, really) appears to be the modern proof of stability of multimarket equilibrium. *It is not, however, that modern proof at all. One must guard very carefully against reading a historical text against a context that misconstrues it.* Looking for Liapunov functions in the work of Allais leads a modern reader to "see" a proof of a time-decreasing (Liapunov) "characteristic function" when in fact no such proof is presented. What Allais is concerned to show, rather, is that in a neighborhood of equilibrium, that function is a decreasing function of its argument, but that argument is not "time," and no differential or difference techniques are used in Allais's analysis.

How, then, does Allais show that his function decreases if markets are not in equilibrium? He begins with Lemma I (1943, p. 487), which he identifies as "variation avec le prix de l'excès de la valeur de la demande sur celle de l'offre" (variation with price of the excess of the value of demand over that of supply). He here attempts to show that – and this is the first use of this term in economic theory – "*au voisinage [neighborhood] de l'equilibre, et pour des prix croissants, la valeur de l'offre croît plus vite que celle de la demande*" (in a neighborhood of equilibrium, and for increasing prices, the value of supply increases more quickly than that of demand) (p. 488, italics in original). Put another way, in the case of the usual markets, holding all other markets fixed, whether in equilibrium or out, and allowing the one market to adjust, near equilibrium the law of markets (prices move with excess demand) reduces the value of that excess demand, and this is true as long as that market is not in equilibrium. Notice, however, that this argument is based on the specific form of the supply and demand relationships, that these assumptions are not made explicit, and that the structure of the proof is to consider markets *one at a time.*

What is necessary, of course, for a proof is a demonstration that if other markets are allowed to react to the adjustment in the first market, the induced disequilibria themselves are meliorated. This is discussed in "Lemme II – répercussion sur les autres marchés" (repercussions in other markets) (p. 489). Allais breaks up the value of the excess demands into those that move directly with price and those that move inversely with price. He argues that

si en effet sur un marché donné la répercussion de la variation du prix a une incidence plus faible sur les valeurs des demandes que sur celles des offres, cela signifie que, d'une manière générale, l'incidence de la variation du prix considérée est plus faible sur les déterminations des demandeurs que sur celles des offres, d'où l'inégalité $[0 < \delta \mathcal{B}^{y} - \delta \mathcal{B}_{i}^{y} < \delta \mathcal{B}_{i}^{x} - \delta \mathcal{B}^{x}]$. [p. 489]

(Indeed, if on a given market the repercussion of the variation of the price has a weaker effect on the value of demand than on the value of supply, that means that, in general, the effect of the price variation is weaker in the determination of demand than in that of supply, so that one has the inequality...where δ represents a "small change" in the variable in a neighborhood of equilibrium.)

In other words, Allais separates (1) those commodities the values of whose excess demands move in one direction as price rises and (2) those commodities that move in the other direction. The problem clearly is to show that the value of all excess demands in all the markets, taken in the aggregate as the algebraic sum of the two commodity groups' values, is falling as long as all markets are not in equilibrium. To accomplish that demonstration thus requires an argument to show that those values that fall "outweigh" those that rise. Allais discusses this in a series of cases in which he breaks up the value movements into those goods whose excess-demand values move directly with the price movement in market i and those whose excess-demand values move inversely with the price movement in market i. This certainly functions in the manner of the Hicksian division of commodities into the substitute and complement groups, though Allais nowhere makes any assumption about the character of the goods in terms of substitutability. What he has then established is an argument to the effect that each market, *taken individually*, will lead to a reduction of the deviation from equilibrium. Moving through each market in this way will allow the conclusion that, near equilibrium, $\delta \mathcal{K} < 0$, or that the characteristic function will decrease as long as equilibrium has not been established. What remains to be shown, however, is that all these adjustments can be effected simultaneously in the sense that the adjustment in market j in response to the disequilibrium in market i will not in fact lead to a further perturbation in market i in a deviation-amplifying manner.

This step is not taken. Instead, Allais's argument goes on to state that if the result is true in $n-1$ markets, then by the global budget constraint (Walras's law) the result must be true in the nth market as well:

Dans le cas d'une économie walrasienne, lorsque l'égalité de l'offre et de la demande est réalisé pour $(n-1)$ bien elle est également vérifiée pour le n^{e} bien en raison de l'équation globale du budget $\sum(\mathcal{B}_{i} - \mathcal{B}) = 0$ qui reste constamment vérifiée. [p. 492]

(In the case of a Walrasian economy, when the equality of supply and demand is realized for $(n-1)$ goods, it is equally realized for the nth good because of the global budget equation...which remains always true.)

Walras, not Arrow-Block-Hurwicz

It is important to be clear that Allais's analysis of the stability of equilibrium was different from that of Hicks in the sense that stability itself was well defined as a property of equilibria, and the issue was to establish that a Walrasian market equilibrium was stable. Hicks, recall, simply argued that "stable" was equivalent to an equilibrium's being a "maximum"; that was what produced the Hicksian stability conditions as second-order conditions. Allais, in contrast, appeared to understand that a *formal* proof of stability required an argument that discrepancies from equilibrium would be eliminated by the market activity itself. His arguments were designed to demonstrate that a measure of the discrepancy, his "characteristic function," took on smaller and smaller values as market forces acted in disequilibrium states and that the change was proportional to the discrepancy.

Note, however, the problem that Walras himself addressed. As Patinkin (1965, p. 535) argued,

[Walras] realized that a tâtonnement on one price which brings it to equilibrium will generally, because of the interdependence of the system, disturb the equilibrium of other markets. But he argued that the direct pressure of excess demand in a given market definitely pushed its price toward its equilibrium level, while the changes in other prices "exerted indirect influences, some in the direction of equality and others in the opposite direction...so that up to a certain point they cancelled each other out. Hence the new system of prices...is closer to equilibrium than the old system...; and it is only necessary to continue this process along the same lines for the system to move closer and closer to equilibrium" (Walras, *Elements of Pure Economics,* 1954, Jaffee translation from the definitive 1926 Paris edition).

Put this way, Allais was simply formalizing the argument of market-by-market adjustment originally presented by Walras, with a sophisticated treatment of the intermarket interdependences, and an argument that the destabilizing movements would be outweighed by the stabilizing movements.

It is very difficult to "unsee" the "true" theorem associated with this demonstration. Because we "know" that the tâtonnement, in its presentation as a set of simultaneous autonomous differential equations for the multimarket system, will lead globally asymptotically to an equilibrium if Walras's law holds, if the system is continuously differentiable, and homogeneous in prices and income, and gross substitutability prevails, it is hard to disconnect Allais's argument from the later proofs. Allais, of course, assumed a global budget constraint, or Walras's law. His demand and supply functions were drawn as though they were quite well behaved and thus could be taken to provide excess-demand functions that would be continuously differentiable and homogeneous. In order to claim that Allais gave the first real proof, then, it is sufficient to assert that he assumed gross substitutability. That is, in fact, the claim put forth by Grandmont (1989, p. 2):

The conditions postulated by Allais to show that the Lyapounov function decreases along a tâtonnement are essentially that when the price of a commodity (good or service) goes up, excess supply goes up, i.e. excess demand goes down, which is essentially gross substitutability.

The argument is that Allais assumed gross substitutability. In fact, Allais did write "... *au voisinage de l'équilibre, et pour des prix croissants, la valeur de l'offre croît plus vite que celle de la demande.* [There are four footnotes to this clause.] On retrouve ainsi une propriété que l'on peut considérer comme établie par l'experience" (... in a neighborhood of the equilibrium, and for increasing price, the value of supply is increasing faster than that of demand. One thus has found a property that one can consider as established as well in experience) (1943, p. 488, italics in original). The four footnotes, however, make clear what is going on. The first, footnote number 5, concerns the fact that individuals should have similar tastes and wealth: "Si les psychologies et les ressources des individus étaient identiques, on aurait..." (If the psychologies and the resources of the individuals were identical, one would have...). The second, number 6, says "La démonstration faite n'est valable qu'au voisinage de l'équilibre" (The proof is valid only in a neighborhood of equilibrium). The third, number 7, argues that when all individuals are essentially the same, then the equilibrium will be stable. Finally, the fourth footnote, number 8, states that individuals may be sufficiently similar for them to be taken as essentially identical if one considers them to be statistically associated with a median individual.

In other words, Allais based his argument on the assumption that aggregate excess demands would behave exactly as individual excess demands. But because *individual* excess demands for a good are taken to move with the price of that good in accord with substitutability (Allais does believe that demand curves slope downward, etc.), he infers that market excess demands can be so described.

The tool Allais uses to establish stability, his characteristic function, is the discrepancy between the supply and demand curves, the values of supply and demand. Certainly there is no discrepancy in equilibrium, for that condition defines equilibrium. And second, it is certain that if the discrepancy can be made to decrease faster the farther away one is from equilibrium, equilibrium will be achieved. This is no Liapunov function, however, because it is not continuously differentiable. It is, in fact, a simple geometric representation of the usual picture of an excess demand, demand minus supply, near equilibrium, together with an argument that if individuals are similar and curves are linear, then demand and supply curves will look "nice"; of course, in this case the equilibrium will be stable.

The issue is, for assessing "priority," whether the Allais argument actually used a Liapunov function. Unambiguously, the answer is no, because such a function must be continuously differentiable.[12]

The Whig prism through which it is all seen

I shall take a brief detour here to sketch the "modern" treatment of the stability of the competitive equilibrium in economics, for I am arguing that this current treatment has forced the past (e.g., Allais's work) to look a certain way.

If the ith market is characterized by a tâtonnement adjustment process, so that the price of the ith good moves with excess demand for that good, and excess demand is a function of all prices of all n goods, then we have

$$\dot{p}_i = E_i(p_1, p_2, p_3, \dots, p_n) \quad \text{for} \quad i = 1, 2, 3, \dots, n$$

The excess-demand function is assumed to be continuously differentiable, to be homogeneous of degree zero, and to satisfy Walras's law. Thus, if $p = (p_1, \dots, p_n)$ and $E = (E_1, \dots, E_n)$, then $\sum p_i E_i(p) = 0$, or, in vector notation, $p \cdot E(p) = 0$. Assume that $p^* = (p_1^*, \dots, p_n^*)$ is the equilibrium price vector (a vector of relative prices if there are actually $n+1$ markets, or alternatively we can have $\sum p_i = 1$ or $p_n = 1$ if there are n markets, etc.), and define the function $V(p) = \frac{1}{2} \sum (p_i - p_i^*)^2$. That is, let V be a measure of the Euclidean distance of the actual price vector from the equilibrium price vector. V is certainly a Liapunov function, because it is a continuously differentiable function of the state variables (prices) that is everywhere nonnegative and is zero if and only if the state is an equilibrium state.

Differentiating V with respect to time to see whether the system's state variables, along trajectories, approach equilibrium, we have

$$\dot{V}(p) = \sum \dot{p}_i(p_i - p_i^*) = \sum p_i E_i - \sum p_i^* E_i = -\sum p_i^* E_i$$

where the last equality is true by reason of Walras's law. The issue thus is one of the positivity of the equilibrium-price-weighted excess demands. Modern proofs, since Arrow, Block, and Hurwicz, depend on gross substitutability and homogeneity to infer such positivity of the last expression. Note that this expression is the negative of the sum of the values of excess demands, or, because excess demand is demand minus supply, this is the value of supply minus the value of demand. And if the value of supply exceeds the value of demand, then V is decreasing. This is the connection to the interpretations of Allais's argument as being based on a Liapunov function, for Allais's work is a demonstration, based on particular assumptions, of the relationship between the value of supply and that of demand. Those values are not the values discussed here, for the values are not equilibrium price weights.

This bit of modern analysis can be used to say that Allais "almost" used Liapunov analysis, or that his work could be presented as if he had used Liapunov analysis, or that he was doing Liapunov analysis without really knowing it, or that he "was a hair's breadth away" from Liapunov analysis, or that he had an imperfect understanding of Liapunov analysis, and so forth. This reconstruction of a text, this reading of Allais's 1943 work, is a reading of the past from the present in a thoroughly Whiggish manner. We "see" the Liapunov function because we know that the argument that Allais was constructing can be worked using Liapunov analysis. We know that his theorem is provable by a technique that seems to be that toward which his arguments strained. Yet though Allais seemed to use a Liapunov function, in fact he did not. His characteristic function was not necessarily continuous, let alone differentiable as a function of time. Nowhere was there an explicit dynamic system introduced, and the Liapunov function was not defined on the motions of the system. Although it is possible to reconstruct Allais's argument in modern terms, as Negishi did so clearly and well in 1962, it is misleading to suggest, as Belloc and Moreaux have done, that Allais either used Liapunov's second method or proved the stability of the competitive equilibrium in the sense of Arrow and Hurwicz. Allais himself has not made such a claim; his 1943 book can stand on its own considerable merits.

Then was Yasui first? [13]

Before leaving this topic, I would like to note the contributions of Takuma Yasui, pointing out that this Japanese economist was one of the first, if not the first in print, to recognize [14] the importance of Liapunov's stability theory for analyzing the stability of economic equilibria.

Yasui is generally regarded as the progenitor of the tradition of mathematical economics in Japan; the "first generation" of students he influenced comprised Morishima and Ichimura,[15] and their students, also under the Yasui influence, included Inada and Negishi. Yasui's importance was recognized by Shigeto Tsuru (1964) in his "Survey of Economic Research in Postwar Japan" and in its successor article in 1984, less accessible but more detailed: "A Survey of Economic Research in Japan, 1960–1983."

Tsuru states that after Yasui's graduation from Tokyo University in 1931, he concentrated on Walrasian analysis and published a series of studies in the general equilibrium tradition by 1938. His attempt to deal with dynamic analysis was put off course by his reading of Hicks's *Value and Capital,* and he began to take a new interest in stability theory. During the war, "his preoccupation with such abstract theoretical matters was not conducive with his promotion at Tokyo University; and he moved to Tōhoku University, Sendai, in 1944" (Tsuru 1984, p. 295).

As Yasui (1985, p. 1) notes, "I published in 1948 a paper entitled 'The Dynamic Stability Conditions of Economic Equilibrium' which was written without seeing Samuelson's *Foundations of Economic Analysis.* (At that time Japan was occupied by the U.S. Army and any foreign book could not be imported.[16])" That paper, which appeared in *Keizai Shichō,* September 1948 (in Japanese), "applied the matrix theory of Frobenius and made an innovative discovery that the stability condition for the difference-equation type reduces itself mathematically to the conditions elucidated by J. Schur and A. Cohn" (Tsuru 1984, pp. 295–6).[17]

Yasui then tackled the larger task of nonlinear stability analysis, and around 1949 he began

to consult the library of the department of mathematics everyday, and examined one after another a lot of volumes of mathematical journals, mostly German, French, and English, hoping to come across what I needed. . . . Among the fifty articles which I listed . . . a paper with the title "Problème général de la stabilité du mouvement," by A. Liapounoff, in view of its title and content, looked most interesting and fitted to my purpose. So I took up Liapounoff. [Yasui 1985, p. 2][18]

Concerning Yasui's "A General Theory of Stability" (1950), Tsuru correctly notes that Yasui "never chose to even have a summary of it published in English. Thus it is generally conceded that priority in the 'rediscovery' of Liapounoff's theory resided in an article by Arrow and Hurwicz in 1958" (Tsuru 1984, p. 296). Yasui's article is difficult to locate in American libraries; it was published in 1950 in Japanese as "Antei no ippan-riron," *Rironkeizaigaku (Economic Studies Quarterly).*[19]

Yasui (1950) began by considering equations of the form

$$dx_i/dt = X_i(x_1, x_2, ..., x_n) \quad (i = 1, 2, ..., n) \tag{1}$$

Such equations have, without loss of generality, equilibrium solutions of the form $x_i = 0$, for all i. Yasui's analysis initially showed the connection between stability of the first and second kinds, as introduced by Samuelson.

In Part II of the article, Yasui linked the discussion of stability with the theory of quadratic forms, in the manner of Liapunov. He introduced the quadratic form $V(x_1, x_2, ..., x_n)$, which he called the complementary function to X in equation (1). Differentiating V with respect to the variable t, and letting V_1 be that derivative function containing terms only of degree 2 or less, then V_1 is a quadratic form also. Yasui showed that if V is positive definite, and V_1 is negative definite, then the stationary solutions $x_i = 0$ of equation (1) are stable in both the first and second Samuelson meanings; that is, they possess stability of both the first and second kinds (Yasui 1950, pp. 18–19). The proofs of this, and related propositions, were rather detailed; they introduced the salient Liapunov theory into the mathematical economics literature.

The next pages provided examples. Yasui showed that in the constant-coefficient case, where $X_i = a_{i1}x_1 + \cdots + a_{in}x_n$, the function V could be taken as $V = \frac{1}{2}(x_1^2 + x_2^2 + \cdots + x_n^2)$, a positive definite complementary function. The associated function V_1 is the quadratic form $\Sigma \Sigma a_{ij} x_i x_j$. Thus, stability analysis of the constant-coefficient equation system is equivalent to a study of the properties of the induced quadratic form; the eigenvalues of the differential equations and the definiteness of the quadratic form induced by the equation's constant coefficients are equivalent tools to analyze stability of the equilibrium motion of the system.

This example is extended in Part III of the article to the full treatment of the matrix equation $dX/dt = AX$. Yasui briefly examines issues of repeated eigenvalues, and eigenvalues with zero real parts, by means of the Liapunov theory. Although Yasui tackles no specific economic problem with the theory, he does "unpack" the concept of stability and provide its modern meaning; that, of course, was Samuelson's objective in his early 1940s *Econometrica* articles. The Liapunov theory allowed Yasui to present a unified perspective on the dynamic system, its eigenvalues, and its associated quadratic forms.

Yasui appears to have been the first economist to call attention to the importance of Liapunov's contribution to stability theory, and Yasui was the first explicitly to "import" Liapunov theory into the economics literature. The fact that Yasui's paper was written in Japanese and was not readily accessible to English-speaking economists is, of course, important, but it should not be allowed to obscure the influence of his interest in dynamic-theory work on individuals like Morishima and Negishi, whose own contributions to the literature on competitive dynamics were far more influential and wide-ranging than those of Yasui.[20]

This said, it must be recognized that Yasui did not use Liapunov theory to "solve" a problem previously unsolved. He used the theory to simplify previous results. Further, his connection to the developing literature was remote in terms of distance and influence. His was not the work that introduced Liapunov theory to economists who were linked to the line of papers that resulted in the articles of Arrow, Block, and Hurwicz. The question remains, then, about the first "real" use of the theory.

Solomon Lefschetz[21].

If Allais was not the first to "use" Liapunov theory, because he did not use it, and Yasui used it, but not to solve a new problem, then how exactly did that theory come to economics? Certainly it was used by Arrow, Block, and Hurwicz in the late 1950s, but what was the path by which those theorists came to the theory? As suggested earlier, the answer involves looking into the biography of the individual responsible for introducing Liapunov theory to the American *mathematical* community: Solomon Lefschetz.

Lefschetz was born in Moscow in 1884, though his parents moved to Paris shortly after his birth. He was educated in Paris and graduated from the Ecole Centrale des Arts et Manufactures as a mechanical engineer in 1905. Like von Neumann, whose first love, too, was mathematics, Lefschetz trained with a regard for and a concern with employment opportunities. Nevertheless, "at the Ecole Centrale there were two Professors of Mathematics: Emile Picard and Paul Appel, both world authorities. Each had written a three volume treatise.... I plunged into these and gave myself a self-taught graduate course" (Lefschetz 1970, p. 344). But that self-teaching was to come years after his graduation; what intervened was a short-lived career as an engineer in the United States, to which he had emigrated in 1905. He obtained a position at the Baldwin Locomotive Works outside Philadelphia, but in 1907 moved to work for Westinghouse in Pittsburgh. There, in 1907, he fell victim to an industrial accident: A transformer explosion resulted in the loss of both of his hands.

Although he returned to work, his increasing dissatisfaction led him, in 1910, to obtain a fellowship at Clark University to seek a Ph.D. in mathematics. As he later recalled, he assiduously studied the Picard[22] and Appel volumes, and "with a strong French training in the equivalent of an undergraduate course, I was all set" (Lefschetz 1970, p. 344). For his dissertation, he sought "to find information about the largest number of cusps that a plane curve of given degree may possess" (Lefschetz 1970, p. 344). He received a summa cum laude doctorate in 1911.

His mathematical career led him initially to the University of Nebraska, then to the University of Kansas, and eventually, in 1923, to an appointment as an associate professor at Princeton University. It was at Kansas that he had what he would later describe as his two major ideas, the first in algebraic geometry, and the second in topology, this latter associated with his attempts to establish generalizations of the Brouwer fixed-point theorem. For the purposes of this history, however, these mathematically important issues can be slighted; instead, I want to make it clear that Lefschetz, by the early to middle 1920s, was established at one of the preeminent mathematical research schools in the United States. Beginning in 1932, he held the Fine Research Professorship (succeeding Oswald Veblen), which involved no assigned duties whatsoever, and so he could and did range extensively over the mathematical landscape. He was an editor of the *Annals of Mathematics* from 1928 to 1958, and during that time that journal became the leading mathematical journal in English. Further, he continued to use his Russian-language fluency to monitor, for the American Mathematical Society's *Mathematical Reviews,* mathematical work in the USSR. But in a manner similar to the way wartime work had an influence on the mathematical-statistical economists Koopmans, Friedman, and Dantzig, the mathematician Lefschetz found that his interests were "channeled" by the war effort.

With some reticence, he noted that "then came World War Two and I turned my attention to Differential Equations. [Later, with] the Office of Naval Research backing (1946–1955) I conducted a seminar on the subject from which there emanated a number of really capable fellows..." (Lefschetz 1970, p. 349). As his former colleague A. W. Tucker remembered,

[His last switch in interest] came about during World War II, when he was asked to be a consultant to the Navy on problems of nonlinear differential equations. He went on to another career in that area, especially studying global properties. Much of this work was done after he retired [in 1953]. [Tucker 1985, p. 350]

This work developed from a collaboration

with Nicholas Minorsky[23] who was a specialist on guidance systems and the stability of ships and who brought to Lefschetz' attention the importance of the applications of the geometric theory of ordinary differential equations to control theory and non-linear mechanics. From 1943 to the end of his life, Lefschetz' main interest was centered around non-linear ordinary differential equations and their application to controls and the structural stability of systems. [Griffiths, Spencer, and Whitehead 1988, p. 8]

The perspective on Lefschetz's role in "bringing Liapunov to America" is reasonably clear: (1) Lefschetz was exceptionally well placed within the American mathematical community. (2) He was fluent in Russian and in fact was the primary translator of Russian-language abstracts for the American mathematical community.[24] (3) He had a strong interest in stability theory and the qualitative theory of ordinary differential equations from at least 1943, when he was a consultant to Minorsky's navy group.

Lefschetz was to play the leading part in disseminating these applied mathematical ideas. In 1943 he translated, for Princeton University Press (in the Annals of Mathematics Studies, No. 11), the book *Introduction of Nonlinear Mechanics,* by N. Kryloff and N. Bogoliuboff, founders of the Kiev school, noted earlier. Further, in 1949 he caused to be published, in that same Princeton series (as No. 17), the photoreproduction of the 1907 French version (which had been translated from the Russian by Edouard Davaux) of Liapunov's original thesis: The 1907 French paper was titled "Problème genéral de la stabilité du mouvement";[25] the Princeton photo-reproduction carried the same title as that 1907 French translation of the Russian original. Additionally, Lefschetz himself was writing in the field, and by 1946 he had prepared the *Lectures on Differential Equations,* and by 1949 he had supervised the translation, from the Russian, of the immensely important *Theory of Oscillations,* by A. A. Andronov and C. E. Chaikin, again for the Princeton University Press. That work provided the first extensive discussion, in English, of the idea of structural stability, though, as noted, it did not examine at all the issues of the Liapunov indirect method of stability analysis that was to lead to the solution of the problem of "stability of a competitive equilibrium."

In that book's Introduction (p. v), Lefschetz noted that Andronov and Chaikin "are both members of the Institute of Oscillations founded about a decade ago by the late Soviet physicist L. I. Mandelstam." For economists today, the major interest in that book is its thoroughgoing treatment of cycles and its appendix on structural stability, which connected to a later appendix on the Van der Pol equation; that analysis was used in subsequent decades as a paradigm for studying the structural stability problem. All the references to Liapunov are present, but there are no references to or analyses of the "second" or "indirect" method of demonstrating stability of a given system of differential equations, or a nonlinear equation. Though this might appear curious for a book published in 1949, it is not surprising at all when one realizes that the book was a translation of a Russian treatise of 1937, by then considered old.

Finally, Lefschetz "institutionalized" these interests of his in the geometric theory of differential equations. In the immediate postwar period he returned full-time to Princeton:

In 1946 the newly established Office of Naval Research funded a project on ordinary non-linear differential equations, directed by Lefschetz, at Princeton University. This project continued at Princeton for five years past Lefschetz' retirement from the university in 1953. [Griffiths et al. 1988, p. 8][26]

Among the Ph.D. students who worked with Lefschetz at Princeton during that period we particularly note Richard Bellman, who received his degree in 1946, and Donald W. Bushaw, who received his degree in 1952. Bellman became an important proselytizer for the new stability theory, and his immense energy, which helped to create the field of dynamic programming, led him to write numerous expository papers on Liapunov theory and stability analysis that were increasingly accessible to engineers and economists in the early 1950s. His position at the RAND Corporation surely led to his connection with the mathematical economists who also had an association with RAND. Bushaw collaborated with the economist Robert W. Clower (they had been friends as undergraduates at Washington State University[27]) on the book *Introduction to Mathematical Economics,* which was published in 1957, though their collaboration had developed in articles on dynamic problems in economics before the early 1950s.

Their "Price Determination in a Stock-Flow Economy" (Bushaw and Clower 1954) has an excellent bibliography that includes references to a 1951 translation of a 1939 paper by the Russian I. Malkin that introduces Liapunov stability ideas and to the 1949 Russian text on the qualitative theory of differential equations by Nemyckiĭ and Stepanov. These are the earliest references to this Russian literature on stability and control that I have been able to locate in the standard economics literature, and the Bushaw connection to Clower via Lefschetz was the mechanism.[28] Bushaw (1989) has noted that the Nemyckiĭ–Stepanov book "was especially important" when he was learning stability theory, and he and John McCarthy edited one version of the English translation.

What we have, then, is one kind of answer to the question about the mechanism by which Liapunov theory came to be utilized in the economics literature on the stability of competitive equilibria. Economists began to use mathematical tools once those tools became widely used by those working in applied mathematics, engineering, and other applied sciences. Outside economics, the rediscovery of Liapunov theory, or, better, its reintroduction into the theory of differential equations, was associated with increased interest in the applied mathematics community in dissipative dynamic systems, especially their qualitative behavior, or the asymptotic properties of their motions. Issues of control, guidance, and stability became extremely important in war-related research in applied mathematics, and that lent immediacy to the interest in Liapunov theory. The period from 1946 to the early 1950s saw wider dissemination of the results and knowledge of that theory; the path led from the wartime workers to the university mathematicians, to the applied mathematics community and engineers, and thence to the mathematical economics community.

Are precursors possible?

When we speak of a precursor, we seem to suggest that at time $t-2$ an individual presented an analysis that can be reconstructed, from a "perspective" placed at time t, as "essentially equivalent" to an analysis "first" done at time $t-1$. What I have here problematized is the notion that the ideas of "first" and "essentially equivalent" have any meaning independent of the "perspective." As our perspective changes, we "know" different things; the things we see as similar and different change. Once one has "seen" the well-known gestalt psychology drawing of the young woman in a fur coat, she cannot be "unseen" after one notices the alternative, an old crone, nor can the gestalt urn be "unseen" as faces. My younger son, having been at age eight years reminded that at age three he confused the words "pigeon" and "midget" as "pidget" can at age thirteen no longer see a little person without seeing a strutting bird as well. It is no different with mathematical work.

We can, of course, reconstruct the past as we wish, read the past in any one of a number of ways. Indeed, we are forced to provide such readings. We are the readers, and our histories, both social and personal, are the contexts for our readings. We impute similar contexts to our own readers: I would construct this paragraph differently for a historian-reader.

Precursor studies seem to function, then, as legitimizers of a historian's interest in certain past contributors, or possibly marginalized members of a particular scientific community. Rhetorically, calling A "B's precursor," where we can assume a reading community's interest in B, legitimizes an interest in A, if A was not previously well known. In like manner, if a previously unknown B's current contribution can be reconstructed as the fully articulated version of the already famous A's almost-analysis, then A's "precursorness" may further enhance a glorious reputation. "It's all in Marshall," after all. Or is it all in Allais?

To the 1950s

The Soviet mathematical approach to dynamic systems, and Liapunov's second method, came to the attention of the Western mathematical community through the interest and energy of Solomon Lefschetz, whose own interest was spurred by Minorsky. The route of the theory on its way to economists is also fairly clear once it is recognized that by the end of the 1940s the material was accessible to a graduate student in mathematics interested in dynamics or stability or the qualitative theory of ordinary differential equations. The Poincaré–Birkhoff tradition in dynamics, which influenced the stability analysis of Samuelson, and thus a generation of mathematical economists trained from his 1947 book, became less important in the 1950s as the mathematics of dissipative systems was reconstituted by Liapunov theory. The new material was important to engineers concerned with matters of guidance and control and was available to them and to the applied mathematics community in a variety of translations, research memoranda, and lecture notes by the late 1940s. It gradually entered into the mathematical economics literature in the early 1950s, and one of the ways in which it appeared was through the Lefschetz–Bushaw–Clower connection.[29]

It might be concluded from this discussion that we should be unsurprised that Liapunov theory began to be used commonly in economics by the late 1950s, because stability analysis of competitive equilibria was itself a topic that was of current interest, and the level of mathematical sophistication among economists was greater in the 1950s than it had been in the early 1940s when Samuelson's papers on dynamics first appeared. But was the interest of economists in the stability of equilibrium really such a simple meshing of the concerns of two communities?

It was certainly true that the way in which the mathematical stability literature was being reconstructed by the new Liapunov theory encouraged economists to participate in the new dynamics community, for whereas the older material had been written for mathematicians and mathematical physicists,[30] the Liapunov theory, as it was presented in books like that of Andronov and Chaikin, was presented by means of applications to simple engineering systems. Further, the systems used in the late 1930s by economists to model market systems were dissipative systems. There were no variational systems in the economists' tool kits; as Mirowski (1989a, b) has made clear, it is important to acknowledge the fact that conservation laws do not exist in economics. The equations of motion that were taken to describe or construct a theory of multimarket price adjustment were autonomous differential equations with no constraints on the motions (as would be true of a Hamiltonian system). Consequently, the Liapunov indirect method appeared to be what was needed to explore the asymptotic, or stability, properties of the competitive multimarket price-adjustment model.

Stability theory was a mathematical theory developed to analyze a particular set of applications in physics and engineering. As economists came to structure their own discussions of the stability of the "economy" or "economic system" in terms of mathematical models of markets and competitive market systems, the mathematical theory of Liapunov was increasingly available to solve the well-defined formal problem. It was not the case that this was a tool searching for a problem to solve.

Koopmans once wrote that

the difficulty in economic dynamics has been that the tools have suggested the assumptions rather than the other way around. Until we succeed in specifying fruitful assumptions for behavior in an uncertain and changing economic environment, we shall continue to be groping for the proper tools of reasoning. [Koopmans 1957b, p. 183]

It is this kind of argument that I believe is called into question by the historical notes presented here. *It is a deep misconception that tools arise to solve problems, where those problems are contextually distinguishable from the tools themselves.* In the case of stability theory, and Liapunov analysis, the problem context shifted as the tool was understood better, and the tool was refined by its success in solving, or failing to solve, particular problems. In the 1930s, dynamic analysis was conceptualized as tracing the evolution of key economic variables through time and distinguishing between static and dynamic models. In the 1940s, stabilization and control themes organized dynamic economic analysis, and there was a not-unrelated shift in the mathematical theories used to unpack the economic arguments. That is, the economic conceptualizations selected the tools, *and* the mathematical tools selected the economic conceptualization. Once one sees a mathematical system of interrelated differential equations, with equilibria some of which can be attractors of arbitrary motions, and once one sees that one can sometimes steer a system to a particular equilibrium over time if the equilibrium is stable, then one's idea of the economy itself changes if the economy is a "system." The new mathematical tool did more than change the particular problem; it changed the economy itself as the economy had come to be differently problematized. There is, as Koopmans recognized, an interaction between tools and reasoning, but it goes deeper than his essay suggested. It is not the case that there are "problems," "tools," and "ways to reason about problems," where only the latter two items interact. In fact, all three concepts form and reform each other.

PART II

From history to interpretation

CHAPTER 5

The brittleness of the orange equilibrium

I want you to remember that words have those meanings which we have given them; and we give them meanings by explanations.
Ludwig Wittgenstein (1960, p. 27)

The proof. . . changes our concepts. It makes new connexions and changes the concept of these connexions.
Ludwig Wittgenstein (1956, p. 166)

Mathematical economists are members of an interpretive community (Fish 1980), and it is sometimes suggested that the creation of mathematical texts in economics is associated with that community's desire to avoid serious issues of interpretation: Mathematics is thought to produce a text that allows little or no variability in a reader's response (e.g., a real number is not a metaphor).[1] My argument, however, will show that a mathematical text *established* one of several competing interpretations and forced readers to select one image from a set of images; mathematical work has, in at least one case, shifted economist-readers' use of a word.

At issue is the word "equilibrium" and how its meaning evolved in a sequence of papers published between 1939 and 1954. Although "equilibrium" is a term that appears in the hard core of the neo-Walrasian program, and "hard core" suggests linguistic fixity, that connotation is misleading. I am not, of course, interested in the "true" meaning of equilibrium. I am instead interested in how an interpretive community read the word "equilibrium" over a fifteen-year period. In McCloskey's terms (1983, 1986), one must examine the rhetoric associated with some writings about equilibrium. In contrast to his case studies of purchasing-power parity and Robert Fogel's historical analyses, I want to study change, to paint over the austere Lakatosian landscape with the bright colors of language.[2]

Value and Capital

Two passages from Hicks's *Value and Capital* prefigure many later themes:

If a small rise in price does not make supply greater than demand, when all its repercussions have been allowed for, then there will be no tendency at all for

99

equilibrium to be restored. The market will move away from equilibrium rather than towards it. [Hicks 1939, p. 66]

A market is in equilibrium, statically considered, if every person is acting in such a way as to reach his most preferred position, subject to the opportunities open to him. This implies that the actions of different persons trading must be consistent. [Hicks 1939, p. 58]

Hicks offers two images of "equilibrium." The first is associated with mechanics and is impersonal in tone and hard in texture (e.g., "in balance," "equally opposed forces"). The second brings to mind individuals acting as if in harmony one with another, and it is called forth with language like "coordination of activity," "the invisible hand," "rational agents," and so forth. The first of the preceding passages speaks of a "market," the latter of a "person"; the two different ways of characterizing equilibrium arose from two different traditions.[3]

Hicks recognized that the market equilibrium was associated with Marshall, whereas the more individualistic alternative was associated with Walras and Pareto: "In deciding to treat the general theory of exchange before dealing with production, we are following the example of Walras rather than Marshall" (Hicks 1939, p. 57).

1. In one case studied by Hicks, individual persons trade, and perhaps they reach equilibrium:

Of course, this ideal state of equilibrium never exists; but a sense of mutual advantage is perpetually bringing about approximations to it, by prompting both of any two men whose scales of marginal significance do not coincide, directly or indirectly to effect exchanges and readjustments until they do.... When a state of equilibrium has been reached – that is to say, when the conditions for exchange and readjustment no longer exist.... [Wicksteed 1945, pp. 144–5]

Thus, it is not just the distinction between Marshall and Walras that is at issue, but the distinction between Marshall, on the one hand, and Wicksteed and Edgeworth, on the other.

2. In the other case, production creates supply, which is a force opposed to demand; supply and demand together determine an equilibrium position of rest for the economic system:

When demand and supply are in stable equilibrium, if any accident should move the scale of production from its equilibrium position, there will be instantly brought into play forces tending to push it back to that position; just as, if a stone hanging by a string is displaced from its equilibrium position, the force of gravity will at once tend to bring it back to its equilibrium position. The movements of the scale of production about its position of equilibrium will be of a somewhat similar kind. [Marshall 1961, p. 346]

Hicks's language induced two images of equilibrium. *For Hicks, indeed, the two ways of imagining equilibrium defined the tension that his book was presented to resolve.* That is, he believed that his method of analysis added a Marshallian dynamic theory to the static theory of Walras and Pareto. That static theory could not address problems in monetary economics, for the business cycle literature was concerned with the time paths of processes that worked themselves out in a monetary economy. Static or mechanical equilibrium notions failed to encompass the ideas of monetary theory. Consequently, Hicks's stability analysis tried to reconcile the two images of equilibrium. His ideas of perfect and imperfect stability were a flawed[4] attempt to blend the imagery of agents acting to make themselves better off with the image of a state of rest of the set of relative prices in the economy. Thus, by 1939 there certainly were two distinct sets of images used to characterize equilibrium. In stating this as a fact, I am not committed to stating that this disjunction did or did not originate with Hicks, nor am I saying that there was any conscious tension in the minds of economists between these two sets of images. I am simply noting the discrepancy and identifying its dimensions.

Paul Samuelson

Paul Samuelson's mathematical training was discernible in his earliest writings, in which "equilibrium" was defined in the language of dynamic systems. Consider "Dynamics, Statics, and the Stationary State" (1943), which was an applied companion piece to the two-part *Econometrica* (1941–2) paper "The Stability of Equilibrium" (in which he introduced both dynamics and the correspondence principle). These papers form Part II of his book *Foundations of Economic Analysis,* which appeared in 1947.

In this 1943 paper Samuelson states that there is a problem in distinguishing between "statics" and "dynamics"; he develops his argument by citing writers who had, like Marshall, been confused by the distinction. He writes: "We may say that a system is dynamical if its behavior over time is determined by functional equations in which 'variables at different points of time' are involved in an 'essential' way" (1943, p. 59). Samuelson attributes this definition to Frisch (1936). The Frisch-Samuelson definition was introduced by an important paragraph:

In defining the term dynamical, at least two possibilities suggest themselves. First, it may be defined as a general term including statical as a special rather degenerate case. Or on the other hand, it may be defined as the totality of all systems which are not statical. Much may be said for the first alternative; the second, however, brings out some points of controversy in the literature and will be discussed here. This decision involves no point of substance, since only verbal problems of definition are involved. [Frisch 1936, p. 59]

This important passage has a simple meaning, as well as a much more complex meaning:

1. The simple idea is as follows: From a mathematical point of view,
    consider any general dynamic system of the form $F_i(x_1, x_2, ...) =$
    0; if x_i is of the form dx_i/dt, then in the sense defined by the con-
    ditions of the implicit-function theorem, F_i can be simplified as
    $dx_i/dt = f_i(x_1, x_2, ...)$, for $i = 1, 2, ..., n$. Thus, a static system
    of the form $f_i(x_1, x_2, ...) = 0$ is a special case of the general (pos-
    sibly dynamic) system; the specialization requires that for all i,
    $dx_i/dt = 0$.
2. Alternatively, define the set of all nonstatic systems as the set of dy-
    namic systems. Then "nonstatic" means that $F_i(x_1, x_2, ..., x_n) = 0$,
    where the x_i may be time-dependent. Then if no x_i is time-depen-
    dent, we have the static system $f_i(x_1, x_2, ...) = 0$, which equation
    does not involve time directly.

Suppose we adopt the second definition of a static system. Because such
a system is fundamentally nondynamic, we must have that equilibrium is
defined by $f_i = 0$; the balance of forces defines the equilibrium. Alternatively, if we adopt the first point of view, the static system is the limiting
case, or the special case, of a degenerate dynamic system. "Equilibrium" is then interpreted as the limit of the dynamic behavior of the system. That is, a solution of the dynamic system involves time, so as time
is allowed to pass out of the picture, as it were, or is integrated out by a
limiting process, or if we wait until time is no longer meaningful to the
statement of the problem, $\lim_{t \to \infty} x_i(t) = \tilde{x}$, the equilibrium.

To reiterate, for the system $dx_i/dt = f_i(x_1, x_2, ..., x_n)$, we can define
"equilibrium" $\tilde{x}$ in two ways:

1. If $x_i(t)$ is any motion or solution of the system, "equilibrium" is
    defined by $\lim_{t \to \infty} x_i(t; t_0) = \tilde{x}$; in this case of the degenerate dy-
    namic problem, equilibrium is linked to the eventual playing out
    of certain behaviors over time. We "settle into" equilibrium, or
    we can conceive of "agents reaching equilibrium" over time. These
    images lead to characterizations of equilibrium that associate ideas
    like "coordination" and the "process whereby agents..." with
    the idea of *equilibration*; the activity of achieving equilibrium
    plays a larger role than does the terminal state of rest.
2. If $\tilde{x} = (\tilde{x}_1, ..., \tilde{x}_n)$, where $\tilde{x} = \tilde{x}(t; t_0)$, $f_i(\tilde{x}) = 0$ defines "equilib-
    rium." Here, "equilibrium" is characterized by the satisfaction
    of a set of static conditions; we speak a language of "equilibrium
    conditions," "balances of forces" of supply and demand, "mar-
    ket clearing," and so forth. Even if the equilibrium conditions
    are maximization conditions for households and firms, there is
    no mechanism that could establish the position of equilibrium.

Thus, by the early 1940s, Samuelson had clarified the distinction between statics and dynamics. The formalization that he used to present and organize his analysis was that of dynamic systems, taken in part from the work of A. J. Lotka, George David Birkhoff, and others (see Chapter 3). That comprehensive theory obliterated the distinction between equilibrium as a behavioral outcome and equilibrium as a mechanical rest point. In the class of models that Samuelson used to present his analysis, the two images of equilibrium were merged: either could characterize the state of the system $f_i(x_1, x_2, \ldots) = 0$, $i = 1, 2, \ldots, n$, and any distinction truly involved "no point of substance... but only verbal problems of definition."

Samuelson's work on dynamics was but one part of a larger theme that concerned him in that period: finding "meaningful theorems of observational significance" (1941, p. 97). By that he meant that the observations in economics, those things that were shown by data, were changes in equilibrium positions resulting from changes in a parameter; to use later econometric language, Samuelson was concerned with the identification problem. If a price was in equilibrium before and after a parameter change, it was not necessary to say anything about the equilibrium save the predicted direction of the price change induced by the parameter change. Except for his interest in comparative statics, Samuelson was uninterested in the equilibrium position. Neither was he interested in untangling the differing interpretations of the statement that "a position of an economic system is an equilibrium position." He believed that the two conflicting interpretations of equilibrium were illusory, for if one were careful in defining (mathematically) the notion of a static system, then both interpretations would collapse to a single formal definition.

To reiterate, Samuelson's approach to analysis was to emphasize maximization and the correspondence principle:

Within the framework of any system, the relationships between our variables are strictly those of mutual interdependence. It is sterile and misleading to speak of one variable as causing or determining another. Once the conditions of equilibrium are imposed, all variables are simultaneously determined. Indeed, from the standpoint of comparative statics, equilibrium is not something which is attained; it is something which, if attained, has certain properties. [1947, p. 9]

In Samuelson's work, the distinctions between the uses of and the images associated with the word "equilibrium" were lost in the mathematical structure; that structure allowed one to talk of "equilibrium positions characterized in the following manner," but it did not have a grammar for usages like "the equilibrium arises from" or "equilibrium is achieved when."

As Hahn notes,

Samuelson does not appear to have committed himself to a formal description of what we are to understand by intertemporal equilibrium.... In particular, he maintains that in general there is no privileged motion of the economy (no sequence) that we want to designate as equilibrium and the stability of which deserves particular attention. Rather it is the asymptotes of "each and every motion of the system" (Samuelson 1947, p. 330) that he proposes to study. [Hahn 1983, p. 33]

That is, the behavior of the system, specifically how it responds to change (comparative statics), is of more importance than any particular reference point designated "equilibrium."

This suggests that Samuelson, having reduced the study of equilibrium to a study of the properties of the solution to a set of equations (which solution was assumed in all cases to exist), was unconcerned with equilibrium as an organizing concept and, rather, used the properties of systems as that organizer. He reminds one of the approach of physicists, not mathematicians:

[In] a series of papers on the partial differential equations of mathematical physics [the mathematician Richard] Courant's primary concern was *existence*. The significance of this concern on the part of mathematicians is sometimes questioned by even quite sophisticated physicists. They are inclined to feel that if a mathematical equation represents a physical situation, which quite obviously exists, the equation must then of necessity have a solution. [Reid 1976, p. 95]

Like physicists mistrustful of mathematicians, Samuelson believed that his equations characterized "reality" or the "real economic situation." Samuelson linked "equilibrium" and the mathematical analysis of solutions of equation systems; his work was a stepping-stone to the papers by McKenzie (1954) and Arrow and Debreu (1954).

Arrow and Debreu

The text for this discussion is "Existence of an Equilibrium for a Competitive Economy" (Arrow and Debreu 1954; cf. Weintraub 1983). Who were the readers of the Arrow–Debreu paper in 1954? The readers of *Econometrica* in 1954 did not have the Xerox machine available, nor did they have discussion papers "on line" for circulation of research work prior to publication.[5] For 1954, we may presume that the function of a scientific journal was to propagate new research findings and to serve as the repository of record for the settling of priority claims to new results. The Econometric Society was not large in 1954, so the journal of that society was not read by large numbers of economists. The members were a mixed group, with young, postwar-trained economists probably predominating. The research traditions were not heavily mathematical; there were few places where training in the calculus was required, and a student who had some knowledge of calculus was placed on the mathematical track.

The early part of the paper provides many clues to its authors' assumptions about their readers' interests and backgrounds. The first paragraph begins with "L. Walras," which defines the Continental tradition in economics and places the article in opposition to the Marshallian partial equilibrium approach. The second paragraph provides some reasons for studying the problem and justifies itself to its readers on the basis of both descriptive and normative considerations: "The view that the competitive model is a reasonably accurate description of reality, at least for certain purposes, presupposes that the equations describing the model are consistent with each other" (Arrow and Debreu 1954, p. 265).

Also, because every competitive equilibrium is Pareto-efficient, and every Pareto-efficient allocation can be considered to be a competitive equilibrium, an interest in efficiency-promoting social actions requires analysis of the existence of equilibrium for competitive economies. Thus, the fourth paragraph of the introduction presents, in ordinary language, the major theorems and the assumptions that entail those conclusions, and the fifth paragraph comments on those assumptions. The sixth introductory paragraph specifies what the reader needs to know to read the paper: "Mathematical techniques are set-theoretical. A central concept is that of an abstract economy, a generalization of the concept of a game" (p. 266). The introduction ends with this sentence: "The last section contains a detailed historical note."

The initial Arrow–Debreu paragraphs located the 1954 readership and the manner in which the readers would partition themselves among ways of reading. The introduction provided a guide for the interested reader who had little mathematical skill beyond rudimentary mathematical analysis; such an individual would note the "Walrasian tradition," acknowledge the reasons for proving the existence of equilibrium, think a bit about the economic assumptions that were used to get the theorem proved, and then skip over to the two-page historical note. That note tied the 1954 paper to a series of past contributions by economists whose work would have been casually known to all readers of the journal.

The introductory paragraphs were thus inclusionary; they invited all readers of the journal to participate in the article, to construct the text for their own purposes. The material in Section 1 of the article, however, restricted readership, served an exclusionary function.

Three paragraphs into that section (p. 267) the reader met with

1.2.1 $x \leqq y$ means $x_h \leqq y_h$ for each commodity h;
      $x \leq y$ means $x_h \leqq y_h$ but not $x = y$;
      $x < y$ means $x_h < y_h$ for each component h.
      R^l is the Euclidean space of l dimensions....
      $\Omega = \{x \mid x \in R^l, x \geq 0\}$....

Any reader unfamiliar with the emergent notational conventions in linear algebra would have been baffled by these lines and possibly would not even have noticed the difference between the symbols $\leq$ and $\leqq$. This notation and its set-theoretic background were not part of an economics curriculum in 1954; in the mathematics curriculum, this vector-order notation was specialized to the theory of games, which was not an established mathematical subdiscipline in the early 1950s.

Equilibrium was formally defined by

1) y_j^* maximizes $p^* \cdot y_j$ over the set Y_j, for each j;
2) x_i^* maximizes $u_i(x_i)$ over the set:
   $\{x_i \mid x_i \in X_i, \; p^* \cdot x_i \leq p^* \cdot \zeta_i + \sum_{j=1}^{n} \alpha_{ij} p^* \cdot y_j^*\}$;
3) $p^* \in P = \{p \mid p \in R^l, \; p \geq 0, \; \sum_{h=1}^{l} p_h = 1\}$;
4) $z^* \leq 0$, $p^* \cdot z^* = 0$, where $x = \sum x_i$, $y = \sum y_i$, $\zeta = \sum \zeta_i$, $z = x - y - \zeta$.

These four conditions define the Arrow–Debreu equilibrium. The first condition states that at the equilibrium price vector p^* and input–output vector y^*, profits are maximized. The second condition says that at the equilibrium price vector p^* and consumption vector x^*, utility is maximized. The third condition defines feasible prices, and the fourth condition states that at the equilibrium price vector, all markets clear in the sense that net excess demand is zero on all markets.

The approach that Arrow and Debreu take to showing that the competitive model has an equilibrium in the sense of the preceding paragraph is to apply the notion of a Nash equilibrium for noncooperative n-person games. A Nash equilibrium is defined by the idea that at an equilibrium, each agent is maximizing his or her payoff, given the equilibrium actions of the other agents.

The proof of the existence of equilibrium is presented in a straightforward manner:

[Each] of the first m participants, the consumption units, chooses a vector x_i from X_i, subject to the restriction that $x_i \in A_i(\bar{x}_i)$, and receives a payoff $u_i(x_i)$; the jth out of the next n participants, the production units, chooses a vector y_j from Y_j (unrestricted by the actions of the other participants), and receives a payoff $p \cdot y_j$; and the last agent, the market participant, chooses p from P (again the choice is unaffected by the choices of other participants), and receives $p \cdot z$. [p. 274]

Informally, each consumer makes a restricted consumption choice and receives a provisional utility payoff, which leads to demands for goods and supplies of factors; each firm makes a restricted input–output choice, which leads to a provisional profit payoff, which leads to supplies of goods and demands for factors. The fictitious market-maker chooses prices in the markets and compares the demands and supplies that are induced in those markets by the actions of the agents who are reacting to the prices that the market-maker chooses. That is, the "center" selects market prices, all agents make their choices on the basis of those prices, and their choices lead to supplies and demands. The center compares supplies and demands and changes prices accordingly. Does this process of price → supply–demand → new price → . . . ever lead to a price → supply–demand → same price? If so, that "maintained" price is an equilibrium. In other words, an equilibrium price, were it to exist, would be one that would mediate among the conflicting desires of the agents, who then would have no incentive to take further action.

This proof strategy forces the reader to accept the idea that an equilibrium is a set of prices and quantities that will not be "objected to in practice" by the agents in the economy. The supply–demand balance serves only as the mechanism by which agents compare notes to see whether they are going to be satisfied; the language is not "equilibrium *is* a supply–demand balance," but rather "when in equilibrium, supply and demand are in balance." Still another way to put it is to go back to the definition and note that conditions 3 and 4 are necessary for an equilibrium, but conditions 1–4 are the necessary and sufficient conditions for the equilibrium. *In the Arrow–Debreu model, the coordination of agents' plans through optimization is necessary for equilibrium, and the clearing of markets as a balance is necessary for equilibrium, but they jointly are necessary and sufficient for equilibrium.*

The "supply–demand balance" is thus what remains of the older images of balance beams and forces. It serves, simply put, as a reference point for some fictitious market-maker to tell the players to keep on playing, for they are not yet coordinated. If, indeed, all agents were to get this information for themselves, from their own actions, then the supply–demand balance idea would not be associated with equilibrium except after the fact; that is, if the message "lack of coordination" could be triggered directly by the lack of harmony among agents' plans, and that message would lead to a revision of those plans in a self-correcting manner, then there would no longer be any need for the "market" to function as an information-dissemination device that says "keep on trading."

Conclusion

The positivist argues that the idea of equilibrium is associated with some aspect of the real world and that the task in the scientific analysis of competitive equilibrium is to create better, or more realistic, models of equilibrium; the test of the theory of equilibrium is thus verisimilitude, correspondence with the real world in which equilibrium is to be found. The post-positivist, the pragmatist, maintains that there is no meaning of "equilibrium" except as that word is used by the community of economists who read and write texts in which the word "equilibrium" appears; the meaning of "equilibrium" is derived from the use to which the word is put by the community of readers of texts on equilibrium analysis. More directly, as "equilibrium" is dependent for its meaning on the context in which it is found, the meaning of "equilibrium" changes over time as the texts change. No meaning has a privileged status because of its presumed correspondence to the true equilibrium out there in the world.[6] "Equilibrium" is associated with a Wittgensteinian language game, and the meaning of the word is dependent on the players of the game and the rules that they decide to play by at a particular moment in the history of economic thought.

The foregoing exercise paid attention to a rhetorical issue. We saw that analysis of a shift in the meaning of the word "equilibrium" was associated with a change in the images called forth in the reader's mind when the word "equilibrium" appeared on the page. We saw that the image change was induced by a mathematical proof strategy and that the mathematical tool itself foreclosed a set of language options, effectively terminating a particular line of inquiry. Although I have been presenting this argument as if it were entirely original, it is not that at all. The quotations from Wittgenstein should suggest to the alert reader that even for mathematics, the rhetorical analysis was done by Wittgenstein. For an absolutely first-rate discussion of these points and a full discussion of two other case studies of mathematical language games in "real" mathematics, see Bloor's Chapter 5, "Mathematics: An Anthropological Phenomenon" (Bloor 1983).

The fundamental shift in the imagery of equilibrium was created by the Arrow–Debreu linking of an equilibrium price vector in a general equilibrium model with a Nash equilibrium, which was really the fixed point of a mapping from prices "given" to prices "induced by the actions of agents." Thus, the equilibrium metaphor shifted from a balance between market forces to a price that, once established by the desires of the agents, would not be modified as long as the desires of the agents remained unchanged.

The ordinary language of economic analysis was, in this case at least, modified by the metaphors associated with a mathematical theorem.[7] The influence of mathematical economics on the corpus of standard economic analysis goes deeper than is usually acknowledged by both friends and opponents of the mathematization of economics.

Discussion

Student: I have listened to the arguments you have been presenting, teacher, and I must tell you that I can hold my comments to myself no longer. You have argued as though there has been a change in the way we talk about equilibrium. You have traced the various ways that the word "equilibrium" has been embedded in models and theories. You have argued that there are images, which change over time, associated with the word "equilibrium." But nowhere have you had the courage to say that one use, or another, is the correct use. Your unwillingness to say whether equilibrium as used by Samuelson is an improvement over its use by Hicks pushes scholarly objectivity to its limits. You must, sooner or later, commit yourself to some position.

Teacher: On what must I commit myself?

Student: To the view that one use of "equilibrium" is correct and another is not correct, or is at least less nearly correct.

Teacher: Why must I assert that one use of a term is correct?

Student: Because our theories are not whimsical. We construct theories to explain the real world, to help us predict phenomena in the real world. "Equilibrium" is a characteristic of the world, and we want models and theories to explain that phenomenon.

Teacher: Where is equilibrium?

Student: What?

Teacher: Where is the equilibrium that you want to explain by the use of theoretical analysis? Is it in my garden, or is it in France? Where may I observe it?

Student: Every time you observe a price you are observing an equilibrium, because that price is a market outcome.

Teacher: Then why call it an equilibrium instead of just a price?

Student: I call them equilibrium prices because they do not change.

Teacher: What about a price of wheat that changes when there is a drought?

Student: Supply has changed, so the equilibrium price changes.

Teacher: It sounds to me more like you have a theory about prices that leads you to call some prices equilibrium prices and others not. Your equilibrium is a theoretical construct, not a feature of reality. In general, equilibrium is a feature of our models, not the world: You should agree with Dorfman, Samuelson, and Solow (1958, p. 351) that "it is the model we are analyzing, not the world."

Student: But what about the truth of the theory? Are you not the least concerned with the truth or falsehood of your theory of equilibrium? Surely you cannot call a tree an "equilibrium" and then argue that an equilibrium has leaves. Don't you think that economics must explain the real world if it is to be useful?

Teacher: Why are you distinguishing between "the real world" and a "useful theory"?

Student: Because I want to know whether my economic theories are correct. How can the theories be judged true or false if there is no reality independently to confirm or disconfirm those theories?

Teacher: Reality does not disconfirm theories; theories are disconfirmed by data or observations or evidence. There is a lot of evidence around, and the choice of what evidence is appropriate to the discussion generated by a particular theory is a feature of the discussion, not "reality."

Student: You cannot possibly believe that there is no world out there, a world of people working at jobs, factories producing goods, governments taxing and spending, central bankers fighting inflation, and so forth. That is the economy, the real world of relevance to economists, and the world that our theories must explain.

Teacher: Of course, I am not denying that there are objects in the sense that we talk about objects. I am simply saying that our theories are "in" language and that our explanations are "in" language, not "in" stones or trees or factories. Our explanations are conversations we have with ourselves and with each other, not monologues directed to rocks and machines.

Student: But don't those explanations have to be connected to reality, to the rocks and machines and unemployed workers?

Teacher: Perhaps, or perhaps not. The only point I wish to emphasize is that there is nothing productive to be said about those connections, about the truth of theoretical propositions.

Student: Are you saying that there is no criterion that can distinguish between truthful and untruthful propositions or explanations?

Teacher: My argument is simply that the success of the enterprise, the human activity, we call "science" does not depend on "Truth" at all; rather, it is contingent on the propositions and statements and claims and arguments and counterarguments that are created by individual scientists.

Student: I cannot believe you mean what you are saying. If your science, or in this case economics, stands totally apart from the real economy, why should I bother with it? Why should I study an economics that cannot explain real events?

Teacher: In any useful sense of the term "explanation" I am sure that economics explains various data and observations and facts and phenomena. I am perfectly happy agreeing that there are many truths, but nothing that can be called Truth. There is no characteristic shared by true propositions that can be abstracted from those propositions and called an attribute – Truth. Aside from saying that proposition A is true and proposition B is true, and both A and B are true, there is no attribute that is shared by A and B and all the other true propositions; at least nothing can be said about them that is philosophically interesting.

Student: What are the implications for science? You argued that there are some.

Teacher: For the practice of science, for the way individual scientists go about doing science each day, I do not believe that there are any implications of this at all! For metascience, or the ways we talk about the activity of science, I believe that the major implication is that science, or Science, is not an enterprise defined by success in uncovering Truth, nor does Science stand in any privileged position with respect to Truth, for if there is nothing useful to be said about Truth, there is no reason to defend Science as a Truth-seeking and -finding enterprise. The justification for Science, or the various sciences like botany, chemistry, economics, physics, and so forth, must be different from their "ability to search for Truth and find it." The success of physics is independent of Truth and should be discussed with reference to the various true propositions that physicists can utter, the prediction successes of physicists, and the contingent theories and experimentation in which physicists engage.

Student: For economics, this means that there is no meaning to be attached to "the economy," I presume.

Teacher: Not so. It is just that we do not justify, or rather appraise the merit of, our theories, our research programs, on the basis of the Truth of those theories, the degree to which they correspond to "the reality of the economy," as it were. Just as in physics, we find theories plausible or not, interesting or not, *true or not,* independent of the success of the theories in possessing the attribute called Truth.

Student: But why should the method of conjectures and refutations, the usual process of scientific investigation, lead to all the interesting or plausible or true propositions about the economy, about economics? Why, in other words, should the use of mathematics, statistics, theory, testing, *et hoc genus omne* be taken to define the appropriate way to do economics?

Teacher: They should not be so taken.

Student: Should astrologers, and Wall Street chartists, be thought of as productive economists?

Teacher: Be careful. If you are talking about the profession "economist," I think that it is at least in part defined by a common training of its members, a common language, and so forth. These issues are well known to sociologists of science, who study the scientific communities. Your question could mean something a bit different, however, and that is, Can an astrologer ever speak a true proposition about the economy or uncover a true proposition about economic phenomena?

Student: Can poets be sources of interesting propositions about the economy in the same sense that econometricians are sources of interesting propositions about the economy?

Teacher: An answer might turn on the meaning of the phrase "in the same sense," for if you refer to the ability to utter true propositions, I must say that the poet and the econometrician are symmetric in my view of things; neither, because of their expertise, has an inside track on the Truth (which is uninteresting), whereas each can utter plausible but different truths. The truths that Marx wrote down about child labor in England early in *Capital* do not differ in their truthfulness from the truths that Milton Friedman wrote about in his studies of the consumption function; the prose of Marx was close, in places, to poetry – the prose of Friedman was never close, in any place, to poetry. Did the high comic style of Veblen prevent his uncovering, and writing, true propositions, interesting propositions, useful propositions? Does the austerity of Lucas's theoretical writing make his ideas more true? I think the answer to both questions is no.

Student: Progress is thus associated with the augmentation of the stock of contingent truths, and useful and interesting propositions.

Teacher: Nicely said.

CHAPTER 6

Stabilizing dynamics

Almost no one has had the courage to do a careful anthropological study of formalism. The reason for this lack of nerve is quite simple: a priori, before the study has even started, it is towards the mind and its cognitive abilities that one looks for an explanation of forms. Any study of mathematics, calculations, theories, and forms in general should do quite the contrary: first look at how the observers move in space and time, how the mobility, stability and combinability of inscriptions are enhanced, how the networks are extended, how all the informations are tied together in a cascade of re-representation, and if, by some extraordinary chance, there is something still unaccounted for, then, and only then, look for special cognitive abilities. What I propose here, as a seventh rule of method, is in effect a moratorium on cognitive explanations of science and technology.

Bruno Latour (1987, pp. 246-7)

The usual history of stability analysis in economics, as presented in, for example, the text by Arrow and Hahn (1971), suggests the following:

1. The economic analysis of the early to middle 1930s that was concerned with dynamics and dynamic problems contained a rich and full range of arguments, ideas, concepts, and language that expressed the variety of what were called dynamic theories.
2. Simultaneously, the mathematical literature had developed a full and detailed language, a formal structure, for discussing and analyzing dynamic systems.
3. The mathematical theories were, by the middle 1930s, in a form suitable for a recasting of some of the arguments that economists had been developing.
4. From 1939 through the early 1940s, Samuelson was the individual primarily responsible for linking the mathematical and economic literatures on dynamics.
5. The period from the early 1940s to the late 1950s was one in which the mathematical analysis of the stability of equilibrium increasingly defined the content of economic dynamics; problems of dynamics were recast as problems of establishing whether a system was stable or unstable.

113

6. The mathematics necessary to determine the stability of particular systems became increasingly known and disseminated among mathematicians in the 1940s and early 1950s.

7. The means of demonstrating the possibility of stable equilibria, Liapunov techniques, were increasingly available to economists by the middle 1950s.

8. Arrow and Hurwicz established the conditions under which the competitive equilibrium would be stable in the late 1950s.

9. Scarf and Gale showed that those conditions were quite strong, and thus the stability of the competitive equilibrium was not necessarily demonstrable for any particular model.

But there are many other ways to tell the story.

A Lakatosian rational reconstruction

As I have argued elsewhere (Weintraub 1985), the neo-Walrasian research program was constituted in its modern form by the early 1950s. The program had, among its hard-core elements, propositions involving concern with equilibrium states of interrelated multiagent systems. Heuristics that asked that analysts model problems as optimization problems with constraints, and outcomes as equilibrium outcomes of such problems, necessitated that the equilibria of models be robust with respect to small changes in initial conditions. That is, given a model and its equilibrium state, the model would be useful to the extent that a perturbation of its structure, defined by its parameters, would likewise lead to an equilibrium outcome. Stability analysis was precisely concerned with this issue. Thus, the development of the neo-Walrasian program was aided by the development of stability theory.

As a subprogram, stability analysis was driven initially by the question, Is the competitive equilibrium stable? This question was answered in the affirmative by Hicks, who showed that optimization and stability went hand in hand. Samuelson showed, however, that Hicksian stability was not the same notion as was required for more general systems, and Samuelson created the "true" or mathematical definition of stability and showed its relation to the Hicksian definition. Other writers in the 1940s, individuals like Lange, Metzler, Patinkin, Allais, and Yasui, pushed out the knowledge frontier as they showed in more and more detail, and with more and more clarity, the relationship between the economics of equilibrium states and the mathematical property of "being a stable equilibrium state." In the late 1940s and early 1950s, the mathematical community developed and disseminated information about the mathematical techniques necessary for demonstrating that a particular model possessed a stable equilibrium state. The program came to fruition in the late 1950s when Arrow and Hurwicz proved that the competitive equilibrium was stable under a range of economic specifications; they developed a variety of sufficient conditions for a competitive equilibrium being stable. Shortly thereafter, however, Scarf and Gale showed that those conditions were self-limiting, because other reasonable economic models could be shown to be unstable or to possess unstable equilibria (Hands 1984).

Developed in this way, the story I have been telling is one of a research subprogram that could be called the "stability program" and that was associated with a sequence of papers and books from Hicks to Scarf. The heuristics involved searching for a model of the competitive general equilibrium system for which a stable equilibrium could be found. This subprogram was linked with the "hardening of the hard core" of the neo-Walrasian research program, for the neo-Walrasian program required a coherent model in which the hard-core propositions could be shown to be not inconsistent. Because one of the primary propositions of that hard core was the statement that outcomes are equilibrium results of optimization problems, a strong coherence check on the value and worth of the neo-Walrasian program was provided by a check of the robustness of the core propositions in the following sense: Because the heuristics asked that models be developed with equilibrium states as outcomes, those states would be relatively more useful if they were robust with respect to small respecifications of the model. Thus, stability of the competitive equilibrium was sought by analysts seeking to encourage general equilibrium treatments of a variety of economic problems.

The story, then, is one of progress as problem gave rise to problem gave rise to problem, and anomaly or counterexample gave rise to new theorems in a sequence that seemed to end, in triumph, with the papers by Arrow and Hurwicz. The original problem of showing stability was seen to have been solved. But then, in fact, the program immediately degenerated as Scarf and Gale showed that reasonable economic models, with well-defined competitive equilibrium states, were unstable. Paraphrasing the words of a later commentator, Frank Hahn (1970), what had been achieved was no more than the compilation of a collection of anecdotes about how prices might adjust in abstract markets. Put in Lakatosian language, the stability program took shape around 1939, progressed until around 1958, and degenerated immediately thereafter.

Better, perhaps, than the language of research programs is the language of proofs and refutations, which suggests that in a sequence of papers between 1939 and 1958, the original conjecture that "the competitive equilibrium is stable" was shaped, reshaped, refined, and recast by a sequence of mathematical papers that produced, eventually, a theorem. That final theorem had the following form: If the competitive general equilibrium model of Arrow and Debreu is such that prices move in accord with excess-demand tâtonnements, and excess-demand functions (1) are continuously differentiable, (2) are homogeneous of degree 1 in prices and income, (3) satisfy Walras's law, and (4) possess weak gross substitutability, then the competitive equilibrium is stable.

Moreover, this theorem was shown to be but one of a variety of attainable theorems, but the original conjecture was shown to be false, as Scarf and Gale produced models of competitive general equilibrium systems that possessed equilibria that were totally unstable (Hands 1984). The final theorem and proof used lemma incorporation, monster-barring, and other proof strategies discussed by Lakatos (1976) in his historical reconstruction of the proof of the Euler conjecture.

Deconstructing the reconstruction

I have just provided an account of a large and diffuse literature, one created by many individuals in many places over a twenty-year period; my rendering of the history showed the unity and wholeness and organic coherence of the work. That vision is, of course, imposed on the history by my deliberate choice to "rationally reconstruct" the history. Using the Lakatosian framework commits the storyteller to a series of choices in the writing of the history. One is forced, before setting the words to the paper, to create a "program" that is the major actor in the story. This requires the historian to look at the material, ascertain common elements in the various texts, moves, and countermoves, and abstract from them all a linking unity. That skeleton is termed the hard core of the program, and the maneuvers that allow theory or paper B to follow from A are termed the heuristics of the programmatic core. Thus, if one can get B from A by the rule "create B-like stuff from A-like stuff," then were that to be the heuristic, certainly B would follow "Lakatos-rationally" from A.

The point, of course, is that the perspective gained from a rational reconstruction is only one perspective. Indeed, Lakatos asked that the "above-the-line" reconstruction be compared with a "below-the-line" discussion, which would show how the actual events would fail to conform to the rationally reconstructed story. This history was actually "constructed-performed" by Lakatos (1976) in his *Proofs and Refutations*. The rational reconstruction of the history of the Euler conjecture in geometry, presented in conversation between a teacher and students as a series of moves and countermoves, was linked by footnotes to the actual history.

Because "historical" material itself does not coerce the writer to reconstruct the activity as a sequence of rational moves by anonymous actors, such a predilection for telling the stories of sequences of "scientific work" would appear to be a result of prior belief in the identification of science with reason itself, with a belief that progress in science can be identified and discussed in terms of increasing truthfulness. As Latour and Woolgar (1979, p. 107) point out,

historians, as portrayed in historical texts, can move freely in the past, possess knowledge of the future, have the ability to survey settings in which they are not (and never will be) involved, have access to actors' motives, and (rather like god) are all-knowing and all-seeing, able to judge what is good and bad. They can produce histories in which one thing is the "sign" of another and in which disciplines and ideas "burgeon," "mature," or "lie fallow."

At the heart of the claim that rational reconstructions of scientific work are necessary to understand the work itself is a belief that Nature or Reality itself constrains the texts in such a manner that the texts can be read or reread as a sequence of moves in which Science gets closer and closer to the Truth about Nature or Reality. In effect, then, a Lakatosian framework predisposes the historian to select the elements of the narrative to confirm the coherent progress (in terms of successor papers solving problems posed in predecessor papers) of scientific research programs. Alternatively, failing to find progress, the historian establishes the counterclaim that a program degenerated because it failed to solve the problems necessary for its continued success.

I do not want to reopen, in these pages, the debate about realism, relativism, pragmatism, and so forth, that has so determined the intellectual life of the postmodern era. I have little to contribute to the big themes so clearly addressed by Rorty, Derrida, Habermas, Bordieu, Latour, Fish, and others.[1] I think, however, that *it is too little appreciated how our notions of writing histories of science, and particularly histories of economics, would have to change were we to take seriously the claim that the rational reconstruction of scientific activity, or, in this case, the rational reconstruction of sequences of economic writings, cannot be elicited from the texts themselves.* Put another way, we have written the history of economics from the rationalist point of view, which says that we historians *discover* the true history, where that true history is one in which papers are linked to other papers in terms of their truth claims, and theories are developed to solve problems that previous theories failed to solve. Other histories, those in which, say, Keynes's theory of liquidity preference would be related to his own sexual history, or in which the success of Friedman's monetarism would be related to the clarity of his prose and the power of his voice in oral argument, are ruled nonhistorical.

This kind of idea is not new, except in economics. Replacing "ethnography" with "economics," we can appreciate the comments of Clifford Geertz (1988, pp. 140, 144):

To argue (point out, actually, for, like aerial perspective or the Pythagorean theorem, the thing once seen cannot then be unseen) that the writing of [economics] involves telling stories, making pictures, concocting symbolisms, and deploying tropes is commonly resisted, often fiercely, because of a confusion, endemic in the West since Plato at least, of the imagined with the imaginary, the fictional with the false, making things out with making them up. The strange idea that reality has an idiom in which it prefers to be described, that its very nature demands that we talk about it without fuss – a spade is a spade, a rose is a rose – on pain of illusion, trumpery, and self-bewitchment, leads on to the even stranger idea that, if literalism is lost, so is fact. [The new work based on such ideas] spells the end of certain pretensions. There are a number of these pretensions, but they all tend to come down in one way or another to an attempt to get round the unget-roundable fact that all [economic analyses and histories of economics] are homemade, that they are the describer's descriptions, not those of the described.

We must seek to leave "discovery" in the history of economics in favor of interpretation, or hermeneutics:

[Gadamer's] "universality of hermeneutics" refers to the fact that enquiry involves tradition-bound theoretical presuppositions in the social and natural sciences. Nowadays, we are more familiar with this contention in the form of three distinctive lines of argument, all linked to the notion of interpretation: 1) The first centers around the denial of brute facts. In essence, it holds that data beyond the challenge of rival interpretations are unattainable by science. 2) The second refers to the circularity of interpretation. It implies that any interpretation of an event or text ultimately depends on yet another set of interpretations, thus leading to an infinite regress of meaning. 3) The third can perhaps best be described in terms of Wittgenstein's notion of a language game. It conceives of interpretation as a condition for the possibility of data in general, and emphasizes the interconnection and interdependency of various levels of interpretation. [Knorr-Cetina 1981, p. 138]

What I am suggesting here is both easy to understand and difficult to relate to the substantive corpus of writing in the history of economic thought. From Blaug's magisterial *Economic Theory in Retrospect* to Samuelson's "Out of the Closet: A Program for the Whig History of Economic Science" (1987), producers and consumers of the history of economics have accustomed themselves to read the past from the perspective of the present, which in economics has led to a concentration on issues of precursors, harbingers, logical slips, factual errors, misuse of evidence, and all manner of past writing that illuminates the present state of economics, or helps us understand what we currently believe. It was in that sense that Walsh and Gram (1980), in their outstanding presentation of classical and neoclassical general equilibrium analysis, could use a two-sector general equilibrium model throughout the book to illuminate the issues that concerned writers as diverse as Quesney and Smith and Ricardo and Marx and Walras.

What such history writing has in common is that it takes up the challenge of presenting the history of science, in this case economic science, as an exemplar of rationality itself.

Science history without rationality

If rationality is associated with the idea that science is the exemplar of rational thought, of the growth of knowledge, then the history of science is the history of reason itself. This view was developed in the writings of the French philosopher Gaston Bachelard:

The conceptual basis of...Bachelard's philosophy of science [was] developed in a series of books written from the 1920s through the 1950s. According to Bachelard, reason is best known by reflection on science, and science is best known by reflection on its history.... The proof of [this latter statement] lies in the repeated refutation of a priori philosophical ideals of rationality by historical scientific developments.... There are, then, no viable accounts of rationality except those derived from the historical developments of scientific reason. To understand reason, philosophy must "go to the school of science."... The rationality that philosophy tries to discover in the history of science is no more fixed and monolithic than that history itself. [Gutting 1988, pp. 159–60]

Bachelard's view led him to focus on the breaks that science created in the human experience; the recategorization and reconceptualization that science induces define the process that is described by the Western notion of change, which has been transformed into the idea of scientific progress. For Michel Foucault, who was deeply influenced by Bachelard, this uncovering, developed in his explorations of discursive practice in an almost archeological analysis, was rooted in a similar attempt to provide a history of reason, although he concentrated on a historical period before reason could be uncovered by attention to science. Foucault did not have science, but had only practice and description, to unpack reason's history.

Writing the history of a science like economics from a perspective other than Whiggish compilation of successes goes against the grain, not only of standard historiography but also of a larger Western tradition. Such a revisionist project threatens those who believe that any reconstruction other than rational reconstruction of the history deconstructs the objective nature of the activity that the history attempts to describe. The frightened believe that rational practice must be described rationally, must be reconstructed rationally, else reason itself be subverted by description.

To see that this is not, in the memorable phrase of Barbara Herrnstein Smith, a straw herring, consider the rules for writing the history of economic thought promulgated by Don Walker (1988, pp. 101–2) in his presidential address to the History of Economics Society:

First, we believe that the writings of economists should be judged on the basis of whether or not they were original.... Second, we believe that a writer's work should be judged on the basis of whether or not it was important.... Third, we judge economic writings in the light of modern economic knowledge [in the sense that] we use current knowledge to detect sound arguments and defective arguments.... Fourth, we believe a writer's work should be evaluated for its logical consistency.... Fifth, we criticize a writer for asserting that he achieved something that he did not.... Sixth, we praise a writer if he explained reality well and criticize him if his work was unrealistic.[2]

But in fact, what is feared is illusory. The anxieties in the closet or underneath the bed of the historian of economics are private vices, not public facts. To ask how the Negishi survey article constructed a history of stability theory is not to say that Arrow and Hurwicz contributed less. To ask, and write, about the stabilizing function of mathematics on the language games played in dynamic economics is not to denigrate mathematics. To deconstruct the evolutionary metaphor rooted in the mathematics that Samuelson assimilated from A. J. Lotka and E. B. Wilson is not to deny the magnitude of Samuelson's genius.

Stabilizing discourse

With the foregoing considerations in mind, I want to suggest that there is another way that the sequence of papers on dynamics and stability can be read, and that is as an attempt, by members of a particular community, to narrow the possibilities for disagreement among community members. This is unobjectionable as a reading, for it is even part of what the primary figures of the subdiscipline said they were attempting to do. What I would like to suggest, over and beyond this form of the claim, is that there were numerous other implications of this strategy that need to be uncovered to understand in more detail the moves and countermoves in the sequence.

Let us agree that there were, indeed, rampant confusions abroad in the 1930s among economists concerning the nature and meaning of equilibrium. At the very least, there were political ramifications to claims that the economy was or was not in equilibrium. To argue, for instance, that the economy was inherently "unstable" was perhaps to claim that the capitalist system was inherently unstable; capitalism's "contradictions" would lead to a systemic economic collapse, and a move to socialism would be required for the next stage of economic development. From this perspective, concern with the nature and meaning of equilibrium, and the possibility of stability of the system's equilibrium path, would be of political importance.

Were the 1930s a time in which the system could be described unambiguously as in or out of equilibrium? I think not. Observing the international trade collapse, and private wealth collapse, and unprecedented levels of unemployment, arguments were still being offered to suggest that the economy was finding its own natural level, or suffering from a temporary adjustment to a new equilibrium position. Keynes, of course, was beginning to suggest, as early as his 1930 Macmillan Committee testimony, that the economy was not self-righting in the neoclassical sense (which he termed the classical sense) and that the economy could continue in semipermanent slump. In the language of later writers, Keynes suggested that the economy was in equilibrium, but that equilibrium was one in which unemployment was very high: Equilibrium (in the sense of equality between aggregate supply and aggregate demand) could be consistent with any level of unemployment at all.

Now, the neoclassical synthesis, which attempted to wed Keynesian macroeconomics to neo-Walrasian general equilibrium analysis, or to instantiate Keynesian macroeconomic theory, or significant portions of that theory, in the belts of the neo-Walrasian program, required *all* markets to be in equilibrium in order to permit the claim that the economy was in equilibrium. That led to the fundamental problem that had to be "solved" by the neoclassical synthesis: How was one to combine market clearing in all the economy's markets with the notion that the labor market, in reporting very high levels of unemployment, apparently was not clearing?

There are various responses one could make to this dilemma:

1. One could deny that the labor market was not clearing. That view would lead one to argue that the levels of unemployment were in fact equilibrium levels of employment and that it was a voluntary choice of leisure that was revealed to be preferred in the labor market. In popular myth, "those people are just too lazy to work for wages, albeit low wages. They would rather receive welfare, or unemployment, or stay on the dole." This is the kind of analysis associated with the "new classical economics" and Robert Lucas's claim (1985) that all unemployment is best modeled as voluntary unemployment, because all observed states of the economy must be modeled as equilibrium states, and so forth.

2. One could argue that the labor market would clear if only some impediment or other to its clearing were not present. That view would lead to the notion that union demands for high wages lead to unemployment,

or minimum-wage laws lead to unemployment, or unemployment compensation leads to unemployment. Such a view merges into the first view if structural imbalances (e.g., unemployed workers in West Virginia, and vacant jobs in Texas), and barriers to mobility (a taste for family land, costs of relocating, etc.) prevent the matching of workers with jobs.

3. One could deny the sense, or observation, that markets do in fact clear. That view would lead one to say that the synthesis itself is perversely misguided in its interest in wedding the Keynesian princess to the neo-Walrasian troll. This position was taken by the post-Keynesians.

4. Finally, one could agree that markets must clear in equilibrium, and that the labor market is not in equilibrium, and that there is a tendency to equilibrium in general, but argue that the movement to equilibrium is weak, vulnerable to obstruction, and on occasion subject to systemic failure. That is, the economy could be "off" the demand or supply curves for labor, and so the normal tendency to return to equilibrium might not be present. That explanation left Keynesian unemployment in the realm of "generalized market failure" (e.g., distributional shifts, monopoly on one or both sides of the labor market, governmental interference, income effects, monetary policy failures, etc.), thus ceding the theoretical ground to neo-Walrasian theory, and leaving the realm of practical policy measures to Keynesians interested in remedying the market failures. In substance, this is the position outlined by Don Patinkin (1965) in his *Money, Interest, and Prices,* which created the neoclassical synthesis as we understand it. In its fully historicized form, the argument was first offered to economists by Axel Leijonhufvud (1968) in his book *On Keynesian Economics and the Economics of Keynes.*

To repeat, there were at least these several potential strategies available to relieve the tension between the depression levels of unemployment ("depression levels of unemployment" themselves are associated with the rhetorical shift that constituted certain workers' behavior as "unemployed involuntarily" and required action to be taken) and the theoretical perspective holding that individual behavior, mediated by market interaction, leads to coordinated, or equilibrium, outcomes. But of the strategies outlined earlier, it was the fourth strategy that allowed the community of economists simultaneously to preserve the theory and the phenomenon.

The neoclassical synthesis allowed the existence of both a general equilibrium and unemployment in the labor market: The synthesis could allow there to be an equilibrium that was not easily, or simply, attained. What was needed to effect that result was simply the idea that there were two kinds of equilibria – easily attainable ones, and others not easily attained. That disjunction permitted, even encouraged, the distinction between stable and unstable equilibria, and thus it created the concern with conditions under which the competitive equilibrium would or would not be stable.

This set of observations makes sense of one of the most curious features of the history of stability theory in economics, and that is how the development of that theory did not follow the logic of the mathematical theory in which it eventually was to be embedded. That is, in all modern historical reconstructions of general equilibrium theory it is argued that there are three "problems" whose solutions defined the creation of modern general equilibrium theory: First, there is the problem of the existence of a competitive equilibrium. Second, there is the problem of the efficiency or optimality of the competitive equilibrium. Third, there is the problem of the stability of the competitive equilibrium.[3]

The formal logic suggests that first one must develop a model, then characterize the equilibrium (the efficiency problem), then establish the existence of such an equilibrium (the existence problem), and then establish the robustness of that equilibrium (the stability problem). Looking at the dates usually provided for the solutions to those problems, we see that Arrow and Debreu separately demonstrated efficiency in 1951. They jointly, and McKenzie independently, solved the existence problem in its modern form (modulo Wald and von Neumann) in 1954. Finally, Arrow and Hurwicz established the stability results in 1958. This sequence apparently confirms the formal logic and suggests that the mathematized analysis drove the community's work.

The difficulty, however, is that the concern for and attention to stability, and the robustness of the equilibrium over time, predated the concern with either the existence or efficiency of the competitive equilibrium. The literature associated with Frisch, Tinbergen, Hicks, and finally Samuelson was associated with understanding the conditions under which an equilibrium would be stable, so as to permit the conjunction of equilibrium theorizing and unemployment analysis. Such analyses led Hicks to distinguish among equilibria on the basis of their intertemporal linkages and thus to locate "Keynesian" concerns not in Part I of *Value and Capital* (1939), which concerned static equilibrium and stability analysis, but rather in Part II, with its analysis of intertemporal equilibrium in the sense of expectations and temporary equilibrium. Samuelson solved the linkage problem by showing that if there were multiple equilibria, stable and unstable equilibria would alternate, and thus the presence of more than one equilibrium would allow scope for policy to move the economy from one to another, for the economy would not necessarily move of its own rules of dynamic adjustment. Lange (1944) allowed equilibria to exist, but showed how instability could appear if monetary authorities should behave in perverse ways. And finally, Patinkin (1965), the true architect of the theoretical structure we have been calling the neoclassical synthesis, assumed that existence was not problematic, but rather argued that Keynesian concerns could be located in the disequilibrium in the labor market; it was Patinkin who presented the lengthy analysis of the nature and meaning of Walras's tâtonnements, the dynamic adjustment mechanism at the center of the mathematical theory that was coming to represent stability theory in economics.

Convergence and divergence

The issues I have broached can be given an alternative twist if we recognize that the "facts" of the economy being stable or not, and the labor market being in equilibrium or not, are actually constructions. The fact is that controversies are possible when there are alternative constructions, or when the meanings of the artifacts created in the particular communities are not, or have not yet been, stabilized. What constitutes the claim that the economy is not in equilibrium when there is a high level of unemployment? Socially, the meaning of this claim is jointly negotiated by economists concerned with macroeconomic issues and those concerned with the conceptualization of the economy as a coordinated system. Out of that negotiation, a process of argument, written and oral, the presentation and development of evidence of one sort or another, and so forth, there is a reconceptualization of the system: The meanings of "equilibrium," "the economy," "employment levels," and "unemployment levels" are stabilized in the sense that individuals use these phrases and ideas in mutually understandable and agreeable ways. As Latour and Woolgar (1979, pp. 176–7) point out,

facts and artifacts do not correspond respectively to true and false statements. Rather, statements lie along a continuum according to the extent to which they refer to the conditions of their construction.... Our argument is not just that facts are socially constructed. We also wish to show that the process of construction involves the use of certain devices whereby all traces of production are made extremely difficult to detect.

Once the statement begins to stabilise, however, an important change takes place. *The statement itself becomes a split entity.* On the one hand, it is a set of words which represents a statement about an object. On the other hand, it corresponds to an object in itself which takes on a life of its own.... At the point of stabilisation, however, there appear to be both objects and statements about those objects. Before long, more and more reality is attributed to the object and less and less to the statement about the object. Consequently, an inversion takes place: the object becomes the reason why the statement was formulated in the first place.... The history of its construction is also transformed from this new vantage point: the process of construction is turned into the pursuit of a single path which led inevitably to the "actual" structure. Only through the skill and efforts of the great scientists could the setbacks and red herrings and blind alleys be overcome and the real structure revealed for what it was.

With respect to the stability literature, what we see is that by the end of the 1940s or the early 1950s, the economy itself had changed in the only meaningful sense in which that claim can be sustained: That is, discursive practice about the economy had been altered to allow simultaneous maintenance of the two claims that the economy was in equilibrium and that there were socially unacceptable levels of unemployment associated with either systemic market failures or specific failures in the labor market. The content of the neoclassical synthesis was precisely that particular reconceptualization, that change in discursive practice.

The mathematization of equilibrium and stability, the papers from Samuelson on through Arrow and Hurwicz, stabilized that discourse and renegotiated the meaning of the economy text. The restriction of "dynamics" to "dynamic system," and the constriction of "stable" to "locally stable equilibrium motion of a dissipative dynamic system," permitted concurrence, initially within the small community of mathematical economists, on the meaning of the claim that unemployment was a disequilibrium position associated with a "usually" stable competitive equilibrium. The neoclassical synthesis was literally unthinkable before the availability of the mathematization of equilibrium and stability; as consensual meaning was extended to wider and wider communities by the increased understanding of the mathematized framework in which those ideas were made manifest, the neoclassical synthesis, too, was more and more widely spread. In consequence, for example, post-Keynesian attacks on that position could not receive a real hearing because they appeared to reject the generally stabilized meanings of the community in favor of meanings introduced by Keynes in the 1930s to modify discursive practice about unemployment (e.g., Keynes's introduction of the distinction between voluntary and involuntary unemployment). Post-Keynesians were increasingly isolated as the linguistic practices in which they engaged were more and more marginalized by the larger mathematically literate community. Their writings, on Keynes's essential meaning, remind us of those about whom C. Vann Woodward (1986, p. 26) wrote:

Lost causes, especially those that foster loyalties and nostalgic memories, are among the most prolific breeders of historiography. If survivors deem the cause not wholly lost and perhaps in some measure retrievable, the search of the past becomes more frantic and the books about it more numerous. Blame must be fixed, villains found, heroes celebrated, old quarrels settled, old dreams restored, and motives vindicated. Amid the ruins controversy thrives and books proliferate.

Constructing meaning

There will be, no doubt, objections to the view I am presenting here. Primary among them will be the objection that empirical experience is not so invisible as the foregoing account appears to suggest. Surely, it will be claimed, meanings are not so loosely contrived, so free to differ and be seen as differing by various individual economists. Surely, it will be argued, Patinkin was constrained by the facts of the economic data, and he had to consider those data, that empirical knowledge, in his account, knowing that his account would stand or fall on the basis of its accord with those data.

How are meanings negotiated in scientific practice? How do particular proposals, presented as contributions to an ongoing discussion, with citations of papers, marshaling of data, and so forth, come to be considered knowledge? How is the scientific reality, the reality of the economy, created?

Thus within the negotiation of meanings that turn individual proposals into inter-subjective realities, we find ambient nature passively constraining possible meanings through active experience that is inseparable from the language use.... Similar constraining processes occur in all discourse communities.... Various discourse communities appeal to various kinds of experience as touchstones for their negotiations of communal meaning.... Science, however, has taken empirical experience as its major touchstone, so that in the process of negotiation of meaning, empirical experience not only constrains the range of possible meanings but is actively sought in the attempt to establish stable meanings from the negotiation. [Bazerman 1988, p. 312]

The idea, so abhorred by the hardheaded positivists among the historians of economics, that meanings are negotiated and constructed seems to turn on the idea that if meaning is negotiated, it is fluid, and subjective, and thus not real; subjectivism is rejected, then, because realness is a given, like Dr. Johnson's kicked rock. Our not-so-straw man (Walker 1988, p. 110) has argued that

subjectivists intermittently need, it seems, to be shocked by the realities of life and death, work and suffering, into a realization of what is obvious to everyone else in the world, namely that it is real and what has happened in the past is not malleable and cannot be altered to fit our interpretations of it. The same is true of the texts we study.

But the point, of course, is that the meaning of death, even, is socially negotiated; the death of the Shiite warrior who dies in battle has a personal meaning different from that of the death of the infidel with whom he battles. And their own personal meanings are different from mine. A belief in an afterlife changes the meaning of death. And, of course, a belief in the obligations of work in the Protestant tradition changed the meaning of work.

Our economy is no less real because its meaning must become stable through the activities of those who study it and talk and write about it and form the community that informs the conceptualization called the economy. To say that economists negotiate the meaning of the economy is not to claim that the economy does not exist: It is not comprehensible to me what such a claim could even mean; we have no language to discuss such silliness. No, it is rather that the activities of economists are precisely concerned with stabilizing the meanings of propositions that express ideas about inflation, say, or equilibration of the balance-of-payments deficit. Models and theorems and evidence of various natures, empirical and formal and definitional, are adduced to convince other members of the concerned community that some meanings are preferable for the agreed purposes, where those purposes themselves must be renegotiated from time to time: Are we interested in controlling inflation, or are we interested in controlling unemployment, or the trade balance, or none of these at all, but rather in controlling the forces of governmental regulation of the economic sphere?

Conclusion

My perspective is that noted by Knorr-Cetina in her important 1981 monograph. She asked (p. 137),

[can] the practice of natural and technological science be distinguished from the symbolic, interpretive, "hermeneutic" practice of the social sciences, and of social life itself[?] I hold that it cannot. In fact, my goal is to underline the essential similarity between the two modes of production of knowledge which have become so painstakingly separated.

Based on the history I have constructed, a history of a line of mathematized argumentation about the stability of the competitive equilibrium, I have tried to suggest that the papers in that sequence could be well understood as an attempt to impose order and to create knowledge; I have tried to show that that process was a social process of negotiation and argument. That a rational reconstruction of the sequence of works fails to make good sense of the papers I have examined should come as no great surprise once it is clearly seen that ex post rationalizations, though they stabilize the previous history, do not themselves present their knowledge contemporaneously with the historical action and actors. We are wise after the fact, where the wisdom is the clarity of reason.

CHAPTER 7

Surveying dynamics

*The state of the economy, for instance, cannot be used unproblemati-
cally to explain science, because it itself is a very controversial outcome
of another soft science, economics. As we saw earlier, it is extracted
out of hundreds of statistical institutions, questionnaires, polls and surveys, and treated in centers of calculation. Something like the Gross
National Product is an nth order visual display which, to be sure, may
be combined to other paper forms, but which is no more outside the frail
and tiny networks built by economists than stars, electrons, or plate
tectonics.*

Bruno Latour (1987, p. 256)

In the period following the publication of Samuelson's articles on stability
and equilibrium, a period that included the 1940s, the literature concerned
with economic dynamics permeated several different subliteratures, one
being that on the microfoundations of macroeconomics, which I have
discussed elsewhere (Weintraub 1979). A second subliterature was that of
endogenous business cycles, which attempted to trace out the time paths
of economic variables. By the late 1950s and early 1960s that work had
been linked to the 1930s literature on capital theory, as well as classical
writings, thereby creating the modern literature on growth theory. In a
third grouping, the writings were more directly concerned with understanding the implications of modeling economic systems, usually multimarket systems, as dynamic systems in the sense in which Samuelson had
brought the term into common use in the economics literature; those contributions are now read as concerning the problem of the stability of the
competitive equilibrium.

The preceding chapter suggested that this last literature can be reconstructed as imposing an order on the larger dynamics literature, an order
that constricted the discourse by mathematizing the field in a particular
fashion. That move was, I argued, not the main objective of the economists who wrote in that period, although they were aware that the mathematics of dynamic systems could and did make coherent a number of previously confused analyses. Even though the economists had not "planned"
matters, but rather had hoped that the problems could be solved, at some
later time the literature would appear orderly to them. That is, practitioners

128

looking back at work in their own scientific subfield seem inevitably to produce a "memory history" in which the false starts and confusions drop away from communal attention around the time that the subject passes into a more settled phase. *At the time the field appears to insiders to be settled and self-contained, it becomes possible to reconstruct the past work in such a manner that activity "led" somewhere and that the sequence of papers "produced" knowledge, whereas prior to that time the field could not have been seen as "coherent."* That is, from the present we look back and see order, but that order was not always evident to those who were in the field at the time. At some point, order emerges, discourse stabilizes. At that point, the field becomes coherent in a public sense, as its language use has been transformed and has been understood to have been so transformed.

In many scientific fields, and in economics, one of the ways in which such a transformation is publicized is with a survey article. As a literary form, and as a historical document, the survey article is not well understood. Only recently have scholars begun to examine the nature and function of survey papers in science.[1] In economics there has not been that kind of attention to research surveys. This chapter will be concerned with that issue and will focus on one particular research survey: For the literature on dynamics and stability, we look back to 1962, when Takashi Negishi wrote a paper for *Econometrica* called "The Stability of a Competitive Economy: A Survey Article." Reading this article today, it appears that Negishi "defined" the subject in the sense that what was surveyed by Negishi has been retained in history, and what was not so surveyed has nearly disappeared from history. Because an exceptional survey article, as the Negishi article was, provides access to a research topic, and because for nonspecialists the survey itself is taken to define the subfield surveyed, its role in economics discourse is important, though that importance is seldom noted in historiographic or methodological discussions.

In this chapter I shall "read" the literature through the Negishi spectacles and examine the ways in which the reader of the period was meant to understand the stability literature surveyed. I shall argue several points concerning this reading. First, it will emerge that there are alternatives to Negishi's interpretations of the paper sequences, and this suggests that the history Negishi presented might be different from a history we might now construct; although this seems incontrovertible, it reinforces one of this book's main arguments: that the history of economics is constructed, not found.[2] Second, but related to the previous point, is that the "success" of a survey may be so great that the field comes to be defined as that which was surveyed. Thus, we may not be aware, today, of the alternative conceptualizations possible at the time of the survey's construction, for we see through the survey's lens. The survey truly constructs history.

Third, it will be seen that a survey's focus on the "completed" literature, or the theorem at the end of all the proof attempts, or the end product of the sequence of papers, overvalues that end result vis-à-vis the other papers; put bluntly, a literature becomes valued primarily for the moves that can be made to its knowledge product. The Whiggishness of this kind of historical writing forces restricted readings on past documents and requires the survey author, and readers, to appraise the past on the narrow criterion of "contributing to progress in solving the problem," even if the problem was not to be stated until some date later than the contribution.

This having been said, we recognize that a survey article is not a history. But in a field like economics, a survey's facts become historical facts, because there is no sifting by historians[3] for at least several generations. But by the time historians begin to examine the historical record, the survey has itself been taken to define the record. Put another way, the survey is almost contemporaneous history, and it is usually written by a participant or a near-participant. It then takes on the character of an "archival treasure," primary source material, and is thus privileged.

This raises the final issue I shall examine: How does the contemporaneous context constitute the text? And how does that constitution differ from that provided by a more distant reading? I shall, in addressing these last questions, provide a "literary" reading of the stability literature: I shall argue that the Negishi survey effectively documented the transformation of the contests for meaning that had invigorated the literature of the 1930s and early 1940s, contests about the static–dynamic and equilibrium–disequilibrium polarities, contests framed in terms of the value of models that represent the economy as being, for instance, either in or not in a state of "static equilibrium." The two polarities gave way by the early 1960s, I shall argue, to the more restricted but nonetheless overarching master trope "stable–unstable."

In the pages that follow, I shall attempt to address these concerns. But the starting place must be with the Negishi survey article itself.

The audience for the Negishi survey

Before examining the Negishi article, I want to comment on the characteristics of the possible readers of that article, for it was that group that had to construe the arguments of the paper in one or another fashion.

Apparently there was a grant to the Econometric Society from the Rockefeller Foundation to commission a series of survey articles; Negishi's was the second, following that by Hendrik Houthakker: "The Present State of Consumption Theory." The Negishi paper appeared in 1962, and by the 1960s, of course, the kind of training that economists received in graduate schools had changed significantly from that of the 1950s: The immediate postwar debates about the proper role of mathematics and mathematical economics in economic theory had settled down; controversy had been replaced with a sustained belief that mathematical training was necessary for individuals interested in economic analysis.[4] Certainly a reader of *Econometrica,* the premier journal publishing the new mathematical economics at that time, would be expected to have known basic mathematics (multivariate calculus and linear algebra) and to have had an appreciation for the role of mathematical argumentation.[5] It is less certain, of course, that such a reader would have been familiar with all aspects of the mathematical usages that appeared in economics. In other words, a normal professional reader would have known techniques at a fairly sophisticated level, but would not be expected to have known the use of those techniques outside of particular subspecializations.

That said, there are two groups of readers who can be distinguished, namely, academic economists and students, and the members of the two groups would have read the survey to different purposes. Indeed, there were two classes of subscriptions to *Econometrica,* standard (associated with membership in the Econometric Society) and student; even with library subscriptions, which would serve both the economist and student groups, there really were but two identifiable reader perspectives. For faculty, the paper would have appeared as an attempt to encourage professionals[6] to keep up with developments outside of their specializations, and the fact of the survey itself would suggest to those readers that the results surveyed were important to a variety of subdisciplines (otherwise the Rockefeller Foundation would not have commissioned a survey devoted to that specific topic); the editorial decision to commission was itself a decision to legitimize the importance of the work to be surveyed. Additionally, the article served the function, for the professional, of allowing an overview of a technical area in which professional competence was required, but in which such competence could be acquired only by means of strenuous effort. Thus, a teacher, in a graduate program that had recently come to require students to demonstrate competence in mathematical economics, would have a source for instructional material, a source from which a lecture or two might be constructed. The article could appear on reading lists, and the instructor could be reasonably certain that the same article would appear on reading lists at other competitive schools. The survey thus allowed a professional to identify the concerns of other professionals in an open way. One would not need to be a member of the "dynamics community," or a general equilibrium theorist, to learn that that community believed itself to have triumphed in finally establishing proof of the stability of a competitive equilibrium. The articulation of the results in a commissioned survey paper affirmed the importance of the results, and the fact that it was published in a journal that commanded respect validated the argument that stability theory was important enough to merit a commissioned survey.

Graduate students were also part of the Negishi survey's audience. My education in the middle 1960s included reading a variety of survey articles, and certainly my Ph.D. program was not alone in including the Negishi survey on graduate reading lists in the period from the middle 1960s to the early 1970s, at which time much of its content was subsumed in the textbook *General Competitive Analysis,* by Arrow and Hahn (1971). Indeed, Peter Newman's two-volume *Readings in Mathematical Economics* appeared in 1968, and that compendium canonized several papers as necessary for understanding the work done in certain areas. Newman anthologized, in his "Part III: Adjustment Processes in the Theory of Static Equilibrium," papers by Smithies (1942), Lange (1944), and Metzler (1945), all written prior to the Arrow and Hurwicz papers of 1958-9; Newman concluded the series of reprints with the Negishi survey and the Gale (1963) instability counterexample. Thus, the "line," as presented by Newman, was defined by the precursors, the survey reporting success, and the concluding announcement of the limitation of that success.

Graduate students in the early 1960s were less likely to have had undergraduate training in mathematics than are today's graduate students, although most were aware that the top graduate programs had quantitative options or electives. The advanced survey articles, as students used them, provided an overview of areas barely mentioned in introductory graduate courses. A survey such as that by Negishi would have been read not only for its coverage of the topic but also for its identification of gaps in the literature, unsolved problems, or possible researchable (dissertation) topics. Because the normal journal article seldom "contextualized" a line of research, any comments about unsolved problems that remained, or any discussion of work left undone, usually was to be found in the concluding section of the research paper. Such a presentation often left a graduate student convinced that only the author or the author's own Ph.D. students were sufficiently competent to undertake that research. Graduate students often would rather read a survey article than the original papers for the very good reason that the survey gave some sense of the subject and made it easier to assess. If passing an examination was the issue, the context and progression of ideas on stability aided the student's memory. At the next educational stage, finding a researchable problem for a dissertation, an upper-level graduate student usually simply received a research problem from a thesis advisor. For students in graduate programs in which thesis advisors were not necessarily strong research scholars (a case that often obtained in the early to middle 1960s, when there were increasing numbers of graduate students, but faculty had not yet been added in large numbers from the smaller Ph.D. cohorts of the 1950s), the survey article itself could have had an impact on the selection of research topics by potential research students.

The structure of the Negishi survey

The opening paragraph notes that it was only in the 1950s that the theory of Walras was reformulated mathematically and the existence-of-equilibrium problem was solved, and "it was not until the paper by Arrow and Hurwicz [1958] was published that the stability problem of a competitive economy was investigated systematically within the framework of general equilibrium analysis" (Negishi 1962, p. 635). That sentence asks the reader to understand that attempts before 1958 to do general equilibrium stability analysis could not have been "systematic." A belief that, say, Hicks had attempted such a systematic investigation was thus challenged: The record would henceforth be one in which Hicks might best be left unread, because he had been unsuccessful. What Negishi did in that sentence, and what his readers must certainly have understood him to be doing, was to suggest that the recent successes of Arrow and Hurwicz validated the entire preceding line of inquiry and that the term "systematically" would itself have to be construed differently thereafter. In other words, Hicks would be demoted to "unsystematic," whereas Samuelson would be identified with "partial equilibrium analysis."

Negishi goes on to say that he will first discuss the general nature of the problem, then give a short review of the literature, and then define a model and present the various results for that model. He notes again that the first systematic treatment of the problem was provided by Arrow and Hurwicz (1958) and by Arrow, Block, and Hurwicz (1959), the latter paper being "the most important." He also notes that the contribution of "Allais [1943], which has been almost neglected so far, must also be noted" (Negishi 1962, p. 636). He thus creates reader expectations that the past will be searched for precursors and that approval and acclaim will be distributed based on the similarity of past work to the successes of the present.

The next section, which is a general discussion of the stability problem, begins by stating that

the stability problem is concerned with the question of what happens to the time paths of economic variables, such as prices and outputs, which are generated from certain dynamic adjustment processes. If they converge to some equilibrium position, the relevant dynamic process is said to be stable. [Negishi 1962, p. 637]

The first sentence contextualizes stability theory as concerned with movement in real time, and the second sentence defines stability with respect to an atemporal concept of equilibrium. It must not be lost through understatement that this move represents an obliteration of the separate categories of "dynamic analysis" and "stability analysis." To do dynamics is to do stability analysis. The rich dynamics literature of the 1930s, and earlier, was by this view only in part truly dynamic. Questions of change that could be framed in terms of instructional change were not to be called dynamic at all, but rather would have to be placed in some other context and grouped with other concerns. There was but one way, moreover, to do stability analysis:

Different adjustment processes have different stability properties, so that a system involving one adjustment process may be stable while another system, identical in the static aspect with the former but coupled with a different adjustment process, may not. . . . Each dynamic system presents its own stability problem, though all can be analyzed by common mathematical tools. [p. 637]

Negishi notes that this way of thinking forces concerns with trade cycles and economic growth into the stability-theory framework, but his concern in the survey is only with "behavior of the short run market clearing adjustment process toward temporary equilibrium within a 'week' in the sense of Hicks" (p. 637). Such a concern with the short period, an artificial time framework, not only divides off capital theory and growth theory and business cycle analysis from his survey, and thus from the subject matter of stability theory, but also further enables Negishi to insulate his discussion from concern with expectations and adjustment of price and expected price simultaneously, as in the papers by Arrow and Nerlove, Arrow and Enthoven, and Arrow and McManus over the early 1950s. Notice, again, that this move is one in which a large and diffuse literature is resectioned, with much of it being discarded. Perhaps "discarded" is too strong, but the move to dynamic systems and the contextualizing of dynamic theory as stability theory of a (short-run) competitive equilibrium position will lead to theorems of less and less generality.

The next subsection (2.2) presents a case for stability analysis as an investigative logic based on arguments about the nature of the economic system, and it works by means of the implicit assumption that the system can be discussed apart from its representations. It is this apparent disjunction between the "system" and the "model" that drives Negishi's main arguments. I shall return to this section of the Negishi paper later, with attention to its details, for it is this section that carries the major burden of the author's position.

Section 3 of the Negishi paper is titled "Historical Remarks," and it is here that we can see how the canonical literature is established within a program or research tradition. After the obligatory mention of Walras, and an aside on Wald's existence argument, Negishi briefly discusses how the "Hicksian stability condition, though useful in comparative statics, remained static in nature since it was obtained without fully exploring the dynamics of the market adjustment process" (p. 643). Here he also notes that Mosak and Sono did essentially the same kind of work. The next bit discusses the Samuelson critique of Hicks and the introduction into economics of explicitly dynamic considerations concerning stability of adjustment processes. The papers he cites are those that explored the relationship between the Hicksian conditions and the (Samuelsonian) true dynamic conditions – the names here offered are Samuelson, Lange, Metzler, and Morishima. Finally, it is pointed out that "Samuelson and his followers did not, however, take full advantage of the implication of the assumptions underlying the perfectly competitive model." A footnote states that "perhaps Allais [1943] who worked independently of Samuelson and others may be an exception in this respect" (p. 643). Negishi goes on, however, to claim that

the nature of the competitive economy in its relation to the stability of equilibrium was first fully explored by Hahn, Arrow and Hurwicz, and Negishi.... Our understanding of stability in the large, i.e., global stability, with due attention to the nonnegativity of prices, was developed by Arrow, Block, and Hurwicz and many others such as McKenzie, Nikaido, Nikaido and Uzawa, etc. [p. 644]

This passage sets out the claim for progressivity, for the growth of knowledge; it is not that earlier concerns were lost in subsequent developments, but rather that earlier work was imperfect and required clarification and development. We see in this recitation of names, specifically the names of the authors of papers (Nikaido, and Nikaido and Uzawa), a Whig history in the making. The interesting historical questions must be, on this construction, the influences on Arrow, McKenzie, Nikaido, and others.

The remainder of the Negishi paper, though interesting, is not of concern here. But for completeness I note that the fourth section develops a model of a competitive multimarket economy and sets out several dynamic adjustment processes, tâtonnement and nontâtonnement, for that model system. Section 5 concerns the theorems developed by Arrow, Block, and Hurwicz on global stability under gross substitutability. Section 6 reconstructs the argument by Allais and shows that his 1943 work could be developed into a modern (circa 1962) stability argument. The seventh section develops the Scarf counterexample, which limited the tâtonnement process stability to cases in which gross substitutability was almost required. That is, the stability theorems were all sufficient conditions that systems be asymptotically stable, and the Scarf example suggested that the class of sufficient conditions could not be weakened in any real, substantive way. Sections 8–10 examine alternative adjustment processes, called nontâtonnement, Edgeworth, and Hahn processes, and survey the stability theorems proved for such systems. A final section (11) is subtitled "Suggestions for Further Studies" and points out that the literature contained many processes whose stability had not at that time been examined, or whose stability properties, while being studied, had not been fully delimited. A reference list of sixty-four items completes the paper.

Creating the canon

I wish to begin by discussing an idea about the growth of scientific knowledge. A particular passage taken from the sociologist of science, Bruno Latour, will help split off one of the clearer issues, the role of a survey in "canon creation," from some of the more troublesome issues concerning survey articles:

Since the status of a claim depends on later users' insertions, what if there are no later users whatsoever? This is the point that people who never come close to the fabrication of science have the greatest difficulty in grasping. They imagine that all scientific articles are equal and arrayed in lines like soldiers, to be carefully inspected one by one. However most papers are never read at all. No matter what a paper did to the former literature, if no one else does anything else with it, then it is as if it had never existed at all. You may have written a paper that settles a fierce controversy once and for all, but if readers ignore it it cannot be turned into a fact; it simply cannot. [Latour 1987, p. 40]

I submit that a potentially important paper, because it was not noted in the Negishi survey, came to be considered unimportant. It is well to be clear here: For a paper not to have been cited or otherwise mentioned in the Negishi survey may have reflected a considered judgment by Negishi that the paper was not sufficiently important, or influential, in the sequence of works that he wished to highlight. Such differences of opinion about the importance of a paper are hardly unusual in scholarly enterprises. Nevertheless, that judgment led to a belief that the Liapunov methods were first introduced into the economics literature by Arrow and Hurwicz in 1958, when in fact they had been introduced earlier.

Specifically, I want to discuss a 1954 paper from *Econometrica,* which published most of the papers Negishi cited, titled "Price Determination in a Stock-Flow Economy" (Bushaw and Clower 1954). The import of the paper was that whereas flow-adjustment mechanisms could be unstable even in the linear case under not unreasonable assumptions, the addition of stock-adjustment mechanisms could lead to stabilized systems (essentially because stock mechanisms "average out" past deviations). More important, however, is the fact that Clower and Bushaw *explicitly used, cited, and discussed the second or indirect Liapunov technique for demonstrating asymptotic stability of the competitive equilibrium.*

In Chapter 4 I argued that Takuma Yasui had written, in Japanese, on the Liapunov theory as early as 1950 and that Morishima had discussed the theory and referred to Liapunov's 1907 paper, also in 1950, in Japanese. Nevertheless, it is not surprising that Negishi made no mention of those papers in his survey; he did cite a paper by a Japanese economist, written in English: Sono's article in the *Osaka Economic Papers* (1955), which was in the same tradition as the papers by Yasui and Morishima. Thus, it would appear that Negishi was in the business of citing works that led to other works in the sequence of "knowledge-accreting" papers. Given his audience, mostly English-speaking, it was reasonable to leave Yasui and Morishima outside the story of the introduction of technical mathematical work to the economics literature.

I am not asking here about precursors, nor am I interested in assigning credit for being the first to cite the Liapunov technique. Rather, what I wish to stress is that the Clower–Bushaw paper was lost in a way that the 1956 paper by Enthoven and Arrow, say, was not lost. Mathematically, the Enthoven–Arrow paper, titled "A Theorem on Expectations and the Stability of Equilibrium," was primitive compared with the Clower–Bushaw treatment, which used Malkin's approach to stability via Liapunov functions. But the Enthoven–Arrow paper lives on in the Negishi survey and is in fact reprinted in the Arrow and Hurwicz (1977) collection of papers.

Now, there are various reasons why one paper lives and another dies. On the basis of the fact that Arrow and Hurwicz "solved" the problem, it would seem likely that earlier papers by Arrow would get cited, and a paper by Clower would not. But in fact, Arrow and Hurwicz (1958), in their bibliography, and in the text in the section on the definition of global asymptotic stability, cited the Bushaw–Clower book (1957), which contained discussion of their paper, and did not cite the Enthoven–Arrow paper. There was no self-aggrandizement at work at all; Arrow and Hurwicz were scrupulously fair to their sources as they knew them.

I want to suggest that Negishi's notice and mention of the Enthoven–Arrow paper and his lack of note of the Clower–Bushaw paper suffice to explain why the former became a part of the "history," whereas the latter dropped from sight, even though Arrow and Hurwicz used and correctly cited the Clower–Bushaw paper. Of course, the Clower–Bushaw paper was not exactly related to the sequence of papers that ended in the global stability theorem of Arrow et al. (1959). Yet the survey acted to identify lines of early work that served as precedent in some fashion or another. Negishi's mention of Allais's 1943 work created, later, a source for claiming that Allais had been a precursor in a significant manner to the later Liapunov-based literature. And Negishi's failure to mention Clower–Bushaw precluded that work from likewise being taken as "significant" in a precursor sense.

This is not at all a denigration of Negishi or his judgment. His own tasks in 1962 were not necessarily "historical." Yet for readers years later, his survey does constitute the historical record and in so doing presents itself to us now as history. One of the tasks of a survey article is to define the official content of the subfield surveyed by leaving out what is deemed unimportant by the surveyor. If the work is successful, researchers and students need not spend time studying papers that appear to deviate from the Whiggish history implicit in a particular line of papers, a significant sequence that culminates in the solution to some problem or other often not even articulated before the sequence terminates. The Clower–Bushaw paper disappeared from professional view until such time as a historian "rediscovers" it.[7] Canon creation is a complicated process, and the role of the research survey is central to defining what is and what is not important in the literature.

Once we recognize that that literature is itself the historical record, we are forced to the understanding that we construct history just as we construct theories and theorems and statistical evidence and reality and trees and personal identities and chicken curry – we construct to some purpose or another. The Negishi survey is one sort of construction of a past, and of a research line. It makes little sense to ask of the historian, reading the Negishi survey, whether Negishi got the history right, because the history was in fact being constructed by the survey. Where is the modern historian to read the historical record if not in the sources that make up that record? But that record is not "given" from outside history; it is constructed to become that history. We do not have a "stability literature" so entirely independent of the Negishi survey that we are able to compare the Negishi survey with some true record. The survey, at least in part, constructed the record and helped to define the terms on which any record could be constructed later. It was not that Negishi's paper so much created the canon, but rather that it created the terms on which canon creation was afterward to be done. That that was not Negishi's intent is irrelevant; the survey functions in that way when it is successful, and it is successful if it is persuasive and influential in the community that practices what the survey surveys. My task, then, is to ask of the Negishi survey not, Was it correct and true? but rather, How did it work?

Stabilizing dynamics

Only partially connected to the issue of assigning credit, and defining the canon, as it were, is the important role that the survey plays in validating the coherence of the texts and ideas surveyed. The Negishi survey began, recall, by discussing the reasons why stability analysis was important, and thus left the reader with the impression that those reasons for working on the problem were in fact shared by all the authors surveyed. The history section further reinforced that impression as the history was presented as a sequence of A did 1, then B did 2, so then C did 3, and so on. Finally, in order to discuss the works surveyed in a common framework, Negishi presented a model of his own creation that allowed him to reinterpret all the work of the economists surveyed as one or another subspecialization of the basic Negishi model.

In the terms set out in the preceding chapter, I submit that the survey worked by succeeding in two major tasks: *(1) The Negishi survey article stabilized linguistic practice, and (2) it recorded a transformation in which economic discourse about dynamics changed to mathematical discourse about the stability of the competitive equilibrium.*

I am not here concerned with the issues associated with that transformation itself. That historical argument is the substance of Part I of this book. Rather, I am here interested to show how the survey article itself established the facticity of that transformation. At issue is the following: The rich discourse about dynamic problems of the economy, and the complicated analysis that a dynamic economy required economists to master, was transformed over the period from the mid-1930s to the mid-1950s to a particular language game in which the rules required the analyst to specify a mathematical general equilibrium model, to determine whether or not it possessed a competitive equilibrium, and then to establish the stability of that equilibrium. Playing that game necessitated familiarity with the new general equilibrium analysis of Arrow–Debreu, and McKenzie, and an understanding of the ways in which dynamic theory – the qualitative theory of dissipative differential equations, actually – could model economic market independence. To repeat, I am not here concerned with the truthfulness of that transformation, but rather its presentation in the Negishi survey; at issue are the manner and shape of that representation.

Leaving such broad concerns, how, in particular, does Negishi's survey accomplish the constructive task of economy-making? I shall examine one passage, of two paragraphs, in some detail. Negishi wrote that

as Walras observed, the equilibrium we obtain mathematically or theoretically is established empirically or practically in the market by the mechanism of competition. At the beginning of every period, markets are not necessarily in equilibrium, i.e., the supply of and demand for commodities are not necessarily equal, and the market clearing adjustment process begins to work. The competition of buyers and sellers alters prices. Prices rise for those commodities whose demand exceeds supply, and fall for those commodities where the reverse holds. We know from experience that under this process prices usually do not explode to infinity or contract to zero, but converge to an equilibrium such that the supply of and demand for commodities are equal. Hence, the process which we choose to represent reality must display the same stability. We must therefore search for intuitively appealing and widely acceptable conditions or restrictions on the model that are sufficient to ensure stability. [1962, pp. 638-9]

He then went on to note that

the equilibrium once established in this way is continuously subject to changes and disturbances, such as taste, technology, resources, and weather. Suppose the system, which has been in equilibrium, is thrown out of it by some of those changes or disturbances. It is known empirically that the economy is fairly shock-proof. Dynamic market forces are generated which bring the economy back to equilibrium when it is perturbed, i.e., there exists a stable adjustment process when the economy is out of equilibrium. Realistic models should contain such a dynamic equilibrium process. [1962, p. 639]

These paragraphs would have been unobjectionable to economists at that time. But notice first the outline of the presentation of the first paragraph. In accord with the usual conventions of scientific realism, a discursive strategy that distinguishes between "objects" and their "representations," the author splits off experience from our understanding of that experience that is contained by our explanation of that experience. Reality is out there, apart from us, and we can discuss reality and the constraints that that reality imposes on theories quite independently of those theories. We have, in this conception, a direct perception of the essential nature of the problem before it is in any way structured by a theory or modeling strategy. What is most remarkable about this set of statements, and their epistemological commitment, is how undefended they are, how unassailable they appear in the context; they are not supported by argumentation, and no counterarguments are presented to be dismissed. The position is so well understood and so well appreciated by Negishi's readers that no defense is deemed necessary at all. The community of mathematical economists needs no reminder of the problematic nature of this claim because the claim itself is *not* problematic. This is, to be sure, not a new position embraced by Negishi; in some measure it would be a position assented to by a majority of economists today. The point, however, is that assent to this view has consequences for the sort of evidence one admits to support claims to facticity, for the sort of techniques that appear natural, and for the sort of questions that can be admitted to the status of "problems requiring solution."

Specifically, note how Negishi invites the reader to contemplate the economy directly: "empirically or practically in the market," "we know from experience," "the process which we choose to represent reality," and "it is known empirically." This language, a convention in science, serves to settle matters best left outside the article's purview. The economy being what it is, the task of describing it can be unexceptional. The economy is this way, reader, and we both know it. Now we want to construct a model of it. This is certainly a set of interrelated claims with which a Marxist, for instance, would disagree; from that perspective there is a false consciousness that experiences, and describes, a world in equilibrium. In the non-Marxist Robert Heilbroner's sense of the term, this splitting of the world from our representation of it using the equilibrium language constitutes Negishi's ideology. Negishi's claim is an interesting presentation of the ideological basis of neoclassical general equilibrium theory circa 1962.[8]

This language of the real economy being there, and interpersonally available for us as a check of our insights, is a scientific commonplace; indeed, it is what nurtures the rhetoric of statistical testing – we check real data to see if our theories are confirmed or refuted. Reality will constrain what we can or should say. It is not surprising to find this structure in the Negishi research survey. After all, a survey should examine a more or less settled area, else the surveyor cannot be "fair," and the assigning editor will have not a survey but a "contribution."

More to the point is the selection of facts, or what are construed to be problems. On the face of it, Negishi has problematized "getting to equilibrium." The presence of equilibrium is not an issue, and neither is the fact that the prices and quantities move in measurable ways with reference to equilibrium prices and quantities. If prices and quantities are definable, and distinct, they are quantifiable, and thus representable by real numbers. Their movements are functions of time as long as the vision is that of a temporal process. Process itself imagines duration and requires a disjunction from equilibrium. Because "under this process prices usually do not explode to infinity or contract to zero," we have a mathematical model already present, for where in the economy is "infinity" or "zero"? Akron? New York?

We see the economy as Negishi sees it, as a mechanical entity at rest, getting hit with shocks, and returning to rest. No people die in this economy, no one is hungry, no politician shouts for deregulation. Disembodied prices converge or fail to converge in homogeneous unblack markets. The metaphor of the machine is not accidental. As Mirowski (1989a) has been able to show, the neoclassical framework is nineteenth-century energetics in action. This machine works in ways understood by physicists in specific mathematical terms; the physicists constructed the machine, after all. For my purpose, I need only point and say that this is what Negishi is doing here; we see the rabbit, we see the hat, and we see the held rabbit placed in the hat – no magic, just craft.

It is clear that Negishi's economy is constructed out of the mathematical structures that he and those whose work he discusses use to solve various problems. That is, the economy is pictured as consisting of economic agents, called households and firms, who optimize subject to constraints and whose choices are made manifest in numerous interrelated markets. That *is* the economy. This is the stuff of observation, it seems, though we, of course, never observe an agent optimizing, nor do we see firms maximizing profits. If you were to observe me in the grocery store, you would simply observe me picking objects off shelves, placing them in a cart, and eventually paying for the items in the cart. You may argue that I "maximized utility," but that is an inference from my behavior – you did not observe my public act of maximizing. By inviting us to see this economy, Negishi opens a door on a placid scene of vibrating levers and humming flywheels and the occasional whine of an unoiled gear. For those who like the linearity of modernist structures, the invitation is accepted. For the bloody-minded Marxist who sees nonlinear banners, exploitative institutions, and bread-marchers where Negishi sees profit-maximizing firms, the invitation will be declined, with regrets offered, and another journal started.

Three oppositions

The main argument that develops from this set of observations is that the literature on dynamic stability, as it developed from the 1930s to the 1950s, was formed and guided by a set of "oppositions," and those oppositions themselves created the language and conceptual framework that structure how modern theorists think about the economy and the way we model-construct that economy.

The basic point is easy to grasp. I submit that the distinctions between statics and dynamics, between equilibrium and disequilibrium, and between stability and instability have guided the construction of models of the economy and that those binary oppositions are the discursive master terms in a language game that, though it has its roots in classical economics, defines the way economists think about the world they make.

The period of the 1930s, recall, was a time of immense social fluidity as the structures of economic life were shaken by the Great Depression. That time of massive unemployment was preshadowed by the English experience of unemployment in the 1920s. In such a time of fluidity, the urge to reconstruct the new order in opposition to the older, more settled prewar order was hardly resisted. The calls for a return to the prewar gold standard were to come to a point with the Churchill budget of 1925; the desire to return to an earlier, more innocent, more settled Victorian time, a time without Ypres and Passchendaele of recent memory, a time of hope and glory indeed, was connected to a view of a settled past, one of ease and certitude and fulfilled expectations, as contrasted with an unsettled present. History became an activity-bound process of movement and change.

In language, we have the need to articulate this sense of movement between fixity and fluidity. I wish to suggest that the pair of terms, what is in literary parlance the "binary opposition," that structured this sense of newness was "static–dynamic." The linguistic move that was reflected in the concern, in the early 1930s, that there was no good way to speak intelligibly one to another about the perceptual frameworks that were coming to instantiate mutually incoherent visions of economic life necessitated a concern, made public in the literature on the meaning of equilibrium and disequilibrium, with the nature and role of economic dynamics. Dynamics characterized the economics that one wanted to do; statics concerned a settled subject appropriate to an earlier settled period. Now, to be sure, that binary opposition was present, and to large measure it had been borrowed from nineteenth-century physics (Mirowski 1989a), but its power as a metaphor was not inherent in the source, but in the target, for the economists constructed the economy out of their concerns, not the concerns of defunct physicists. The metaphors drew their power not from their origins but from their use.

Economists in the early 1930s understood the issue of statics and dynamics to be a polarity, as an either–or situation. That could not logically be maintained, however, because the two terms were defined each with reference to the other; that metaphorical failure rooted the concerns that were to lead to the Samuelson move of the late 1930s. That is, the idea associated with "static" requires the idea of "dynamic" to give it life. A time of ease is a time of internal movement, at least, but it appears as a time of ease only in retrospect, when unease, disease, intrudes. One is sick relative to being healthy, and one is at rest relative to motion. Absolute stasis is inconceivable. Thus, the idea of a dynamic economics, a theory or set of theories to describe or construct an economy that would allow change and strife and imbalance and fear, which, in short, would allow discussion of the political vision of the economies of the 1930s, necessitated a self-consciousness about the static–dynamic opposition. That worked itself out, as I have tried to show, in the Frisch papers of the mid-1930s, though the metaphors had been present in the borrowed physics of the earlier mathematical economists.

That this polarity was recognized, and later imposed as a history on the theories, can be inferred from Negishi. He notes that "the static theory of general equilibrium, developed by Walras, Cassel, Hicks, Leontief, etc., can be dynamized in many different ways" (Negishi 1962, p. 636). It is not sensible, or possible, to separate the Walrasian contribution as static except with reference to some dynamic version or extension. This reading is profoundly ahistorical, for Walras never argued that his own vision was so limited; indeed, his tâtonnements themselves were a groping *process*. The forcing of Walras into the category of "static," leaving "dynamics" to develop decades after Walras's theory was established, reconstructs Walras as having a static theory of price adjustment! Such a reading was provided by Patinkin (1965) in his *Money, Interest, and Prices,* and it was a strong and convincing reading indeed; the point at issue, of course, was precisely that Walras's static theory could be juxtaposed with Samuelson's dynamics to give rise to a useful static–dynamic distinction, but it could not be sustained of its own accord. The static Walras was constructed by the dynamics of a later age, a dynamics that had to take its meaning from the tension of a distinction not present in earlier times. The Walrasian tâtonnement process was insufficiently dynamic, in later terms, to allow a richness of distinction among dynamic processes. So Walrasian dynamics became static, and static became an opposition to a dynamic that had not been present at the time of the formation of general equilibrium thinking.

The illusion that one could separate statics from dynamics was fostered by the Marshallian vice of drawing supply and demand curves. That is, the conceptual illusion of such schemata is that a salience is afforded one and only one point in the space of all possible points, the point of intersection of the two curves. Only that one price–quantity configuration is special; all other points in the space of possible prices and quantities are irregular, unsustainable, unattainable, or otherwise inaccessible. The partition of the nonnegative price–quantity space into equilibrium and disequilibrium points fosters a separation of interest, for nothing can really be said about most of the possible price–quantity configurations whatsoever, except that those pairs will not ever be wanted, desired, or observed. They stand outside analysis, outside economics, outside language. Equilibrium is real, for it is potentially observable. We have already seen that Negishi noted that "the equilibrium we obtain mathematically or theoretically *is established empirically or practically in the market by the mechanism of competition*" (1962, p. 638, italics added). Put another way, the world produces outcomes that are equilibrium outcomes. But that construal requires disequilibria, which are not observed. The issue of the geometry is not irrelevant here. The continuous curve in the plane, in Euclidean two-dimensional space, which models the supply or demand curve, produces, by the Jordan curve theorem, a division of the space into two parts. If the curves are closed naturally, the enclosed space has an inside and an outside in a natural sense. Space is bifurcated by a planar curve in two-space, as a consequence of the Hahn–Banach theorem. The conjunction of two such curves, meeting in a point, locates a special point only with reference to all those points excluded. The specialness is not intrinsic, but is mediated by the other points not on the curves. Equilibrium is fuzzy in a model with fuzzy curves; the clarity of either–or is lost.

The static–dynamic polarity structures discourse about the economic world we wish to construct, to see, to convince others to act in or on. That disjunction, never given to the economist, but rather always imposed by the economist, must then be rooted in the equilibrium–disequilibrium polarity, for each world, the static and the dynamic, can permit each term of the dyad to function in its linguistic practices. We can construct the static equilibrium vision of the settled consumer's choice, or the dynamic disequilibrium vision of a capitalist crisis; our worlds are rich, and the ways we can speak about them provide the measure of that richness.

Such complexity comes at a price, of course, and that price is paid in the coin of confusion and argument and conversations distinctly non-Habermasian. The communities of neoclassicals and Marxists cannot converse, but what is worse, perhaps, is that the neoclassical theorists themselves cannot understand arguments that cross over from the static to the dynamic. As Negishi remarks,

the models of trade cycles and economic growth generate time paths of outputs, capital stocks, and prices, which are of a dynamic equilibrium type, in which the supply of and demand for each commodity are assumed to be continuously equal in each market. This abstraction from the market clearing process, which may be considered as a shorter run phenomenon than the one under consideration. . . . [1962, p. 637]

The two polarities resolve their tensions, in a community bent on consensus, as a scientific community pledges itself to be, in a revision of discourse that permits conversation to go on. To reiterate the point made at the beginning of this chapter, the Negishi survey effectively documents the transformation of the contests for meaning that had invigorated the literature of the 1930s and early 1940s, contests about the static–dynamic and equilibrium–disequilibrium polarities, contests framed in terms of the value of models that represent the economy in terms such as "static equilibrium model." The two oppositions came to be replaced, or reinterpreted, by the more restricted but nonetheless overarching master trope "stable–unstable."

Because the mathematical theory that coded stability permitted static or dynamic stability ideas to be imposed on phenomena, that mathematical structure subsumed the earlier contests for meaning in the literature. It accomplished that feat by providing a systematic investigatory logic to probe the nature and scope of the stable–unstable distinction. As we saw in Chapter 4, "stable" was linked to a particular motion of the dynamic system in the mathematical structure; in the mathematics it referred to a motion approaching a distinctive motion, called the equilibrium motion, in an asymptotic sense. "Unstable" suggests no such quietude, but in the mathematical instantiation of the ideas, a maintained oscillation around a particular path, much as an undamped pendulum, could be called an unstable motion. As with any newly reinterpreted idea, in the mathematics of stability one had to use what one had inherited linguistically. And what one had bought, in the grammar of stability analysis, was the usage of "one motion gets close to another motion." When it is seen that a motion is a curve in space, it is immediate that there are manifold ways in which one curve can be depicted as close to another: Are two snakes close when they coincide, or only when one coils around the other or crosses over the other several times (but these snakes are infinitely long!), or only when their tails coincide or when they are within mouse distance of each other?

For Negishi, the stable–unstable polarity must respect the ordering of the economists' belief that "prices usually do not explode to infinity or contract to zero, but converge to an equilibrium such that the supply of and demand for commodities are equal" (1962, p. 639).

This is the vision that the mathematics can sustain in language, and the Negishi survey establishes and legitimizes the description of that vision. The marginalized "unstable," in contrast to the normative "stable," is neither exterior to nor subsequent upon its opposite. Rather, the pair work together within the language of economics, and the mathematics sustains the pairing. The Negishi discussion of the various meanings to be attached to "stability" (pp. 640-1), even within tight mathematical formulations, encourages the perception that stable and unstable are contextually formed and reformed.

A concluding note

I have tried to suggest that static–dynamic and equilibrium–disequilibrium gave way to stable–unstable as the master binary oppositions of a particular set of discursive practices in economic theory. These oppositions framed what could be said, just as the language practices generated by them constructed an economy in which some things, but not other things, could be pictured and problematized. The larger community, to be a community, required its members to talk coherently about the economy. Coherence was obtained by sharing a vision of the economy, "seeing" the same object. This required a transformation of experience and an ordering of that experience; that ordering gave substance to the new rules of the language game called modeling the competitive economy. The Negishi survey article played a role in that transformation of economic description. And today, the Negishi survey provides a window on that reshaping of discursive practice.

CHAPTER 8

Conclusion

...but what is Whiggery?
A levelling, rancorous, rational sort of mind
That never looked out of the eye of a saint
Or out of a drunkard's eye.
...All's Whiggery now...

W. B. Yeats (1946, pp. 277–8)

The history of economic thought as usually presented has a frankly Whiggish perspective in the sense that the narrative impels the reader to see how success was or was not reached in the particular paper or papers under discussion. Don Walker, in his recent presidential address to the History of Economics Society, made it explicit that "we judge economic writings in the light of modern economic knowledge...we use current knowledge to detect sound arguments and defective arguments" (Walker 1988, p. 101). Walker's paper and Samuelson's "Out of the Closet: A Program for the Whig History of Economic Science" (1987),[1] define what most economists believe about the nature and use of histories of economics, and the history of science more generally. That is, in a brief caricature, that history must be a moral exemplar showing how scientists came to "get it right," eventually, where the "right stuff" is called Truth. Thus, Walker states that the historian judges economic writings on the basis of criteria of originality, importance (as measured by impact on other, later writers), correspondence to current views, logical consistency, avoidance of false claims, and realism of the theories. For Walker, science (and economic science) progresses over time in the measurable sense that more and more Truth is discovered. The history of science, and so, too, the history of economics, must show to a reader just how that progress is constructed, for if there is no progress in a particular line of work, its study is, to Walker, mere "antiquarianism."

My perspective is different from those of Samuelson and Walker. I submit that the history developed in Part I leads to some doubts about the Whiggish perspective itself. Moreover, I submit that were we to need to face the epistemological issue directly, we would have to address the question whether or not the sequence of papers, the developed stability

149

literature, can in fact be viewed as a more and more faithful representation of the true state of affairs of the economy. Succinctly, what are we to make of the question, Is the economy in a position of stable or unstable equilibrium? From our understanding that there can be only one answer to this question (It depends on what we mean by "economy," "stable-unstable," and "equilibrium") it is clear that the "representation" represents not what is "out there" but rather what the economist creates. Where Marx saw a falling rate of profit, Clark saw a marginal product of capital. Where Pigou saw an excess supply of labor, Keynes saw a particular level of employment associated with the point of effective demand. Where Solow sees a market failure, Lucas sees rational competitive activity.[2] Such "seeing" is a construction, not a representation in the sense of a discursive act that is closer to Truth than any other construction. For me, I cannot confidently appreciate what such an idea of "representation" might mean. As Rorty argues,

the quest for a theory of reference represents a confusion between the hopeless "semantic" quest for a general theory of what people are "really talking about," and the equally hopeless "epistemological" quest for a way of refuting the skeptic and underwriting our claim to be talking about nonfictions.... Debates about theories of reference get their concreteness from attempts to answer the first part of the question, and their philosophical interest from hints that they might somehow answer the second. But nothing can refute the skeptic – nothing can do what epistemology hoped to do. For we discover how language works only within the present theory about the rest of the world, and one cannot use part of one's theory to underwrite the rest of it. [Rorty 1979, pp. 293–4]

From my project, this book, I claim that there is no meaning to be attached to "the economy is in a position of stable equilibrium" or "the economy is not stable," except as that claim is understood as imposing a discursive order on phenomena. It is an invitation from A, who makes the claim, to B, to whom it is spoken or written, to participate in a (Wittgensteinian) language game to be played according to a particular set of rules; or it is an attempt to convince the hearer that a particular way of speaking is useful for some shared purpose such as reducing the misery of laid-off automobile workers and those who no longer qualify for particular "unemployment" benefits. "The economy is inherently unstable" is a claim that if uttered and treated seriously by the hearer may lead to a desire to restructure society along particular collectivist lines, or it may lead one to ask for more decentralized decision making by market agents. The point is that we construct our economy by our descriptions:

[We] make constellations by picking out and putting together certain stars rather than others, [and] we make stars by drawing certain boundaries rather than others. Nothing dictates whether the skies shall be marked off into constellations or other objects. We have to make what we find, whether it be the Big Dipper, Sirius, food, fuel, or a stereo system. [Goodman 1985, p. 36]

I submit that nothing whatsoever is lost, in economics or in the history of economics, by giving up the notion of representation as "discovery of the other." Representation as a constructive invitation, as a presentation of a position or vision or way of speaking to some important end, is not lost at all. We do represent the economy with our accounts, models, theories, stories, and data; but except as a burdensome fiction, those representations do not "describe" except as they create that which is to be described. Except as a confusion, models of the economy do not "depict" except as they instantiate a vision to be shared, and profitably discussed, by a particular community of economists. Representation is a creative, purposeful human act, and communities that can agree on representations and descriptions can jointly act on their created world. Social purpose is served by social behavior, by shared linguistic practices, and by following mutually understood rules of action and interaction. Understanding how this activity is manifest in communities of economists is a legitimate task, worthy of historians of economics.

Notes

2. Economists on dynamics and stability in the 1930s

1 I use "text" in the literary sense, as a written document, not in the sense of "textbook." As later chapters will suggest, there are useful insights to be gained as well from thinking of the economy as a text to be read.

2 My late colleague Joe Spengler once arrived late at a party, and I asked him what he had been doing. He said that he had been doing the corrections to galley proofs for a book on Persian economic thought. When I asked him how he had ever got onto such a subject, he looked wistfully at the ceiling and replied: "I had been doing a book on Indian economic thought, and, well, you know how it is, one thing just led to another."

3 In a chapter in an earlier book (Weintraub, 1985), I used 1930 as a cutoff date for a history of existence-of-equilibrium proofs. In the kind of misunderstanding that constitutes a willful refusal to read in good faith what is written, a reviewer criticized that book harshly for that chapter's failure to discuss the contributions of a couple of economists who wrote before 1930.

4 As an example of what this decision leaves out of my discussion, consider the fact that Gerhard Tintner had, by 1935, become interested in the work being done by both Roos and Evans in applying the calculus of variations to problems in economics. As Karl Fox (1987) notes, "from 1936 to 1942 he published a series of brilliant articles on such topics as maximization of utility over time, the derivation of dynamic demand curves.... Apparently these articles attracted little attention under the disturbed conditions of the time." Because Samuelson does not refer to Tintner at all, I shall not discuss his work either.

5 I shall return to this problem of distinguishing between the two uses of "equilibrium" in my discussion of the imagery associated with those uses, in Chapter 5.

6 Robbins, of course, had intellectual roots in what was then Austrian economics, although Wicksteed was the major influence on his microeconomic analysis. His approach to business cycle theory, which was certainly the subject of his paper noted by Samuelson, was influenced by Wicksell and Hayek and Mises. These influences are well noted by D. P. O'Brien (1991).

7 The first paragraph of the paper gives the exact context of its genesis: "At the Namur meeting of the Econometric Society, September, 1935, a discussion arose regarding Wicksell's concept of the 'natural' interest rate. The discussion subsequently extended to the question of what in general was to be understood by a 'natural' or 'equilibrium' position of a certain set of economic variables. The discussion was continued in private between Messrs. Breit, F. G. Koopmans,

Marschak, Tinbergen, and myself. As an outcome of this discussion I prepared a brief paper on the subject, which was presented at one of the subsequent sessions. The following is a somewhat modified and enlarged version of this paper." Rasmussen (1987), in an excessively hagiographic entry in *The New Palgrave,* notes that Frisch wrote the paper overnight in a hotel room following the discussion and presented it to his colleagues the next day.

8 After these distinctions were introduced in the first three pages of the paper, Frisch used these ideas to examine Wicksell's theory of the natural rate of interest in the final three pages.

9 I shall return specifically to this point in Chapter 5.

10 Such equations have characteristic equations, as do differential equations. However, in the mixed case, the characteristic equations are not polynomials, but rather transcendental equations, like, for example, $x + a \log x = 0$. The eigenvalues λ for such equations yield solutions of the form $x(t) = \Sigma c \cdot \exp(\lambda t)$, but there may be a finite or infinite number of roots to such equations, unlike the simple polynomial case. Finding such roots (and thus finding solutions that had oscillations) was thus a difficult problem in numerical analysis in the 1930s, before the development of computers.

S. Chakravarty (1987) notes that it was a 1930 paper by Tinbergen, on shipbuilding cycles, that first introduced such mixed equations into economics ("Ein Schiffbauzyklus?" *Weltwirtschaftliches Archiv,* 1930).

11 This is one reason that the "new classical" business cycle literature, in its antagonism to Keynesian macroeconomics, has claimed the earlier cycle's literature as its ancestry. But that literature is not of a piece. This topic is lucidly treated by Kim (1989).

12 Frisch's use of "trend" was different from modern usage; he preferred to think of a real series as made up of all sorts of superimposed "trends," whereas we would think of it as composed of all sorts of interacting "cycles." On Frisch's language, see Morgan (1990).

13 Reflecting on that paper, in a recent interview, Tinbergen (1987, p. 125) noted the following: "I think that what interested economists most was not the shocks but the mechanism generating endogenous cycles, and it might well be that we have overestimated the role of the mechanism. Maybe the shocks were really much more important. This problem has never been solved, because the War came along and after the War we were not interested in business cycles anymore."

14 The only reference to this material in *Value and Capital* is to Burnside and Panton (1904, pp. 181–2).

15 I thus disagree with the evaluation of this Hicksian analysis provided recently in *The New Palgrave* by Christopher Bliss (1987), who wrote that Hicks's was "the first ever attempt to analyse the stability of a system of multiple exchange. This was the same question as was examined by Paul Samuelson in various papers in the 1940s." Bliss went on to argue that Hicks's method of keeping all markets except the ith market in equilibrium, and then seeing what would be required to equilibrate the ith, and doing that in turn for all n markets, was

essentially the way that Walras presented his tâtonnements, as a way of establishing that equilibrium could be achieved. Thus, Hicks was presenting not so much a dynamic analysis as an implicit existence proof. That the language of these two approaches cannot be untangled after the mathematics of dynamic systems is taken to define how the problem is posed is the substance of Chapter 5. This, of course, is the reason why "the Hicksian stability condition can be shown to be neither necessary nor sufficient for [Samuelson's true dynamic stability]" (Bliss, 1987, pp. 642-3).

3. The foundations of Samuelson's dynamics

1 This argument, sketched in an early draft, was entirely reworked after Mary Morgan and Phil Mirowski noted the connection between my discussion and the earlier book by Cynthia Eagle Russett, *The Concept of Equilibrium in American Social Thought* (1966). I have drawn on that book's perspective rather extensively in some later sections of this chapter.

2 This book, the first edition of which was published by the Williams and Walker Company, Baltimore, in 1924, was reprinted with corrections from the author's notes as *Elements of Mathematical Biology* by Dover Books, New York, 1956. This is the edition I shall use, and page references are to this reprint edition.

3 "From an original edition of about 2,500 it sold 568 copies in 1925, followed by an average of 234 per year until 1930, when sales dropped off sharply to 73. A small market for the book continued throughout the 1930's, until by 1940 the edition was nearly sold out" (Kingsland 1985, p. 48).

4 As a mathematics student, I learned this as the rumor-propagation model, where the rate ($\dot{R}$) at which a rumor propagates is directly proportional not only to the number of individuals who have heard the rumor (R) but also to the number who have not heard ($\bar{P} - R$) it, so that $\dot{R} = \alpha R \times (\bar{P} - R)$.

5 In fact, the Samuelson idiosyncrasy of writing down general functional equations, but working with difference or differential equations, and interpreting definitions presented generally into the special cases, masks the simplicity of his approach and its analogues in the standard work of the times. The highly abstract presentation in terms of general, time-dependent functional equations is a notational bother; it did allow Samuelson to define a stationary state simultaneously for difference and differential equations, but that was a small gain for the loss of coherence that resulted when the excess of generality forced him to interpret each definition in several special cases anyway. See, for example, the *Foundations,* on "Stability and Dynamics" (pp. 260-9).

6 There are significant issues at stake here, and it is well to point them out apart from the main argument. Philip Mirowski (1989a) argues that the entire mathematical structure of energetics, particularly the mathematics of conservative dynamic systems, took root in the neoclassical "revolution." But because economists took maximization and minimization, but did not have any conservation laws, the neoclassical conception is formally flawed in that the central dogma of neoclassical analysis, the optimization-equilibrium metaphor, misapplies the

mathematical structures appropriate to conservative dynamic systems to dissipative systems. Without going into the controversy over the Mirowski thesis here, I note that that idea was surfaced explicitly, to no effect, in Harvard's own journal by Northrop (1941).

7 Lotka provides references here to Picard's discussion of singular points, using the 1891 edition of Volume I, the 1893 edition of Volume II, and the 1896 edition of Volume III.

8 He gives the footnote citation to the text as follows: "Recherches sur les Equilibres Chimique, 1888, pp. 48, 210; *Comptes Rendus,* 1884, vol. 99, p. 786; Mellor, *Chemical Statics and Dynamics,* 1904, pp. 435–436."

9 Philip Mirowski (1989d) has an extended discussion of the Le Chatelier principle in economics, and the Wilson-Samuelson connection in this regard, in the June 1989 issue of *Studies in the History and Philosophy of Science.*

10 For example, Tatsuo Hatta (1987, p. 155): "Suppose a 'just binding' constraint is added to an extremum problem such that the initial solution is on this constraint. Adding such a constraint affects the solution only after some parameters are shifted. The Le Chatelier Principle states that the (compensated) effect of a shift in a parameter upon the solution of a decision variable is smaller with such an additional constraint than without."

11 Simon suggests that, even more importantly, Lotka set out a program that could be termed "pre-cybernetic": "He sees that [energy transformations] are far from the whole story, and has a strong sense of the significance of entropy for irreversible systems. [In his section] entitled "Intelligence as a Discriminating Agency," [he] compares organismic powers of selection with Maxwell's demon.... I can find no closer approach in his pages to information-theoretic concepts" (Simon 1959, p. 494).

12 Freely rendered as follows: "We say, following Liapunov, that we have a stable solution if for any positive number l, no matter how small, we can assign another positive number ϵ, such that when we take some initial values (at $t = 0$) of the x_i, denoted α_i, [small enough] so that the absolute values of the α_i are less than ϵ, then [we can be assured that] the absolute values of the x_i will be less than l for all positive times t."

13 This section and some of the arguments it contains were suggested both directly by my correspondence with Philip Mirowski and indirectly by my reading of his work. Though I have attempted to do justice to the strength and force of his views, no small section, even one so closely linked to the central thesis of this chapter as this, could do justice to Mirowski's remarkable and remarkably intelligible arguments (Mirowski, 1988, 1989a, 1989b, 1989d). It should be obvious that Mirowski would not agree with all of my uses and interpretations of his writing, despite his attempts to persuade me that my story can be well understood from his perspective.

14 Much of the material on Wilson's career is based on the biographical essay by Jerome Hunsaker and Saunders Mac Lane (1973).

15 All these Wilson letters that I shall cite were provided to me by Mirowski and are copies of letters in the Harvard University Archives, E. B. Wilson Collection, HUG 4878.203, Personal Correspondence.

16 However, the particular point Wilson makes is entirely opaque. Gibbs's equation 133 (Gibbs 1906, p. 100) concerns "the stability of a fluid enclosed in a rigid envelop which is non-conducting to heat and impermeable to all the components of the fluid." The discussion of the equation suggests that at equilibrium a certain expression is zero, but it is positive elsewhere; this is the state of affairs referred to as "stable," and it suggests that equilibrium is associated with a minimum point. The definiteness of a quadratic form then has a real context, not entirely akin to the cost-minimization issue with which Samuelson was concerned.

17 This is an appropriate point to note my debt to the Russett book, which I had not seen until my own work was well under way. Her unraveling of the "equilibrium" story in social theory has provided a foundation for my own attempt here to link economists' renewed interest in equilibrium analysis with broader intellectual currents. It is unfortunate for the history of economic thought that Russett apparently believed that the economists of the 1930s and 1940s had a good understanding of the nature and role of equilibrium theorizing, for she placed little emphasis on economists in her masterful study. Her book is required reading for any economist interested in the development of modern mathematical economics out of general equilibrium theory and systems theory.

18 From Picard (1928, pp. 384–5).

4. Liapunov theory and economic dynamics

1 This three-volume work was published in a third edition in 1928.

2 As I noted in Chapter 3, Samuelson made use, albeit a curiously haphazard use, of Picard's book.

3 This having been said, it should be noted that Andronov was publishing, on occasion, in French and in German during the 1930s: He had papers in the French *Comptes Rendus* in 1929 and 1930 on Poincaré limit cycles and on self-maintained oscillations, and those papers were written in French. Further, he published a paper in a Soviet physics journal in 1935 in French and one in a Soviet math journal in 1930 in German. He also published a paper, in German, in a German physics journal in 1926 (Boĭko 1983, p. 196).

4 The primary original idea of the Moscow school was, of course, the notion of structural stability of a system. Unlike the Liapunov stability ideas, which concerned issues of arbitrary motions defined by the system converging eventually to a well-defined equilibrium motion, structural stability asked instead whether a perturbation of the system's parameters would change the character of the limit behavior of the system. That is, if the system for some parameter values had a limit cycle as the "attractor" of nearby motions, would a perturbation of the system also lead to a limit cycle as an attractor, or would, instead, the limit motion change to a source, or saddle, say. Certainly, real applications to engineered systems would require that the system possess structural stability, else small voltage variation, say, could lead to radically different performance characteristics. These ideas have not, to this day, played any role in economic models.

5 That mathematical work itself fostered a growth industry – "optimal growth models" – in the economics profession in the mid-1960s.

6 I do not know why this book was not cited by Samuelson in his *Foundations of Economic Analysis*. This is certainly one of the very important books in mathematical economics, much praised by Hotelling, especially for the Appendix: "Economics and the Calculus of Variations."

7 Lest this seem too strong, examine the Appendix, where the note on elimination on pages 94–6 specifically states that "when we have the same problem [simultaneous equations to be solved] involving squares, products, or other functions of $x, y, \ldots$, the procedure is the same essentially, though it is not always possible to carry it out by simple methods" (p. 95).

8 Evans was one of the first fellows of that society. Mirowski suggests that because Evans and his student Roos both thought that utility was a little silly, they were rather snubbed by the community of economic theorists. As evidence for this, he notes that Samuelson's mentor, E. B. Wilson, wrote the following to Frank Taussig, also at Harvard, dated May 17, 1934: "Evans' book on mathematical economics seems to me wrongly conceived but I may be mistaken. . . . He seems to treat the whole subject as a series of rather minor problems" (E. B. Wilson Correspondence, Harvard University Archives, HUG 4878.203). I have, however, found a useful citation to the Evans book in Tinbergen's survey, for *Econometrica*, in 1935.

9 Certainly Samuelson had described "true dynamic stability" of systems of the form $\dot{x} = Ax$, where x and A are as before; he showed the eigenvalue results about stability explicitly. The difference was that Samuelson concentrated on local stability analysis, and so was content with establishing results for linearizations of the full autonomous system. He then argued that multiple equilibria, which could be present in many economic models, would be "distinct," and so the local stability of each could be analyzed. His results on such problems suggested that stable and unstable equilibria would "alternate" with each other, so that one would always get to "some" equilibrium in sensible models.

10 This is reinforced by a letter I received from Michel Moreaux, in which he writes that "you can find a brief and excellent account of Allais' contribution in T. Negishi" (Moreaux, 1989).

11 My loose translations of the French may be of some help to readers who wish to keep the argument in view without dictionary in hand.

12 This is crucial, for the nature of a Liapunov function is that one may differentiate it with respect to time and show that its time rate of change is negative. To speak or write of a nondifferentiable Liapunov function is to commit a category mistake.

13 Much of this section is revised, with permission of Duke University Press, from my earlier article: Weintraub (1987).

14 Yasui cited, in his major paper to be discussed later, both Michio Morishima and Sono, a mathematician who wrote on economic dynamics; I have not been able to learn much about Sono's influence, except that his papers were well

known to Yasui. Morishima indeed set up sections of his *Dynamic Economic Theory* (1980, from the 1950 Japanese version) with titles like "Hicks's and Sono's Stability Conditions." Unfortunately, the English-language edition of 1980 omitted all references and bibliographical material.

15 The influence was not directly personal, because both were students at Kyoto, whereas Yasui was six hundred kilometers away at Tohoku.

16 Yasui here agrees with Tsuru's recollection, however, that "I had a copy which Paul had sent to me; and knowing Yasui's interest at that time, I lent that copy to him immediately after I received it. But by then Yasui's paper was in the printer's hands" (Tsuru 1986).

17 Tsuru goes on to note that "Yasui wrote a letter to Samuelson on this and received a reply from the latter which acknowledged Yasui's priority and suggested he write on it for *Econometrica*. But Yasui would not do this, believing as he did that the question of priority in such matters – i.e. a rediscovery of a mathematical theorem for application in economic theory – was not very important in any case" (Tsuru 1986, p. 296). It is also worth noting that although Yasui had not seen the Samuelson book, he did know Samuelson's 1941 *Econometrica* article on stability, from which material on dynamics in the *Foundations* was drawn.

18 Yasui has written that "I was then entirely unaware how great this Russian mathematician was and what rank he held in his profession. In retrospect, it was as if I happened to have angled for a big fish from the dark sea. . . . Compared with such more recent neat expositions as W. Hahn's or LaSalle–Lefschetz's Liapunov books, my paper was assuredly tortuous as well as clumsy, but it was a little solace that no economist of the day paid attention to Liapounoff" (Yasui 1985, p. 2).

19 My discussion of the article is based on a translation prepared by Mr. Shuichi Murata, who was a graduate student in economics at Duke University in November 1985. My understanding of the paper was greatly enhanced by conversations with Professor Aiko Ikeo, of Kokugakuin University, who visited Duke during 1988–90.

20 In fact, Morishima rediscovered some major elements of Liapunov's theory in his 1948 work, which was a dynamization of Sono's static theory; that handwritten mimeographed paper, circulated among Japanese theorists, had a title that translates as "Economic Equilibrium and Its Stability": "One year later I published an abridged version of the report in a journal, which is 'Static and Dynamic Stability Conditions' (again in Japanese) where I repeated the same argument" (Morishima 1986).

21 Unless otherwise noted, material in this section has been developed from the excellent paper "Solomon Lefschetz," by Phillip Griffiths, Donald Spencer, and George Whitehead, dated October 3, 1988. This memoir is to be published, after revision, by the National Academy of Sciences. The biographical sections and the sections on differential equations in this paper were both written by Spencer. I am grateful to Phillip Griffiths for allowing me to examine this paper in its prepublication version.

22 In his obituary for Picard, Lefschetz wrote that the *Traité D'Analyse* "is a mathematician's book, and it helped to form generations of mathematicians" (Lefschetz 1943, p. 365).

23 In the Preface to the 1949 English-language edition of the Andronov and Chaikin book, Lefschetz wrote that "the work of the [Mandelstam] Institute has become known to the world at large through Dr. N. Minorsky's *Introducduction to Non-Linear Mechanics* recently issued by the David Taylor Model Basin" (p. v). It seems clear that it was Nicholas Minorsky who actually transmitted to Lefschetz knowledge of the Soviet work on oscillations.

24 In fact, in each of 1935, 1936, and 1937 he published papers, in Russian, in Russian mathematical journals; see the Bibliography of Griffiths et al. (1988, p. 41).

25 This, of course, was originally published in 1907 in *Annales de la Faculté des Sciences de l'Université de Toulouse*.

26 Although it takes us beyond our time period, we should note that in 1957 the Glenn Martin Aircraft Company formed a Research Institute for Advanced Study (RIAS), and Lefschetz was hired to create its Mathematics Center; that group, which was to include Cesari, Hale, and LaSalle, was the motive force in the rebirth of interest in qualitative dynamic theory, Liapunov theory, and control theory. The group moved as a unit to the Department of Applied Mathematics at Brown University in 1963.

27 Clower recalled that he and Bushaw had both been candidates for Rhodes scholarships and that in their competition year, both had been turned down. He further recalled that Bushaw, who even as an undergraduate had had superior language skills, had read Liapunov in the French version, which had appeared in 1949, and had discussed the ideas with Clower, who had received his B.A. in 1947 and his M.A., also from Washington State University (WSU), in 1949 (Clower, telephone conversation, January 19, 1989). Bushaw recalls that "when we were undergraduates at WSU (then WSC) in 1946–1949, Bob and I spent a great deal of time together (often making a foursome with our respective wives), not only talking about mathematics and economics, but talking philosophy and literature, playing pinball machines, etc. . . . The effects of these amusements on our later collaboration are not clear" (Bushaw 1989, p. 1).

28 The book might have appeared earlier and have had a different impact except that "not long after Bob and I started [that book] he spent several years in Pakistan. We made valiant efforts (involving reams of paper) to keep the collaboration going, but it really didn't work, and not until he returned to Pullman [Washington] did we begin to make good progress again, and then the book did not take long to finish. Without the Pakistan interlude, the book might have come out three years or so sooner" (Bushaw 1989).

29 I have discussed elsewhere the way in which Liapunov theory began to appear through another path, that from the work of some Japanese theorists (Weintraub 1987).

30 The Birkhoff book contained no problems and no real applications outside of celestial dynamics; it was a mathematical work, written for and published by the mathematics community.

5. The brittleness of the orange equilibrium

1 Mathematization is also associated with the professionalization of economics as a social science. A. W. Coats (1985, pp. 1698–9) cites the sociologist Thomas Haskell's observation: "[Professionalization involves] a three-part process by which a community of inquirers is established, distinguishes itself from other groups and from the society at large, and enhances communication among its members, organizing and disciplining them, and heightening their credibility in the eyes of the public. Any act which contributes to these functions, which strengthens the intellectual solidarity of this very special kind of community, is a step towards professionalization" (Haskell 1977, p. 19). It should be clear that the mathematization of economics was a step toward professionalization in this sense. This is another set of arguments concerning mathematization about which I shall have nothing to say.

2 It was my intention in my earlier studies of general equilibrium analysis (Weintraub 1985) to show how the Lakatosian vision required significant augmentation to explain the growth and development of a literature in economic theory. This chapter can thus be read as an exploration of a Wittgensteinian language game, the game of "What is the meaning of equilibrium?": "A asks 'How many slabs?' and B answers with a numeral. . . . Systems of communication [like this] we shall call 'language games.'. . . Children are taught their native language by means of such games. . . . We are not, however, regarding the language games which we describe as incomplete parts of a language, but as languages complete in themselves, as complete systems of human communication" (Wittgenstein 1960, p. 81).

3 I am not unmindful of the force of Mirowski's claim (1988, 1989a) that the central mechanical imagery was simply lifted, as a piece, from classical field theory in physics. Indeed, I think that the broad substance of Mirowski's argument is not only correct but also of paramount importance for understanding modern economics. The details of how field theory worked in particular arguments, such as the ones I present here, are crucial to understanding and corroborating Mirowski's work.

4 Oskar Morgenstern (1941) took Hicks to task for ignoring the published solution to the equilibrium-existence problem (Weintraub 1985, p. 85), and Samuelson, as we saw in Chapters 2 and 3, made an early reputation untangling Hicks's mathematically monstrous distinctions concerning "stability."

5 But it is worth noting that Debreu was alerted to Arrow's interest in the problem of equilibrium when he was asked to referee a Cowles Paper written by Arrow; for Debreu's memory of that origin of their collaboration, see Weintraub (1983, pp. 28–9; 1985, p. 95).

6 This view is, in the literature, most recently associated with the historian Thomas Kuhn (1962, 1977), who documented the manner in which many concept words in science are theory-dependent; the correspondence view, the idea that science is an epistemological enterprise, is the target of Rorty (1979, 1982).

7 In this case, the Nash equilibrium theorem (Nash 1950), which is equivalent to the Brouwer fixed-point theorem (von Newmann 1936) or the Kakutani fixed-point

theorem (Kakutani 1941). It should be recognized that the Brouwer theorem is presented to mathematical readers with an image of some power: The theorem is sometimes called the "cowlick theorem," for if a head is a sphere, and a scalp is convex and compact, then hair is associated with the points of a compact convex set. "Combing hair" is thus a transformation or mapping of the points of the scalp to itself. "Combing" is certainly a continuous mapping. The Brouwer theorem can then be stated as follows: "There is always a cowlick after every combing." (A continuous mapping of a compact convex set to itself always has a fixed point.)

6. Stabilizing dynamics

1 For what it is worth, I am most taken with the position developed by Barbara Herrnstein Smith, a position critical of both objectivism-absolutism and radical relativism, in her *Contingencies of Value: Alternative Perspectives for Critical Theory* (1988).
2 I have refrained from quoting from the latter sections of Walker's paper, wherein he takes on the imaginary dragon he calls "subjectivism" and, having gotten himself utterly confused about what and who that monster is, ends up slicing off his big toe with his broadsword. He concludes this breathtaking auto-bloodletting as follows: "To accept subjectivism would be to revert to unscientific thought, to abandon the clear-minded and rational approach that has led to decades of improvement of the study of the history of economic thought" (Walker 1988, p. 111).
3 Sometimes it is suggested that there is a fourth problem, which is referred to as the problem of "uniqueness" of the competitive equilibrium, but on actual analysis this problem turns out to be part of the stability problem.

7. Surveying dynamics

1 One of the best of these is Greg Myers (1989). See also the two-part paper on review articles by Garfield (1987a, 1987b).
2 It also suggests that the commissioning of survey articles by major journals, such as the *Journal of Economic Literature,* is a topic worthy of examination by historians of economics.
3 This seems somewhat less the case in other sciences, such as physics and biology and medicine, perhaps because, for example, the subdisciplines in the history of physics do concern themselves with "modern" work. In mathematics, history is seldom conceived of as more recent than the 1940s: The recent two-volume *History of Modern Mathematics* (Rowe and McCleary 1989) takes "modern" to mean 1800–1945!
4 Some of this debate, strange to modern eyes, lives on in the footnotes to Koopmans's essay "The Interaction of Tools and Problems in Economics" (1957b), which is still frequently read.
5 Taro Yamane's *Mathematics for Economists* had appeared in 1962, suggesting that by that time the knowledge of mathematics required by economics graduate programs had been well codified.

6 There were few nonacademic members of the Econometric Society, as the list of the fellows of the society, its high-status membership, will document. Nonacademics would have been much less interested in theory, and more interested in applications, because applications provided the sustenance for economists outside the academy.

7 Purely anecdotally, ask graduate students today about stability and Arrow and Clower, and they will talk about Arrow's contribution, but disbelieve that Clower, a distinguished monetary economist, had any significant mathematical background or made contributions to a field as mathematized as stability theory. They are uniformly surprised to learn that he was the first, or nearly the first, to introduce Liapunov theory to economists.

8 See Robert Heilbroner (1990).

8. Conclusion

1 This was the keynote address to the fourteenth annual meeting of the History of Economics Society.

2 All this "seeing" is definitively discussed by Richard Rorty (1979).

References

Allais, M. 1943. *A la recherche d'une discipline économique. Première partie: l'économie pure.* Paris: Ateliers Industria.

1978. *Contributions à la science économique: Vue d'ensemble 1943-1978.* Paris: Centre d'Analyse Economique.

Andronov, A. A., and Chaikin, C. E. 1949. *Theory of Oscillations.* Princeton, N.J.: Princeton University Press.

Arrow, K., Block, H. D., and Hurwicz, L. 1959. "On the Stability of the Competitive Equilibrium, II." *Econometrica* 27:265-90.

Arrow, K., and Debreu, G. 1954. "Existence of an Equilibrium for a Competitive Economy." *Econometrica* 22:265-90.

Arrow, K. J., and Hahn, F. 1971. *General Competitive Analysis.* San Francisco: Holden-Day.

Arrow, K., and Hurwicz, L. 1958. "On the Stability of the Competitive Equilibrium, I." *Econometrica* 26:522-52.

(eds.). 1977. *Studies in Resource Allocation Processes.* Cambridge University Press.

Bazerman, C. 1988. *Shaping Written Knowledge.* Madison: University of Wisconsin Press.

Belloc, B., and Moreaux, M. 1987. "Allais, Maurice." In Eatwell, J., Milgate, M., and Newman, P. (eds.), *The New Palgrave, Vol. 1* (New York: Stockton Press), pp. 78-9.

Birkhoff, G. D. 1927. *Dynamical Systems.* AMS Colloquium Publications, Vol. 9. New York: American Mathematical Society.

1934. "The Work of Poincaré on Differential Equations." *Bulletin of the American Mathematical Society* 40:363-6. Reprinted in G. S. Birkhoff, *Collected Mathematical Papers, Vol. 3* (New York: Dover Books, 1968), pp. 544-7.

Birkhoff, G. D., and Lewis, D. C., Jr. 1935. "Causal Systems." *Philosophy of Science* 2:304-33.

Blaug, M. 1980. *The Methodology of Economics.* Cambridge University Press.

Bliss, C. 1987. "John Richard Hicks." In Eatwell, J., Milgate, M., and Newman, P. (eds.), *The New Palgrave, Vol. 2* (New York: Stockton Press), pp. 641-6.

Bloor, D. 1983. *Wittgenstein: A Social Theory of Knowledge.* New York: Columbia University Press.

Boĭko, E. S. 1983. *Shkola Akademika A. A. Andronova.* Moscow: Nauka.

Bowley, A. L. 1924. *The Mathematical Groundwork of Economics.* Oxford University Press.

165

Burnside, W. S., and Panton, A. W. 1904. *The Theory of Equations.* London: Longmans, Green.

Bushaw, D. W. 1989. Letter to E. R. Weintraub, February 4.

Bushaw, D. W., and Clower, R. 1954. "Price Determination in a Stock-Flow Economy." *Econometrica* 22:328–43.

1957. *Introduction to Mathematical Economics.* Homewood, Ill.: Irwin.

Chakravarty, S. 1987. "Jan Tinbergen." In Eatwell, J., Milgate, M., and Newman, P. (eds.), *The New Palgrave, Vol. 4* (New York: Stockton Press), pp. 652–4.

Coats, A. W. 1985. "The American Economics Association and the Economics Profession." *Journal of Economic Literature* 23:1697–727.

Cohen, J. E. 1987. "Alfred James Lotka." In Eatwell, J., Milgate, M., and Newman, P. (eds.), *The New Palgrave, Vol. 3* (New York: Stockton Press), pp. 245–7.

de Marchi, N. B. (ed.). 1988. *The Popperian Legacy in Economics.* Cambridge University Press.

Diner, S. 1986. "A Renewal of Mechanism: Toward an Instrumental Realism." In Diner, S., Fargue, D., and Lochak, G. (eds.), *Dynamical Systems: A Renewal of Mechanism – Centennial of George David Birkhoff* (Singapore: World Scientific, 1986), pp. 273–84.

Diner, S., Fargue, D., and Lochak, G. (eds.). 1986. *Dynamical Systems: A Renewal of Mechanism – Centennial of George David Birkhoff.* Singapore: World Scientific.

Dorfman, R., Samuelson, P., and Solow, R. 1958. *Linear Programming and Economic Analysis.* New York: McGraw-Hill.

Enthoven, A. C., and Arrow, K. J. 1956. "A Theorem on Expectations and the Stability of Equilibrium." *Econometrica* 24:288–93.

Evans, G. C. 1930. *Mathematical Introduction to Economics.* New York: McGraw-Hill.

Fish, S. 1980. *Is There a Text in this Class?* Cambridge, Mass.: Harvard University Press.

Fox, K. 1987. "Gerhard Tintner." In Eatwell, J., Milgate, M., and Newman, P. (eds.), *The New Palgrave, Vol. 4* (New York: Stockton Press), pp. 654–5.

Friedman, M. 1946. "Lange on Price Flexibility and Employment: A Methodological Criticism." *American Economic Review* 36:613–31.

Frisch, R. 1933. "Propagation Problems and Impulse Problems in Dynamic Economics." In *Economic Essays in Honor of Gustav Cassel* (London: George Allen & Unwin), pp. 171–206. Reprinted and distributed by Universitetets Okonomiske Institutt, Oslo, No. 3, 1933, pp. 1–35.

1936. "On the Notion of Equilibrium and Disequilibrium." *Review of Economic Studies* 3:100–6.

Gale, D. 1963. "A Note on Global Instability of Competitive Equilibrium." *Naval Research Logistics Quarterly* 10:81–7.

Garfield, E. 1987a. "Reviewing Review Literature. Part 1: Definitions and Uses of Reviews." *Current Contents* May 4, pp. 3–8.

1987b. "Reviewing Review Literature. Part 2: The Place of Reviews in the Scientific Literature." *Current Contents* May 11, pp. 3–8.

Geertz, C. 1988. *Works and Lives.* Stanford, Calif.: Stanford University Press.

Gibbs, W. 1906. "On the Equilibrium of Heterogeneous Substances" (first published 1878). In *The Scientific Papers of J. Willard Gibbs* (Vol. 1, pt. 3) (London: Longmans, Green).

Goodman, N. 1985. *Of Mind and Other Matters.* Cambridge, Mass.: Harvard University Press.

Grandmont, J.-M. 1988. "Report on M. Allais' Scientific Work." CEPREMAP Discussion Paper No. 8819. Paris: CEPREMAP.

1989. Letter to E. R. Weintraub, March 14.

Griffiths, P., Spencer, D., and Whitehead, G. 1988. "Solomon Lefschetz, September 3, 1884–October 5, 1972." Unpublished manuscript for the National Academy of Sciences, October.

Gusdorf, G. 1980. "Conditions and Limits of Autobiography" (trans. J. Olney). In Olney, J. (ed.), *Autobiography: Essays Theoretical and Critical* (Princeton, N.J.: Princeton University Press), pp. 28–48.

Gutting, G. 1988. "Michel Foucault and the History of Reason." In McMullin, E. (ed.), *Construction and Constraint: The Shaping of Scientific Rationality* (South Bend, Ind.: University of Notre Dame Press), pp. 153–88.

Hahn, F. 1970. "Some Adjustment Problems." *Econometrica* 38(1):1–14.

Hahn, F. H. 1983. "On General Equilibrium and Stability." In Brown, E. C., and Solow, R. (eds.), *Paul Samuelson and Modern Economic Theory* (New York: McGraw-Hill), pp. 31–55.

Hands, D. W. 1984. "The Role of Crucial Counterexamples in the Growth of Economic Knowledge." *History of Political Economy* 16:59–67.

Haskell, T. L. 1977. *The Emergence of Professional Social Science: The American Social Science Association and the Nineteenth Century Crisis of Authority.* Urbana: University of Illinois Press.

Hatta, T. 1987. "Le Chatelier Principle." In Eatwell, J., Milgate, M., and Newman, P. (eds.), *The New Palgrave, Vol. 3* (New York: Stockton Press), pp. 155–7.

Hayek, F. von. 1931. *Prices and Production.* London: Routledge.

Heilbroner, R. 1990. "Economics as Ideology." In Samuels, W. J. (ed.), *Economics as Discourse* (Boston: Kluwer), pp. 101–16.

Henderson, L. J. 1935. *Pareto's General Sociology, A Physiologists' Interpretation.* Cambridge, Mass.: Harvard University Press.

Henry, C. 1987. "Liapunov Functions." In Eatwell, J., Milgate, M., and Newman, P. (eds.), *The New Palgrave, Vol. 3* (New York: Stockton Press), pp. 256–9.

Heyl, B. S. 1968. "The Harvard 'Pareto Circle'." *Journal of the History of the Behavioral Sciences* 4:316–34.

Hicks, J. R. 1937. *Théorie mathématique de la valeur en régime de libre concurrence.* Paris: Hermann.

1939. *Value and Capital.* Oxford University Press.

1967. "The Hayek Story." In Hicks, J. R., *Critical Essays in Monetary Theory* (Oxford University Press), pp. 203–15.

1977. "Recollections and Documents." In Hicks, J. R., *Economic Perspectives* (Oxford University Press), pp. 134–48.

1982. "LSE and the Robbins Circle." In Hicks, J. R., *Money, Interest and Wages, Collected Essays, Vol. 2* (Oxford: Basil Blackwell), pp. 3–10.

1984. "The Formation of an Economist." In Hicks, J. R., *The Economics of John Hicks* (Oxford: Basil Blackwell), pp. 281–90.

Homans, G. C. 1968. "Henderson, L. J." In Sills, D. (ed.), *International Encyclopedia of the Social Sciences, Vol. 6* (New York: Macmillan), pp. 31–58.

1984. *Coming to My Senses: The Autobiography of a Sociologist.* New Brunswick, N.J.: Transaction Books.

Hughes, S. 1961. *Consciousness and Society.* New York: Basic Books.

Hunsaker, J., and MacLane, S. 1973. "Edwin Bidell Wilson." In *Biographical Memoirs, Vol. 43* (New York: Columbia University Press), pp. 284–320.

Kakutani, S. 1941. "A Generalization of Brouwer's Fixed Point Theorem." *Duke Mathematical Journal* 8:457–9. Reprinted in Newman, P. (ed.), *Readings in Mathematical Economics, Vol. 1* (Baltimore: Johns Hopkins University Press, 1968), pp. 33–5.

Keynes, J. M. 1930. *A Treatise on Money* (2 vols.). London: Macmillan. Republished as Keynes, J. M., *The Collected Writings of John Maynard Keynes, Vols. V–VI* (London: Macmillan, 1971).

1936. *The General Theory of Employment, Interest, and Money.* New York: Harcourt Brace. Republished as Keynes, J. M., *The Collected Writings of John Maynard Keynes, Vol. VII* (London: Macmillan, 1973).

Kim, K. 1989. *Equilibrium Business Cycle Theory.* Cambridge University Press.

Kingsland, S. E. 1985. *Modeling Nature.* University of Chicago Press.

Knorr-Cetina, K. 1981. *The Manufacture of Knowledge: An Essay on the Constructivist and Contingent Nature of Science.* Oxford: Pergamon Press.

Koopmans, T. 1957a. *Three Essays on the State of Economic Science.* New York: McGraw-Hill.

1957b. "The Interaction of Tools and Problems in Economics." In Koopmans, T., *Three Essays on the State of Economic Science* (New York: McGraw-Hill), pp. 169–220.

Kryloff, N., and Bogoliuboff, N. 1943. *Introduction to Nonlinear Mechanics* (trans. S. Lefschetz). Annals of Mathematics Studies No. 11. Princeton, N.J.: Princeton University Press.

Kuhn, T. S. 1962. *The Structure of Scientific Revolutions.* University of Chicago Press.

1977. "The Historical Structure of Scientific Discovery." In Kuhn, T. S., *The Essential Tension* (University of Chicago Press), pp. 165–77. Reprinted from *Science* 136(1962).

1977. *The Essential Tension.* University of Chicago Press.

Lakatos, I. 1976. *Proofs and Refutations.* Cambridge University Press.

Lange, O. 1944. *Price Flexibility and Employment.* Bloomington, Ind.: Principia Press.

LaSalle, J. P., and Lefschetz, S. (eds.). 1962. *Recent Soviet Contributions to Mathematics*. New York: Macmillan.

Latour, B. 1987. *Science in Action*. Cambridge, Mass.: Harvard University Press.

Latour, B., and Woolgar, S. 1979. *Laboratory Life*. Beverly Hills, Calif.: Sage.

Lefschetz, S. 1943. "Emile Picard." *American Philosophical Society Yearbook 1942*, pp. 363–5.

1946. *Lectures on Differential Equations*. Annals of Mathematics Studies No. 14. Princeton, N.J.: Princeton University Press.

1949. "Scientific Research in the U.S.S.R.: Math." *Annals of the American Academy of Politics and Social Science* 263:139–40.

1953. "Russian Contributions to Differential Equations." In *Symposium on Nonlinear Circuit Analysis, Proceedings* (New York: Polytechnic Institute of Brooklyn), pp. 68–74.

1968. "A Page of Mathematical Autobiography." *Bulletin of the American Mathematical Society* 74:854–79.

1970. "Reminiscences of a Mathematical Immigrant in the United States." *American Mathematical Monthly* 77(4):344–50.

Leijonhufvud, A. 1968. *On Keynesian Economics and the Economics of Keynes*. Oxford University Press.

Liapunov, A. M. 1949. "Problème général de la stabilité du mouvement" (trans. E. Davaux) (first published 1907). Annals of Mathematics Studies No. 17. Princeton, N.J.: Princeton University Press. Photoreproduced from *Annales de la Faculté des Sciences de l'Université de Toulouse* 9(2):27–474.

Lotka, A. J. 1956. *Elements of Mathematical Biology* (first published 1924). New York: Dover.

Lucas, R. 1985. *Studies in Business Cycle Theory*. Cambridge, Mass.: MIT Press.

McCloskey, D. N. 1983. "The Rhetoric of Economics." *Journal of Economic Literature* 21:481–517.

1986. *The Rhetoric of Economics*. Madison: University of Wisconsin Press.

McIntyre, A. 1984. *After Virtue* (2nd ed.). South Bend, Ind.: University of Notre Dame Press.

McKenzie, L. 1954. "On Equililbrium in Graham's Model of World Trade and Other Competitive Systems." *Econometrica* 22:147–61.

Mandel, B. J. 1980. "Full of Life Now." In Olney, J. (ed.), *Autobiography: Essays Theoretical and Critical* (Princeton, N.J.: Princeton University Press), pp. 49–72.

Marshall, A. 1961. *Principles of Economics* (ed. C. W. Guillebaud) (first published 1890). London: Macmillan.

Merton, R. K. 1957. "Priorities in Scientific Discovery: A Chapter in the Sociology of Science." *American Sociological Review* 22:635–59.

Metzler, L. 1945. "Stability of Multiple Markets: The Hicks Conditions." *Econometrica* 13:277–92.

Milgate, M. 1987. "E. B. Wilson." In Eatwell, J., Milgate, M., and Newman, P. (eds.), *The New Palgrave, Vol. 4* (New York: Stockton Press), pp. 922–3.

Mira, C. 1986. "Some Historical Aspects Concerning the Theory of Dynamical Systems." In Diner, S., Fargue, D., and Lochak, G. (eds.), *Dynamical*

Systems: A Renewal of Mechanism - Centennial of George David Birkhoff (Singapore: World Scientific), pp. 250–61.

Mirowski, P. 1988. *Against Mechanism: Why Economics Needs Protection From Science.* Totowa, N.J.: Rowman & Littlefield.

1989a. *More Heat Than Light.* Cambridge University Press.

1989b. Letter to E. R. Weintraub, March 23.

1989c. "How Not to Do Things With Metaphors: Paul Samuelson and the Science of Neoclassical Economics." *Studies in the History and Philosophy of Science* 20(2):175–91.

1990. "From Mandelbrot to Chaos in Economic Theory." *Southern Economic Journal* 57(2):289–307.

Moreaux, M. 1989. Letter to E. R. Weintraub, September 6.

Morgan, M. S. 1987. "The Stamping Out of Process Analysis." Unpublished mimeograph, Duke University Economics Department.

1990. *A History of Econometric Ideas.* Cambridge University Press.

Morgenstern, O. 1941. "Professor Hicks on Value and Capital." *Journal of Political Economy* 49:361–93.

Morishima, M. 1980. *Dynamic Economic Theory* (author's translation of M. Morishima, *Dogakuteki Keizai Riron,* 1950). London: International Centre for Economics and Related Disciplines.

1986. Letter to E. R. Weintraub, June 18.

Morse, M. 1946. "George David Birkhoff and His Mathematical Work." *Bulletin of the American Mathematical Society* 52(5):357–91.

Munz, P. 1985. *Our Knowledge of the Growth of Knowledge: Popper or Wittgenstein.* London: Routledge & Kegan Paul.

Myers, G. 1989. "Stories and Styles in Two Molecular Biology Review Articles." Unpublished mimeograph, Modern Languages Centre, University of Bradford, U.K.

Nash, J. 1950. "Equilibrium Points in *N*-Person Games." *Proceedings of the National Academy of Sciences, U.S.A.* 36:48–9.

Negishi, T. 1962. "The Stability of a Competitive Economy: A Survey Article." *Econometrica* 30:635–69. Reprinted in Newman, P. (ed.), *Readings in Mathematical Economics, Vol. 1* (Baltimore: Johns Hopkins University Press, 1968), pp. 213–47.

Newman, P. (ed.). 1968. *Readings in Mathematical Economics* (2 vols.). Baltimore: Johns Hopkins University Press.

Northrop, F. S. C. 1941. "The Impossibility of a Theoretical Science of Economic Dynamics." *Quarterly Journal of Economics* (November):1–17.

O'Brien, D. P. 1991. "Lionel Robbins and the Austrian Connection." *History of Political Economy* 23(5).

Patinkin, D. 1965. *Money, Interest, and Prices* (2nd ed.). New York: Harper & Row.

Picard, E. 1928. *Traité d'analyse, Vol. III* (3rd ed.). Paris: Gauthier-Villars.

Rasmussen, P. N. 1987. "Ragnar Frisch." In Eatwell, J., Milgate, M., and Newman, P. (eds.), *The New Palgrave, Vol. 2* (New York: Stockton Press), pp. 428–30.

Reid, C. 1976. *Courant*. New York: Springer-Verlag.

Robbins, L. 1930. "On a Certain Ambiguity in the Conception of Stationary Equilibrium." *The Economic Journal* (June):194–214.

Rorty, R. 1979. *Philosophy and the Mirror of Nature*. Princeton, N.J.: Princeton University Press.

1982. *The Consequences of Pragmatism*. Minneapolis: University of Minnesota Press.

Rosenberg, A. 1983. "If Economics Isn't Science, What Is It?" *Philosophical Forum* 14:296–314.

1986. "The Explanatory Role of Existence Proofs." *Ethics* 97:177–86.

Rowe, D. E., and McCleary, J. (eds.). 1989. *The History of Modern Mathematics* (2 vols.). New York: Academic Press.

Russett, C. E. 1966. *The Concept of Equilibrium in American Social Thought*. New Haven, Conn.: Yale University Press.

Samuelson, P. A. 1939. "Interactions between the Multiplier Analysis and the Principle of Acceleration." *Review of Economic Statistics* 21:75–8.

1941. "The Stability of Equilibrium: Comparative Statics and Dynamics." *Econometrica* 9:97–120.

1942. "The Stability of Equilibrium: Linear and Nonlinear Systems." *Econometrica* 10:1–25.

1943. "Dynamics, Statics, and the Stationary States." *Review of Economics and Statistics* 25:58–68.

1947. *Foundations of Economic Analysis*. Cambridge, Mass.: Harvard University Press.

1972. "Economics in a Golden Age: A Personal Memoir." In Holton, G. (ed.), *The Twentieth Century Sciences, Studies in the Biography of Ideas* (New York: Norton), pp. 155–70. Reprinted in Brown, E. C., and Solow, R. (eds.), *Paul Samuelson and Modern Economic Theory* (New York: McGraw-Hill, 1983), pp. 1–14.

1986a. Letter to E. R. Weintraub, September 17.

1986b. "Economics in My Time." In Breit, W., and Spencer, R. W. (eds.), *Lives of the Laureates* (Cambridge, Mass.: MIT Press), pp. 59–76.

1987. "Out of the Closet: A Program for the Whig History of Economic Science." *History of Economics Society Bulletin* 9(1):51–60.

Scarf, H. 1960. "Some Examples of Global Instability of the Competitive Equilibrium." *International Economic Review* 1:157–72.

Shackle, G. L. S. 1967. *The Years of High Theory*. Cambridge University Press.

Simon, H. 1959. "Review of 'Elements of Mathematical Biology'." *Econometrica* 27(3):493–5.

1987. "Griffith Conrad Evans." In Eatwell, J., Milgate, M., and Newman, P. (eds.), *The New Palgrave, Vol. 3* (New York: Stockton Press), pp. 198–9.

1988. Letter to E. R. Weintraub, November 2.

Smith, B. H. 1988. *Contingencies of Value: Alternative Perspectives for Critical Theory*. Cambridge, Mass.: Harvard University Press.

Smithies, A. 1942. "The Stability of Competitive Equilibrium." *Econometrica* 10:258–74.

Solow, R. 1988. Letter to E. R. Weintraub, November 4.

Sono, M. 1955. "Positive and Negative Relations and Stability Conditions." *Osaka Economic Papers* 3(3):15–28.

Stewart, I. 1989. *Does God Play Dice?* New York: Basil Blackwell.

Tinbergen, J. 1935. "Annual Survey: Suggestions on Quantitative Business Cycle Theory." *Econometrica* 3:241–308.

1987. "The ET Interview: Professor J. Tinbergen." Interviewed by Jan R. Magnus and Mary S. Morgan, *Econometric Theory* 3:117–42.

Tsuru, S. 1964. "Survey of Economic Research in Postwar Japan." *American Economic Review* (June Supplement):81–101.

1984. "A Survey of Economic Research in Japan, 1960–1983." *The Economic Review* (Institute of Economic Research, Hitotsubashi University) 35:289–306.

1986. Letter to E. R. Weintraub, June 26.

Tucker, A. W. 1985. "Solomon Lefschetz: A Reminiscence." In Albers, D. J., and Alexanderson, G. L. (eds.), *Mathematical People* (Boston: Birkhauser), pp. 349–50.

van der Berg, G. 1988. "Search Behavior, Transitions to Nonparticipation, and the Duration of Unemployment." Unpublished mimeograph, University of Tilsit.

von Bertalanffy, L. 1973. *General Systems Theory* (rev. ed.). New York: George Braziller.

von Neumann, J. 1936. "Über ein okonomisches Gleichungssystem und eine Verallgemeinerung des brouwerschen Fixpunksatzes." In Menger, K. (ed.), *Ergebnisse eines mathematischen Kolloquiums, 1935–36* (Vienna: Franz Deuticke, 1937), pp. 73–83. Reprinted as "A Model of General Economic Equilibrium" (trans. G. Morton, 1946). *Reviews of Economic Studies* 13:1–9.

Walker, D. A. 1988. "Ten Major Problems in the Study of the History of Economic Thought." *History of Economics Society Bulletin* 10(2):99–116.

Walras, L. 1926. *Elements D'Economie Politique Pure* (edition définitive). Paris: R. Pichon et R. Durand-Auzias. Translated by W. Jaffee as *Elements of Pure Economics* (London: Allen & Unwin, 1954).

Walsh, V., and Gram, H. 1980. *Classical and Neoclassical Theories of General Equilibrium*. Oxford University Press.

Weintraub, E. R. 1979. *Microfoundations*. Cambridge University Press.

1983. "On the Existence of a Competitive Equilibrium: 1930–1954." *Journal of Economic Literature* 21:1–39.

1985. *General Equilibrium Analysis: Studies in Appraisal*. Cambridge University Press.

1987. "Stability Theory via Liapunov's Method: A Note on the Contribution of Takuma Yasui." *History of Political Economy* 19(4):615–20.

1988. "The NeoWalrasian Program Is Empirically Progressive." In de Marchi, N. (ed.), *The Popperian Legacy in Economics* (Cambridge University Press), pp. 213–27.

Wheeler, L. P. 1952. *Josiah Willard Gibbs*. New Haven, Conn.: Yale University Press.

Wicksteed, P. H. 1945. *The Common Sense of Political Economy* (first published 1910). London: Routledge.

Wilson, E. B. 1938a. Letter to H. H. Burbank, December 20.

1938b. Letter to P. A. Sorokin, December 20.

1938c. Letter to P. A. Samuelson, December 30.

Wittgenstein, L. 1956. *Remarks on the Foundations of Mathematics*. Oxford: Basil Blackwell.

1960. *The Blue and Brown Books*. New York: Harper & Row.

Woodward, C. V. 1986. "The Lost Cause: Review of Irving Howe's Socialism and America." *New York Review of Books,* January 30, p. 26.

Yamane, T. 1962. *Mathematics for Economists*. Englewood Cliffs, N.J.: Prentice-Hall.

Yasui, T. 1948. "The Dynamic Stability Conditions of Economic Equilibrium" (in Japanese). *Keizai Shichō* (September).

1950. "A General Theory of Stability" (in Japanese). *Economic Studies Quarterly* 1:13–32.

1985. Letter to E. R. Weintraub, December 6.

Yeats, W. 1946. "The Seven Sages." In *The Collected Poems of W. B. Yeats*. New York: Macmillan.

Index